D0421837

ALSO BY JASON MATTERA

Hollywood Hypocrites

Obama Zombies

CRAP**ITALISM**

CRAPITALISM

CRAP

THRESHOLD EDITIONS
NEW YORK   LONDON   TORONTO   SYDNEY   NEW DELHI

CRAPITALISM

CRAPITALISM

ITALISM

LIBERALS WHO MAKE MILLIONS
SWIPING *YOUR* TAX DOLLARS

Jason Mattera

Threshold Editions
A Division of Simon & Schuster, Inc.
1230 Avenue of the Americas
New York, NY 10020

First Threshold Editions hardcover edition October 2014

THRESHOLD EDITIONS and colophon are trademarks of Simon & Schuster, Inc.

For information about special discounts for bulk purchases, please contact Simon & Schuster Special Sales at 1-866-506-1949 or business@simonandschuster.com.

The Simon & Schuster Speakers Bureau can bring authors to your live event. For more information or to book an event, contact the Simon & Schuster Speakers Bureau at 1-866-248-3049 or visit our website at www.simonspeakers.com.

Interior design by Fine Design
Cover design by Chris Sergio

Manufactured in the United States of America

10 9 8 7 6 5 4 3 2 1

Library of Congress Cataloging-in-Publication Data is available.

ISBN 978-1-4767-5041-5
ISBN 978-1-4767-5043-9 (ebook)

To Kendra, the one who makes me smile

Contents

Introduction

Capitalism kicks ass, Crapitalism sucks.

Capitalism and the free market generate jobs, create pathways out of poverty, and keep people like Rosie O'Donnell off food stamps.

Crapitalism has taken the greatest economic system ever known to man and sullied it.

Americans love capitalism. Only pot-smoking Marxists and flea-infested Occupy Wall Street types could oppose an economic system that has built the middle class and made the United States the richest nation ever to inhabit planet earth.

But what Americans don't love—what they loathe, in fact— are well-connected crony capitalists who make millions by picking taxpayers' pockets. These poseur capitalists have turned capitalism into its very opposite. *Real* capitalists don't take bailouts or corporate welfare, or suck from the government contract teat. Real capitalists get rich by providing goods and services that benefit us all. That's good for them, and it's good for us.

But all that good goes up in smoke when business and government hop in the sack together.

When cronyism collides with capitalism you get . . . *Crap*italism.

Crapitalism has forced us to subsidize goods and services that we would never have subsidized otherwise. It's allowed the rich and famous to become even more rich and famous at our expense.

And, most disturbing, it's turned the rule of law on its head by creating two classes of citizens: those who benefit from crony connections and those who don't.

Americans agree. A Rasmussen poll found that people oppose crony capitalism 3–1. So strong is the bipartisan loathing of cronyism that a full 64 percent say they believe government money will be wasted "if the government provides funding for a project that private investors refuse to back." Just 27 percent believe it's ever okay "for the government to make investments in private companies."[1]

Who, then, supports perverting free markets?

Answer: *Crap*italists.

Let's define a Crapitalist: A well-connected friend of the powers that be who scores big bucks at taxpayer expense. From bagging millions in tax dollars for phony "green energy" companies that go bust, to vacuuming public coffers to build glitzy sports stadiums, to utilizing little-known tax credit loopholes to loot $1.5 billion a year for Hollywood movies—Crapitalists know how to use every trick to enrich themselves at taxpayer expense. Rather than playing and winning in the rough-and-tumble world of business competition, Crapitalists use government to rig the game in their favor and leave you and me—the taxpayers—holding the bill. These corporate sissies know their ideas suck, so they try to stack the deck to privatize their profits and socialize their losses.

And there's the rub: crony capitalism is socialism's Trojan horse.

When government gets in the business of picking winners and losers, free market competition—the "muscles" that animate capitalism—begin to atrophy. That's what big government Leftists want. Sadly, it's also what some corporatist Republicans want as well. Republicans like Jeffrey Immelt, the head of General Electric. He's taken cronyism to a stratospheric level, going as far as to call Uncle Sam a "key partner."[2] And later on you'll see he wasn't kidding. GE has lobbied its "partner" to impose regulations, mandates, and other edicts that boost its bottom line. Hell, if you look up the definition of "corporate welfare" in an online dictionary, you may get back "General Electric" as the answer.

To the Crapitalist, ideology isn't nearly as important as who will keep the government gravy train operating at full speed. That's why some fat-cat Republicans are already dropping hints that they would support Hillary Clinton for president over a more populist candidate like Rand Paul or Ted Cruz in 2016, because they know she'd maintain the cozy relationship that Wall Street has enjoyed with D.C.[3]

Real conservatives and libertarians, on the other hand, understand there's a major difference between being pro free markets and pro big business. Those who support free markets believe businesses should compete to win customers. Being pro-business sometimes means turning a blind eye to government bailouts and corporate welfare if they boost profits. The former leads to wealth and prosperity. The latter leads to socialism.

That's why Crapitalists are so dangerous.

Take, for example, billionaire John Doerr and his good pal Al Gore, both partners in the venture capital firm Kleiner Perkins Caufield & Byers. With an estimated $3.3 billion net worth, Doerr lands at number 159 on *Forbes*'s list of richest Americans.[4]

And, as the *New York Times* notes, Gore is "poised to become the world's first 'carbon billionaire,' profiteering from government policies he supports that would direct billions of dollars to the business ventures he has invested in."[5] Their firm has donated at least $2.2 million to political campaigns, most of which has gone to Democrats (shocker).[6]

To put it simply, these are two loaded liberals.

In 2008, Doerr and Gore's firm became a major stakeholder in the "green car" company Fisker Automotive. As Fisker's CEO explained to the *Wall Street Journal*, because of Doerr and Gore's investment "we have all the capital we need to move forward."[7]

Now, if two losers want to blow millions investing on a $107,000 car that runs on electricity—half of which comes from burning *coal,* you morons!—in the name of saving the planet, fine. Let them.

But that's not what happened.

The very next year, Obama's Department of Energy approved Fisker for $529 million in taxpayer-funded government loans. The Obama Energy Department *swears* Gore had nothing to do with the approval of the loan. (If you believe that, I have a crappy electric car to sell you.) However, numerous companies vying for DOE loans said the process reeked of cronyism. Indeed, sixteen of John Doerr's green-tech venture projects received taxpayer-funded loans or grants. "God bless the Obama Administration and the U.S. government," said Doerr. "We have really got the A-team now working on green innovation in our country."[8]

Not surprisingly, lefty loons like Matt Damon and Leonardo

DiCaprio scurried to snatch one up. Even Canadian ankle-biter Justin Bieber got one. His manager made a stir when he gave the teenage crooner a Fisker Karma for his birthday on the *Ellen DeGeneres Show*. For maximum douchiness, Bieber has since chromed out his Fisker, morphing the thing into an obnoxious mirror that blinds fellow drivers whose tax dollars were used to subsidize it.

But there was just one teensy problem on the road to Doerr and Gore's green earth glory. The Fisker Karma turned out to be taxpayer-funded junk.

First, there were the fires—as in, the car *catching on fire*. Fisker claimed the problem was the battery and issued the obligatory recalls. Then, a few months later, *another* Fisker Karma caught fire. This time Team Goremobile blamed it on the cooling fans and recalled 2,400 Karmas.

Then there was the issue of Fisker outsourcing jobs by assembling the Karma entirely in Finland, a revelation Mitt Romney wisely pounced on. "I am ashamed to say that we're seeing our president hand out money to the businesses of campaign contributors, when he gave money, $500 million in loans, to a company called Fisker that makes high-end electric cars, and they make the cars now in Finland."

D'oh!

But best of all was *Consumer Reports'* testing of the Fisker Karma wherein the car literally died right in the middle of the test![9] Think I'm joking? Pull up the YouTube clip and watch for yourself. You just can't make this stuff up.

Fisker Automotive ultimately filed for bankruptcy and was bought up by a Chinese vehicle manufacturer.[10] Meanwhile, taxpayers suffering in the worst economy since the Great Depression are forced to sit back and watch as Crapitalists Doerr and Gore flush millions in taxpayer cash down the turd chute on a green scheme designed to make them millions, minimize their losses, and stick taxpayers with the tab either way.

Crapitalism, pure and simple.

Crapitalists don't just seize taxpayer money for things only patchouli-smelling hippies enjoy, like electric cars. They also use some of America's favorite institutions, like pro football, as lures designed to loot our hard-earned money. Consider, for example, Minnesota Vikings owner Zygi Wilf. Wilf successfully lobbied to force taxpayers to foot more than half the bill ($498 million, to be exact[11]) for a new $975 million showplace stadium where my New York Giants can kick the stew out of his Vikings. Amazingly, the liberal state of New Jersey didn't ask taxpayers to pay a single dime in 2010 to build a $1.6 billion NFL stadium for the Jets and Giants, nor did Massachusetts raid the public treasury to help the New England Patriots built its facility in 2002.[12] But the vast majority of NFL stadiums are publicly funded, with taxpayers subsidizing a jaw-dropping 65 percent of the total costs.[13]

What's up with that?

Why should Crapitalists be allowed to bilk taxpayers to fund teams—many of which suck—so they can get richer?

Crapitalists always cloak their cronyism in the guise of helping society, saving the planet, or doing it "for the children." So it's hardly surprising that Zygi and his ilk claim new stadiums produce an explosion of economic development and jobs. But a boatload of economic studies show such claims are almost always bogus. Indeed, according to Democratic Minnesota state senator John Marty, the cost to taxpayers for Zygi's football profit palace will be around $72 per ticket . . . for the next thirty years. Republican state senator Warren Limmer agrees: "I think the real question is, what is the financial need of someone asking for help from state government to solve their private business problems?" As the senators' comments demonstrate, hatred of taxpayer-swindling Crapitalists should be a bipartisan affair.

But here now you have some poor hammer-swinging construction worker getting fleeced to pay for a stadium he can't even afford to take his kids to so that billionaire Zygi Wilf can fatten his wallet—all while subjecting the nation to the atrocity that is the Minnesota Vikings.

Idiots.

Crapitalists have also sunk their crony claws into the world of movies. Take the iconic filmmaker Steven Spielberg. *Forbes* says that with a net worth of $3.4 billion, Spielberg is the 159th-richest person in America.[14] You'd think homeboy, rolling in that much dough, could fund his own flicks without any taxpayer support. Well, he could. But he decided to milk taxpayers anyway. And with the help of lawmakers, no less!

Spielberg had his eyes on Virginia as a possible location to film his biopic on Abraham Lincoln for years, but it wasn't until the general assembly and the governor offered him a financial package worth millions that he made his decision.[15]

I know, what a strange coincidence.

"Virginia's rich historic legacy, coupled with the remarkable period architecture found in Richmond and Petersburg, make Central Virginia the ideal location for this production," Spielberg said.

Not everyone was pleased with the announcement, however.

"From my point of view, the state giving $5 million to a billionaire to make his movie in Virginia is a luxury our state can't afford right now when we are cutting education, Medicaid and the rest of our safety net," noted one state delegate.[16]

Keep in mind that *Lincoln* grossed more than $180 million worldwide. So not only were Virginia residents shelling out cash for overpriced movie tickets, but they were also subsidizing a film that brought in almost three times its estimated budget.[17]

Of course, Virginia is hardly alone in raiding public funds to attract big-studio production. Around forty states offer similar types of tax credits. And as we'll learn, these Hollywood handouts rarely live up to their economic hype. But politicians will pat themselves on the back because of the photo op arranged alongside their favorite celebrity. Think of it as the most expensive selfie ever—except you're not even in the picture.

Let me let you in on one of Crapitalism's dirtiest secrets. Contrary to what most liberals would have you believe, big business does *not* hate big government. To the contrary, as author Timothy P. Carney points out, "Big business and big government prosper from the perception that they are rivals instead of partners (in plunder)." Think about it. If, say, crushing government-imposed regulations can dramatically raise the prices on small start-up companies entering a market, big companies are all for it! Heck, big companies often *love* regulations, because their deep pockets allow them to easily absorb the financial costs that their smaller, leaner competitors can never afford.

And when big government programs require big government spending, big companies looking for big government contracts come running. Government should not be a corporate sugar daddy handing out our taxpayer dollars to businesses willing to prostitute themselves by bagging crony deals. Why? Because the libertarian and conservative visions of a limited, smaller government will never come to fruition as long as companies have a vested interest in seeing government grow.

And you see, that's what's so messed up about Crapitalism: it snuffs out the magic of true, rock-ribbed American competition. As

University of Chicago economics professor Luigi Zingales puts it, "A truly competitive market has no place for favoritism."[18]

This book is an unapologetic call for a return to real, true, competition-driven capitalism—the kind that has lifted millions of poor people into the middle class, created jobs and opportunities, and helped spark life-changing and lifesaving innovations that bring value and greater freedom to our lives.

But simply loving free markets isn't enough; we must defend our economic freedoms from the crony crooks seeking to pervert them.

That means naming names, reporting facts, and raining shame on the Crapitalists who would rather swipe your tax dollars to fund their loony ideas and cover their financial asses than compete, innovate, and win their way to the top the old-fashioned way, through hard work and competition.

It's time to stop apologizing for the freedom-producing engine that is free market competition.

It's time to protect taxpayers from the lazy limousine liberals who would rather poach your money than earn real profits.

It's time to flush these Crapitalists down the toilet.

Let the flushing begin!

1 Representative Greg Meeks

It's taking care of the things for my family needs in the house. You need to make sure the house is furnished. You need things.

—Representative Greg Meeks

Greg Meeks sucks.

If sucking at life was like working for one of those multilevel marketing companies, Meeks would be Double Emerald Platinum Level Suckface. That any of our tax dollars go to pay his congressional salary is cause for puking.

On the surface, Meeks fronts like a regular Joe.

For example, we're both New Yorkers from working-class neighborhoods: I'm from Brooklyn, and Meeks represents Queens. We both like sports. We both like nice cars. My problem is, I pay for my lifestyle. Greg Meeks? Well, like the auto manufacturer that shares his initials, he requires a lot of taxpayer cash to stay afloat.

Meeks has been in Congress since 1998, so with an annual salary of $174,000 he obviously should be able to afford a pretty sweet ride. And he does—a nice Lexus. Like a lot of members of Congress, he leases it. But unlike many members of Congress, his lease costs the taxpayers around $1,000 a month.[1,2]

Excuse me?

Unfortunately, you don't get to be a Double Emerald dirtbag by just bilking Ma and Pa Taxpayer for a nice whip. By Meeks's standard, his Lexus is our best bargain.

Meeks loves living it up at exotic locales. And I don't mean Jamaica, Queens. Meeks has dropped big bucks, on his campaign's dime, at luxury resorts in Puerto Rico, the Virgin Islands, Panama, Vegas, and Miami, just to name a few. His jet-setting was so blatant even the *New York Times* profiled it in an investigative piece. When you're a liberal and the *New York Times* calls you out, you know it's bad. Meeks defended his travel to the paper, saying, "I do fundraisers where the people with the money are. . . . I am not going to raise the money in my district that I need to be a player here in Washington."[3]

Gangsta!

Unlike other members of Congress, forced to rely on ingenuity, guile, problem-solving skills, and an actual work ethic, Meeks can weasel his way to relevance by hobnobbing through the Caribbean. His constituents must be proud.

Citizens for Responsibility and Ethics in Washington (CREW) puts out a yearly list of Washington's most corrupt. Guess who is a regular? Our boy Government Greg.[4]

Unfortunately, while Meeks's use of campaign cash to live a

lifestyle he wouldn't be able to afford otherwise is distasteful, it is not illegal. Congress has a way of looking out for itself that way. The laws as currently written allow for certain campaign expenditures to be used toward things you and I (and apparently Meeks) wouldn't be able to afford otherwise. But even with all this leeway, Meeks pushes the envelope there, too.

For example, a 2006 audit by the Federal Election Commission found Meeks had improperly used almost $17,000 worth of campaign dollars on personal expenses, including over six grand for a personal trainer. Meeks ended up simply paying a fine, and once again cruised to reelection.[5] Then he got smarter about how to exploit his position.

Unlike regular campaign accounts, Leadership PACs can use money on nice restaurants, fancy resorts, and other expenses as long as you can rationalize it as a "campaign expense." So in 2013, when Meeks dropped over $17,000 with NFL ticket agencies and broadcast networks, it was okay because it was for a "Fundraising Event." Same thing in 2014. He gobbled up nearly $10,000 worth of tickets when the Seattle Seahawks annihilated the Denver Broncos. He calls it campaigning. I call it partying at the Super Bowl.

His Leadership PAC, Build America, can do those things because the laws are superliberal in terms of what LPACs can get away with. Part of the rationalization for having LPACs is so members of Congress can donate funds to other members of Congress, currying favor for their own legislative priorities by essentially buying votes. It isn't unusual for someone to spend almost all their LPAC money on building coalitions and supporting members of their party. It is, in fact, how many members elevate through the party ranks. Remember how Government Greg said he needed to go to those resorts and hold fundraisers so he could become "a player"?

Remember how his working-class neighborhood just wouldn't allow him access to the capital to matter in the Capitol?

In the 2011–12 cycle, Meeks's LPAC spent over $150,000. How much of that do you think, given that Meeks sailed to an easy reelection, went to his fellow Democrats? Maybe $100,000? $75,000 at least?

Nope. A measly twenty grand. Less than 14 percent.

Meeks actually ranked as the sixth-least-generous member of Congress in terms of LPAC donations to other candidates who spent more than $100,000 in the cycle. Even though his campaign didn't need the money, Meeks himself did. That's why he sucks so bad. Even though I personally appreciate that he doesn't use his campaign money to help elect more Democrats, I still get sick at the way he uses his position to hit people up for cash so he can party all over the globe, and live it up here at home.

Meeks bought himself a new home in 2006. Nothing wrong with living the American dream. But Meeks's house was built for him by a developer friend who just so happened to be a campaign contributor. The designer of the house, Robert Gaskin, had not only contributed to Meeks's campaign but had also worked on projects that Meeks had secured taxpayer cash to bankroll.[6]

Meeks paid $830,000 for the house. It is said to be by far the largest in his neighborhood. Kevin Donegan, an appraiser, called Meeks's price "substantially below market" and said Meeks got "a very, very good deal."[7] In fact, months after the house was finished, the city listed its market value as more than $400,000 above the price Meeks paid.[8]

Cha-ching!

Everything about the sale smells. Even the house Meeks sold to purchase this one went to a buyer with a reported annual income of less than $10,000, yet he was somehow able to qualify for a

$400,000 home. Would you believe me if I told you that the lawyer who handled the buyer's closing went to jail ten months later for mortgage fraud?[9]

But Greedy Greg didn't care. That someone with whom he had just completed a high-dollar legal transaction was going to jail wasn't his problem. He had bigger issues to deal with: 800 large is a lot to spend on a house. Especially when, like Meeks, you don't have any cash in the bank. According to the congressman's financial records, on paper Meeks is a broke joke.[10] He claims he has less than $5,000 in his checking account and no investments worth more than a grand. So how does he afford all the high-end houses and vacations?

Homeboy is shady as hell.

If you had just bought a house and needed to furnish it, but didn't have a ton of cash on hand, like our buddy Greg, what would you do?

Go to IKEA and just learn to appreciate the art of bargain Swedish furniture design? Maybe. Take it to Goodwill, Salvation Army, or some other place that allows you to put some stuff in your house without breaking the bank? Perhaps. Maybe if you saw something you really wanted you'd hit up friends and family for a loan so you could get that futon you had your eye on. But not with G-Money behind you.

Meeks did take out a loan—but not from family, or even, you know, a bank. Instead, he "borrowed" $40,000 from a real estate agent crony of his named Edul Ahmad. I say "borrowed" because the loan didn't have a fixed interest rate, it had no set date for repayment, and Meeks never actually signed any documents to secure it. He also failed to disclose the loan on any of his financial disclosure documents until the "handshake deal" was reported by a New York paper. A lot of people think it wasn't a loan at all, but a gift, from a guy who would end up in prison a few years later over a $50 million mortgage fraud case.[11] Those are the kinds of guys Meeks does business with.

For his part, Meeks was cleared by a House Ethics Committee investigation. I mean, who can fault a guy just looking to allow his family a place to sit down? "I was in a new home," Meeks said about the loan. "It's taking care of the things for my family needs in the house. You need to make sure the house is furnished. You need things."[12]

You need things. That entitlement sums up Meeks's congressional career perfectly.

See, you need things. So whatever you need to do to get them is fair game. Accept a gift from some shyster real estate agent? No problem. Use your campaign funds? Sure thing. Take advantage of one of the worst natural disasters in a century for your own personal gain?

You betcha.

We all remember Hurricane Katrina. One of the worst events in recent American history—both in terms of the loss of human life and the government response. In fact, Meeks tried to score cheap political points by adding his name to a letter calling for the resignation of Michael Brown, then head of the Federal Emergency Management Agency.[13]

I'm definitely not here to defend the job Michael Brown did in Katrina. But at least, to my knowledge, Brown didn't try to exploit the Katrina victims for his own personal profit. Meeks did.

In the wake of the New Orleans flooding, a New York nonprofit called New Direction Local Development Corporation, cofounded by Meeks and sharing an address with Meeks's former campaign treasurer, began collecting donations in the name of Katrina relief. They pledged to raise $270,000 for victims of the disaster—all of which would go directly to victims. Or so they said. They threw a benefit concert that brought in $11,210 and delivered the money to Meeks. All told, Meeks's charity raised a little over $30,000 in the name of disaster relief. (If you weren't keeping count, New Direction missed its goal by an astounding $240,000.) So how much went to help victims?

According to tax records, New Direction shelled out a whopping $1,392 to victim expenses.[14] Meeks would later claim he wasn't responsible for the actions of the charity he helped found, and said he doesn't know what happened to the money. Neither do the victims.

Darryl Greene, husband of an original board member of New Direction, is part of Team Meeks. He was also convicted of stealing half a million dollars from several New York City agencies.[15] Perhaps he knows where the money went? Then there's New York state senator Malcolm Smith, who helped cofound New Direction and acquired $56,000 of state funding for it.[16] Maybe he knows where the Katrina money went? The thing is, Meeks's pal Malcolm is a little busy right now: he's fighting charges that he tried to bribe his way onto the New York City mayoral ballot.

Actually, if you're a betting man and want to wager on whom the feds plan to investigate next, just randomly pick someone close to G. Money. Much higher odds than the slot machines! As your luck would have it, the feds are investigating whether Team Meeks rigged the process to snag a multibillion-dollar casino contract for a consortium known as Aqueduct Entertainment Group.[17] The contract was eventually rescinded. The New York inspector general's office released a blistering 308-page report detailing the corruption, which included "secret lobbying and more than $100,000 in campaign donations from the bidders."[18] Malcolm Smith (see above) reportedly bragged about how the casino deal would serve as his "golden parachute" once he quit the state senate.[19] Then there was the involvement of Floyd Flake, one of Aqueduct's early investors.[20] This is the same Floyd Flake who is Meeks's political mentor and held his congressional seat before him.

Rinse, Wash, Repeat.

For his part, Meeks dismissed the allegations of corruption regarding Aqueduct as—wait for it—racism.[21]

But hey—let's not act like Meeks is coldhearted. (Go with me on this.) Just because he used a tragedy to raise money, then never delivered any of the funds to the intended victims, doesn't make him a bad guy. And just because everyone around him is under investigation, well, that could happen to anyone, right? He does have a softer side. In fact, Meeks has personally hopscotched the planet in the name of helping a friend.

The friend? None other than the now-convicted Ponzi schemer Allen Stanford, who defrauded investors of up to $7 billion. Meeks went to Venezuela to try to get Hugo Chávez to launch a criminal probe into one of Stanford's former employees.[22] But I mean come on! He traveled all the way to South America! Have you flown internationally lately? Those meals are *not* that good. A modern-day saint, that Meeks.

Stanford, currently serving a 110-year prison sentence for a "massive Ponzi scheme," helped bankroll the Inter-American Economic Council (IAEC). Remember all those fancy trips Meeks took to the Caribbean? The IAEC paid for six of them.[23] In return, Stanford asked Meeks to, among other things, talk to his good socialist dictator buddy Hugo Chávez about launching a criminal probe into one of Stanford's enemies.

The *New York Post*, in its inimitably understated style, was all over Meeks's malfeasance:

A month later, Meeks went to Venezuela for a string of meetings, including some with Chavez, on a trip that was reportedly hailed as a thank-you for the henchman's deal with former Rep. Joseph P. Kennedy II (D-Mass.) to bring low-cost heating oil to Northeast states. A year later, [Gonzalo] Tirado—who had accused Stanford of running business scams—was charged with tax evasion and stealing.[24]

See! Meeks isn't such a bad guy. He's happy to pitch in and lend a hand to a brother in need . . . especially if that brother in need is likely to go to prison in the near future.

Honestly, this is just the tip of the iceberg on Meeks. He checks so many boxes from the corrupt-pol playbook that he may be about to invent a new verb. From now on, aspiring elected officials with questionable character will aspire to "Meeks" their way through Congress. Both his sister and wife are paid lobbyists. You think that happens by accident? He also appears to be the subject of an ongoing federal investigation[25] targeting New York politicians, though he's likely to skate by on that one as well if his luck holds.[26] After all, Meeks is a guy who willingly associates himself with the likes of Charlie Rangel, the ethically challenged congressman who's a veteran at playing the "race card."

Taxpayers don't detest Meeks because of the color of his skin. We loathe him because of the content of his character. He's the worst kind of Crapitalism kingpin. He cheats taxpayers. And he steals goodwill from every aspiring honest politician out there, who has to suffer by comparison. Greg Meeks sucks. Period.

And he's just the beginning.

2 Representative Maxine Waters

It's time for the bully pulpit of the White House to bring the gangstas in, put them around the table and let them know that if they don't come up with loan modifications and keep people in their homes that they've worked so hard for, we're gonna tax them out of business.[1]

—Representative Maxine Waters (D-CA)

The United States House of Representatives, since its formation in 1789, has been the legislative home to any number of Honest-to-God Great Americans. Abraham Lincoln. Daniel Webster. Henry Clay. Sonny Bono. (Just kidding. Although he was pretty awesome in *Airplane 2*.)

The point is, no matter how lax we make the list of America's Top House Members, Maxine Waters won't make it. She's behind

Lincoln. She's behind Webster. She's behind Bono. Hell, she'd be behind Cher and Chaz Bono for that matter. In her fifth decade of taking tax dollars for a living, Waters has carved out a reputation as the congressional equivalent of your kooky uncle and the most ridiculous cast member from one of those Real Housewives of Crazytown shows. She's insane, which is fine. She even has a reputation as a sort of cult hero among the college kids and the hipsters for her ridiculous pursuit of socialist policies. But she's made millions of dollars for her friends and family as a result, which, you know, is less fine, especially for a socialist.

How insane? We're talking about a woman who still blames the CIA for the drug problems of the black communities. I guess she never bothered to rent *American Gangster* on Netflix. (Maxine, you should do it. It's got Denzel.) A member of the Congressional Black Caucus, she has sponsored legislation that would bring about reparations for slavery. In 2009—or more than a century after anyone actually had any slaves.

During the 1992 Rodney King "Can't We All Get Along" riots— where sixty-three people died and more than one thousand buildings were vandalized—she sympathized with the looters. When asked about the South Korean–owned stores in her district that were robbed by unruly mobs, Waters acted like going out and stealing stuff was the right thing to do. About the looters, she said:

> There were mothers who took this as an opportunity to take some milk, to take some bread, to take some shoes. . . . They are not crooks.[2]

This makes me wonder if, besides lacking a moral compass, she might also lack a fundamental understanding of some basic parts of the English language. Specifically, the word *crooks*. But I guess I shouldn't be shocked that she doesn't think the looters are crooks. The amount of money she's siphoned off the taxpayer teat for her and her family's benefit will piss you the hell off. But when it comes to her family, though, "Money" Maxine can do a whole lot better than snatch bread and shoes off a store shelf.

Remember the whole financial crisis of 2008? The "Too Big to Fail" banks and other financial institutions that cozied up to Uncle Sam and got huge bailouts? Well, it turns out one of the banks with its hands out was a Boston bank called OneUnited, one of the biggest black-owned banks in the country. Maxine the Compassionate, Maxine the Considerate, didn't let the fact that the bank was three thousand miles away from her own district stop her from personally calling the Treasury secretary at the time, Hank Paulson, and asking to set up a meeting between him and members of the National Bankers Association. But when the meeting actually happened, members from only one bank showed up—OneUnited. Just an example of Mama Maxine doing a minority bank a solid, right? Being down with the struggle? Power to the People?

Not quite.

See, Maxine's husband, Sid Williams, is a former board member with OneUnited and owned between $500,000 and $1,000,000 in stock in this bank. Waters was the chairwoman of a powerful banking subcommittee at the time, so getting the meeting for the bank advocates was a huge coup. And so the fact that the bank had "a record of bad investments and extravagant spending" didn't stop the feds from shelling out $12 million in bailout cash to help them out.[3] But it wasn't just that she helped set up the meeting, allowing the bank to get the cash. Money Maxine also got her pal Barney Frank to help change the rules so banks like theirs would get extra help, rigging the system so that OneUnited could count the bailout cash among its preexisting assets *before it actually arrived*. Of the

707 financial institutions to get TARP money, Maxine's husband's bank was the only one to get the special favors it received.[4] She's a hell of a friend. But whom did she help more than herself? You think that stock her husband had would have suffered a bit if the bank didn't get all those privileged perks? We'll never know. And unfortunately, neither will the esteemed congresswoman from California's bank account.

Even worse, Waters kept the whole part about her having a major financial stake in the rescue of this bank under wraps. As left-wing nonprofit Citizens for Responsibility and Ethics in Washington (CREW) wrote in its report on the issue, "Rep. Waters did not disclose her financial ties to OneUnited to Treasury officials when she requested meetings between regulators and bank officials."[5]

According to CREW, the former Bush administration official who helped set up the meeting was pissed that Waters, um, forgot to mention how the bailout would directly benefit her husband's portfolio: "(Learning of the connection) was upsetting to me. We are talking about something potentially explosive and embarrassing to the administration. She should have at least let us know."[6]

The House Committee on Ethics actually conducted an investigation into this deal, as blatant as it was. But, after some cursory hearings and a few claims of racism, Money Maxine was cleared.[7] Because that's the way they do it in the U.S. House.

Of course, the whole bailout process might not have happened had we not had the financial collapse. And one of the biggest reasons for the collapse was the disaster that was the Fannie Mae and Freddie Mac mortgage meltdown. But in 2004, old Maxine had no problems with the institutions' leadership. At a congressional hearing on the matter, Waters lauded Franklin Raines's "outstanding leadership" at Fannie Mae. That's like saying the captain of the

Titanic had excellent night vision. And all it cost you and me was a couple of trillion dollars. No biggie.

Maxine's affection for low-income mortgage assistance didn't stop there—especially when her husband was hired by a guy pimping one of the programs. In 2007, Waters sponsored a bill that would keep seller-funded down payment assistance programs viable, even though the IRS called them "scams."[8] Another example of Waters being a race-baiting Robin Hood? Not exactly. As it turns out, the lobbyist for the program had hired Waters's husband as a consultant. Even after the feds outlawed the practice of the program's "mortgage middleman" as part of their efforts to deal with the housing collapse, Waters sponsored a bill to try to overturn the ban.[9] Stop and think about this. Literally months after the worst economic downturn since the Great Depression, Waters is out there trying to resuscitate some of the problematic practices that caused the collapse in the first place. That her husband was on the payroll, surely, was just a coincidence.

Hooking her husband's former bank up with some federal bailout money and sponsoring legislation to benefit his benefactor were just the latest in a long line of helpful handouts to her freeloading family, though.

Being Maxine Waters's kid is big business. In 2004, the *Los Angeles Times* did a report showing that her "family members earned more than $1 million in the past eight years doing business with candidates, companies and causes she helped." Both her daughter, Karen, and son, Edward, collected fees from campaigns she endorsed, and her husband worked for a company that received a government contract Waters's cronies steered his way.[10]

You'd think being affiliated with Waters would be some sort of political STD, with only distance, time, and a healthy dose of penicillin being able to make it all better. But in fact, people pay good money to get the Maxine Waters endorsement. So Money Maxine, never one to miss a trick, figured out how to cash in on her endorsement by getting her family in on the action. They formed this thing called L.A. Vote, a political organization that sends out a mailer advertising the campaigns that Waters endorses. It's like a Christmas Card from Hell. And all of her demon spawn are getting rich because of it.

L.A. Vote raked in $1.7 million over an eight-year span, fees paid by candidates and campaigns for issues hoping to gain political traction. Of that, Maxine's daughter collected nearly half a million. And her son, Edward, he of the basketball-coach-by-day-and-political-consultant-by-night pedigree, cashed in $115,000. Because being able to break down a zone defense is just like mobilizing your target issue voters, yo!

Of course, when asked about the fairly obvious relationship between the companies and campaigns that were keeping her kids on the payroll and the causes she was supporting, Waters fessed up to everything. And by fessed up, I mean pretended there was no relationship at all. She said, "They do their business, and I do mine."[11] Good one, Maxine.

For as despicable as it is, Waters's operation is actually pretty brilliant. She's like a Godmother, only with fewer Sonnys and more Fredos. By raising money through the mailer, she becomes exempt from other standard fundraising rules, like donation limits. So everyone from California lieutenant governor Gavin Newsom to Senator Barbara Boxer is sending money her way to get on the mailer. Money that only ends up back in her family's pocket.

Of course, that's all someone else's money. Want to advertise in the mailer? That's your problem. But our tax dollars end up feathering the nest of the Waters Family Tree. Maxine's grandson is her chief of staff, not exactly a volunteer position. He gets a nice six-figure salary from the congressional office. A taxpayer-funded salary. We're talking about $700,000 in total thus far.[12] So between that and her kids' profits, Waters's descendants have made more than $2 million off Money Maxine. In her family tree, the roots run deep. And the branches bloom with cash.

But with Waters, it's far more than just endorsements for sale. In 2010 she earmarked $1.76 million for Loyola Marymount University.[13] That was the same year Loyola was listed by the Center for Responsive Politics as a "top donor" to Waters's campaign.[14]

But the whole wink-wink, nod-nod nature of earmarks was too subtle for her. Plus, her Republican colleagues put an end to that practice after they regained control of the House of Representatives. So now Waters just implores folks right to their faces that she wants to be bought off. "Influence us," she told a roomful of bankers in Los Angeles, encouraging them to hire more lobbyists. "Help us understand the intricacies of your business." As the *New York Times* put it, Maxine was "reminding them of her new role as the ranking Democrat on the House Financial Services Committee."[15]

Of course, if someone else makes money, then Money Maxine has a problem. In 2008, Waters suggested, in a hearing full of oil executives during a spike of gas prices, that America should "socialize . . . all of your companies." It astounded and confounded everyone in the room. Namely, the people whose companies she had just overtly threatened to seize. But that's just part of this chick's MO. She sees some shiny thing that someone else has, then snatches it for her own personal benefit. Like bread on a shelf. Or a private company's oil.

What makes Maxine Waters so bad isn't that she has money. Hey—you've abused your position of authority for personal profit.

Congratulations. This makes you virtually indistinguishable from any number of other current members of Congress. The thing about her is—she's definitely a bastard about it.

Maxine Waters is mean. You'd think someone hitching a ride on the back of the American taxpayer, and bringing their whole damn family along with them, would at least be nice about it. Not her.

In 2011 Waters said the Tea Party could "go straight to hell . . . and I intend to help them get there."[16] It makes sense. Of course she hates people dedicated to protecting tax dollars. She's dedicated to *taking* them. But what can you do to try to get your way if the initiatives you promote are, on their face, self-serving, fiscally irresponsible, and otherwise just moronic? I'll give you a hint: it rhymes with "race card."

Among her other hobbies, besides funneling business to family members and being investigated by House ethics committees, Maxine also enjoys throwing around racially loaded language. I just hope she warms up first. I'd hate for her to strain something.

She called former Los Angeles mayor Richard Riordan a "plantation owner."[17] She suggested that until Barack Obama was elected president, the world hated "racist America."[18] And she can wax poetic, and polemic, for days on White Power. In an interview with the *Los Angeles Times*, she said something that explains quite a bit of her mind-set and methods:

> Policy, for the most part, has been made by white people in America, not by people of color. And they have tended to take care of those things that they think are important. Whether it's their agricultural subsidies, or other kinds of expenditures that are certainly not expenditures for poor people or for people of color. And so we have to band together and keep fighting back.[19]

There you have it, America. Blacks and poor people need to band together and keep fighting back. The funny thing is, while Maxine counts any number of the former category in her family, thanks to her blatant and unethical abuse of power, I'm not sure how many more of the latter she currently has to worry about. Maybe that's her deal. Her legislative ideas are a joke. Her effectiveness as a congresswoman sucks. She can't get her way on socializing oil companies or passing slavery reparations. So she does the only thing she can—cheat like hell. Her family has been getting rich for years because of it. And she owes it all to you and me. And also to political correctness. Because when people call her out on it, she cries racist. People who should know better cower in fear. Well, not anymore. Maxine Waters, you are a Crapitalist. It isn't your skin color that concerns me. It's that you exploit and manipulate. You use black and white to make the green. And we're tired of it.

3 Terry McAuliffe

Let me tell you, it's a lot easier to raise money for a governor. They have all kinds of business to hand out, road contracts, construction jobs, you name it.

—Terry McAuliffe, *What a Party!*

You remember the nineties, right? A period of economic prosperity and moral decay a decade that started with Murphy Brown controversially deciding to be a single mother and ending with a White House that served as the basis for the reality show *Temptation Island*. Probably the first name that comes to mind when you think of the nineties is Bill Clinton. And after you remember his name, a flood of other names might surface: Gennifer Flowers. Paula Jones. Monica Lewinsky.

But the name that lingers the longest from Clinton's scandalous Skankadex isn't any of those. Incredibly, from the man who brought us Linda Tripp and that famous blue dress, Terry McAuliffe is the Clinton legacy's biggest stain.

McAuliffe is a longtime political fundraiser for Democrats who brags in his memoir about wrestling an alligator in 1980 to secure a donation for Jimmy Carter. The incident, which landed both McAuliffe and the alligator on the cover of *Life* magazine at the time, would be among his more dignified professional endeavors.

We're talking about a guy who complained after 9/11 that security concerns and, you know, decorum, kept him from traveling and fundraising as extensively as he would have liked to. In his memoir, McAuliffe called himself a "caged rat" after the terrorist attacks and whined because "I was one of our party's most visible spokesmen, and I had to keep a low profile after the attacks. . . . I couldn't travel. I couldn't make political calls. I couldn't make money calls."

Classy, Terry. Families of victims kept candlelight vigil as they worried whether their loved ones were alive. McAwful was upset because he couldn't go raise money and keep his name in the news.

Long before 9/11, though, the man known as "Tricky Terry" was inventing new and unprecedentedly seedy ways to disgrace America.

The *Washington Post* chalks up McAuliffe's friendship with Clinton to the meshing of two outsized personas. In an article about Clinton's presence at a McAuliffe for Governor fundraiser, the *Post* reported, "Confidants said Clinton is drawn to McAuliffe's loud Irish humor and feeds off his endless optimism and energy."

What it didn't mention was how Clinton feeds off McAuliffe's money, too.

When Bill left office in 2001, he borrowed money from McAuliffe to build his mansion in Chappaqua, New York. The $1.35 million raised all sorts of ethical issues for both the lender and lendee, but ethical issues had long stopped bothering both parties.

Like most of the women Clinton would become entangled with while in office, McAuliffe wanted access to the White House bedrooms. But unlike the distinguished members of Clinton's Coital Cabinet, McAuliffe wanted to be paid. The idea of allowing high-dollar donors to the Clinton campaigns access to the Lincoln Bedroom is wholeheartedly attributed to Trashy Terry. Apparently none of the other occupants of the White House had the imagination, forethought, or complete and total moral bankruptcy to rent out two centuries of American history to the highest bidder.

But presidential pajama parties are only the tip of the iceberg for this guy. He raised $275 million for Clinton while Slick Willie was in office. And when Hillary ran for Senate, and later president, McAuliffe was by her side as well. What did he get for his loyalty, and generosity, albeit with other people's money? Well, he's currently governor of Virginia. So there's that.

I still can't believe it. How does one of the country's largest slimeballs get to be in charge of the state Washington and Jefferson called home? Well, it's amazing what you can do with $32 million in campaign donations and a shameless willingness to drop the Clinton name. In his look at all things Washington, author Mark Leibovich devotes quite a bit of time to McAuliffe and his relationship with Clinton. For McAuliffe at least, it appears the two are often inseparable:

> If McAuliffe's signature is fund-raising, his principal identity is as a professional best friend to Bill Clinton. The title of McAuliffe's memoir *What a Party!* might as well be Let Me Tell You Another Story About Me and Bill Clinton. . . . To deprive

McAuliffe of the words "Bill Clinton" would be like depriving a mathematician of numbers.[1]

Why do you think the association with Clinton was so important to the lifetime moneyman? The guy has fundraised for presidents before, but you don't hear him telling Jimmy Carter stories all the time. (Side note—what are Jimmy Carter stories like? And how many of them involve Jimmy swapping tool belts with people on Habitat for Humanity builds as a prank? Forty percent?)

Could it be that access to power was an integral step in Trashy Terry's template? Everywhere he goes, he follows the same playbook. He flaunts his connections with the powerful, uses them to gain access to capital, sets some aside for himself, then sends some downstream to his network of cronies. It can be helpfully summed up by the following, completely coincidental acronym: D.I.C.K.—Demonstrate Intimacy, Cash in, Kick back.

McAuliffe admits as much himself, telling the *New York Times* in 1999, "I've met all of my business contacts through politics. It's all interrelated."

Names like Global Crossing and Telergy may sound familiar to longtime cronyism chroniclers. They serve as great illustrations, among many, of how Tricky Terry D.I.C.K.s over Americans.

Global Crossing was a telecom company McAuliffe sunk $100K into. A year after it went public, McAuliffe cashed out for a cool $8 million. That the company would later go bankrupt, costing investors a reported $54 billion and all ten thousand employees their jobs, was of little consequence to McAuliffe. Nor to the CEO, Gary Winnick. Trashy Terry hooked up Winnick with his good buddy Bill Clinton, setting them up on a golf outing. Winnick would later cut Clinton a $1 million check for his presidential library.[2]

Telergy was an Internet start-up that went bust after the tech bubble burst in the early 2000s—but not before putting McAuliffe on its board in 1999. Winnick, the Global Crossing CEO who was now great pals with Bubba Clinton, invested $40 million shortly after. McAuliffe was paid $1.2 million for his troubles.[3]

McAuliffe has been, and is, a veteran practitioner of the ultimate D.I.C.K. move. But what else would you expect from a guy who, according to his memoir, left his pregnant wife in the delivery room so he could attend a *Washington Post* soirée?

How do you think McAuliffe was able to raise so much money for so many years? McAuliffe wasn't collecting checks. He was selling *access*. He's the ultimate middleman. How else do you think he raised $100 million for this?

If a VW bug and a micro machine had sex, and then the micro machine abused alcohol and illegal narcotics for the duration of its pregnancy, the resulting spawn would look better than one of GreenTech's automotive abortions. It's like a Smart Car that ate too many lead paint chips growing up.

Just like in real life, though, maybe once you found out who the parents are you wouldn't be shocked the kid turned out ugly and slow.

GreenTech Automotive is a company McAuliffe swore would "reinvent the automobile." What it actually reinvented was the modern paradigm by which Crapitalism is practiced. As the *Washington Post* noted, "GreenTech fits into a pattern of investments in which McAuliffe has used government programs, political connections and access to wealthy investors of both parties in pursuit of big profits for himself."[4]

Basically, GreenTech is a hybrid-car company, to use the term loosely. McAuliffe bought 25 percent of the company in 2009 after his failed bid for governor despite some dubious legal issues surrounding one of the principals of the previous version of the company. McAuliffe was looking for a, um, vehicle by which to rebrand himself as a business-savvy jobs creator. GreenTech fit the bill.

McAuliffe bragged about all the jobs that would be located "in the heart of Virginia."[5] What it really produced is "a nearly vacant lot" in Mississippi. That's because then–Mississippi governor Haley Barbour came through with millions of taxpayer dollars in incentives and abatements for the company. McAuliffe and Barbour, coincidentally, are great friends and invested in an upscale D.C. restaurant together called Social Reform, which is hailed as a "bipartisan" dining experience. But the GreenTech deal was standard operating procedure, according to Barbour.

Hillary Clinton's brother Anthony Rodham also bellied up to the taxpayer trough in the GreenTech deal. Rodham, with his illustrious professional pedigree as a former prison guard, led the board of Gulf Coast Funds Management—the company that secured GreenTech's primary investors.

But neither Rodham, nor his company, put up the $100 million GreenTech now boasts in its account. A lot of cash came from China. But why? And why are people still giving money to a company that is employing only about eighty people in Mississippi?

Virginia might be for lovers. But when it comes to GreenTech, Mississippi is for cronies.

This is a company that features a former governor and IRS commissioner on its board. And former president Clinton showed up for the Mississippi plant's grand opening, along with McAuliffe's fellow restaurant investor Barbour. It's the ultimate good ole boy network. That none of them knows anything about cars isn't really a problem. They haven't built any yet. So what's the interest for the Chinese investors?

One of Mississippi's state representatives was quoted as saying,

"At this point, it sounds like they're selling visas."[6] And he doesn't mean the credit cards.

There is actually a federal program that allows wealthy foreigners to invest in American companies and, if the project is deemed economically viable enough, investors will be granted permanent access to U.S. residence for themselves and their families. It's called the EB-5 program, and it appears to be GreenTech's primary product of interest to its Chinese investors.

Secret GreenTech documents revealed the promises they were making to Chinese investors about the access McAuliffe would have to governing agencies. No wonder the money was pouring in.

The Securities and Exchange Commission is now investigating possible claims of fraud related to the program. And several whistle-blowers have also come forward on the EB-5 deal, something U.S. senator Chuck Grassley noted as "unusual."

A Department of Homeland Security (DHS) official, Doug Smith, who exchanged emails with McAuliffe over the visa issue, left DHS shortly after the story came to light. He now works for a political consulting company run by a major donor to the McAuliffe for Governor campaign.[7] Again, a D.I.C.K. move by the master.

This should surprise precisely no one. Ultimately, GreenTech is building a large plant in China, though reports are that they can't even get off the ground there, either. But the investors got their visas. The whole program was a scam, and it seems unlikely to benefit any American taxpayers. Except, of course, McAuliffe.

When asked why, after all his public declarations to the contrary, he located GreenTech in a state other than Virginia, McAuliffe told the truth: "We don't bid on big car plants here and shame on us. . . . You gotta incentivize. Mississippi gave me 200 free acres, they gave me tax incentives, they gave me the infrastructure to lead into the factory. This is what states do all over the country."[8]

You gotta incentivize. For some reason, this doesn't comfort me, nor should it comfort anyone who lives anywhere near Virginia. Terry McAuliffe, the incentivizer. This is the same guy who, when talking about his role as a fundraiser, had this to say in his own damn memoir about the office he currently holds: "Let me tell you, it's a lot easier to raise money for a governor. They have all kinds of business to hand out, road contracts, construction jobs, you name it."

Of course, now that McAuliffe is in office he'll change his ways, right? Would you believe me if I told you that his first appointment (first freaking appointment!) went to a GreenTech lobbyist? But let's not stop there. McAuliffe later appointed a GreenTech fundraiser to the Virginia Lottery. Both of those appointments, however, are not to be confused with the guy he nominated who was under federal investigation for "improperly" lobbying Congress. For real.[9] McAuliffe also vetoed an ethics bill passed unanimously by the general assembly that "would have prevented him from asking for political donations from companies seeking loans or grants from a state economic development fund."[10]

And that's just his first six months as governor.

During the GreenTech rollout, Bill Clinton was asked if he would buy a car from McAuliffe. "Absolutely," Clinton insisted with a straight face. "I would buy a new car from Terry." But then came the punch line. "A used car? I am not so sure about a used car." Clinton guffawed at his own joke, then reportedly wheeled around to repeat to Barbour his clever turn of phrase.[11] The tragic thing about Virginia's governor is, McAuliffe probably loves telling that story, too. Anything that will remind people of his relationship to Bill. Of his relationship to power. Maybe now that he's a governor he won't need Clinton as much as the other way around. Maybe now he won't be such a used car salesman. But for Virginians, it's too late to return the lemon.

years—tying the record for longest sentence ever for corrupt public official.[1] Those are the headlines Detroit gets these days. Detroit used to be Axel Foley from *Beverly Hills Cop*. Now it's Judge Reinhold from *Beverly Hills Cop 3*.

Chris Hansen from NBC's *Dateline* did a piece on Detroit's despair in 2010. Yes, the same Chris Hansen who confronts pedophiles in kitchens. So if you're keeping score at home, if you see Chris Hansen, either you are a pedophile, or you live in the municipal equivalent of one. Hansen called Detroit "a shell of its former self."[2] He then noted some of the sorry statistics saddling Detroit before making this interesting observation:

> One third of the people here live in poverty. Almost half the adults are illiterate, and about 75 percent of kids drop out of school. I could be describing some ravaged foreign nation, but this is the middle of America.

When Chris Hansen, who deals with human filth for a living, compares you to a third-world country, you've got problems. But this is Detroit. A Democrat-controlled town that is paying people to move back into it. It's a city that became the largest in American history to declare bankruptcy. And it also happens to be Mike Ilitch's playground.

Ilitch made his fortune in what I consider one of the most deplorable endeavors ever. He's selling crappy pizza. I'm from Brooklyn. I know pizza. Little Caesars isn't pizza. It's cardboard topped in cheese, tomato sauce, and regret.

The thing is, it was good enough for Ilitch. Millions of no-pizza-palate-possessing Americans sought comfort from their lives in underdeveloped crust and cute corporate logos. And it made Ilitch

4 Mike Ilitch—Pizza Pimp

I'm committed to spend what it takes.

—Mike Ilitch

In its heyday of the 1950s, Detroit could lay claim to being one of the great cities in America. An industry town, producing a product second to none in the world, supported by a quintessentially American work ethic. Its music, culture, and entertainment options were highly valued and sought after. And then all of it went away.

It didn't happen overnight. Union greed, corruption, and a destructive devotion to the Democratic Party have taken a former jewel of the American experience and turned it into a beat-up and discarded soda can, like the many that adorn its littered streets. The former mayor, Kwame Kilpatrick, went to prison on federal corruption charges. Kilpatrick got sentenced to twenty-eight millions. Little Caesars started offering the "second pizza for the same price" deal in the 1970s, and business has been booming ever since. Estimates show that Little Caesars sells more than a billion dollars of pizzas a year.[3] That's a lot of dough.[4]

And fair enough: if you can convince millions of folks to fork over cash for cheese-covered crap, good for you. It's a free, if tasteless, market.

But the way he made his money would be a clue for how he would go about conducting other business, business that cost taxpayers millions—and they wouldn't even get crappy pizza to show for it.

A 1995 article in the *Los Angeles Times* profiling the pizza magnate detailed how Ilitch's pathway to profit lay in franchising the Little Caesars brand. The article attributed the move to a plane trip in 1962, when Ilitch sat next to a businessman from Texas. The best way to expand the operation, the article reports the unnamed businessman as saying, "is to use other people's money."[5]

And by "other people's money," he means yours.

Since that article was published, Ilitch has continued serving up endeavors for the citizens of Detroit to consume, and pocketing fist loads of cash at every turn. Ilitch is now said to be worth almost $3.6 billion. He owns two professional sports franchises and numerous other entertainment-related ventures. But one theme runs throughout his empire—he has used other people's money to build it. And a ton of tax dollars. All at a time when Detroit was going bankrupt.

As *Forbes* points out:

The real tragedy is that Detroit's pain could have been avoided if city officials had not ignored sound economic reasoning in their eagerness to spend other people's money for their own short-term benefit. The unwillingness of the city to live within its means has predictably resulted in disaster.

A disaster that has only added to the pizza pimp's bank account. And it isn't as if the Ilitches have steered clear of political involvement over this time frame. Mike and his wife, Marian, have greased enough palms along the way to keep their tax subsidies rolling in. Both Mike and Marian dished out $5,000 to Democratic senator Debbie Stabenow, plus $10,000 for a Democratic state committee. But Republicans, to paraphrase Michael Jordan, buy pizzas and hand out tax money, too. So they also threw cash to the Republican National Committee and to Mitt Romney in 2012. No matter how 2012 worked out they were covered. Their daughter, Denise, was a huge backer for Obama in 2008 and 2012, and is considered something of a rising star in Michigan's Democratic Party. There was even some talk she would run for governor of Michigan.[6] But Denise decided not to run. Not that it would have made much of a difference for the Ilitch family's access to taxpayer dollars. They've always gotten what they wanted. Little Caesars might not deliver, but for the Ilitches, the city of Detroit always did.

Here's how their taxpayer heist operates.

Two years after that *Los Angeles Times* article was published, Ilitch, owner of both the Detroit Tigers baseball team and the Detroit Red Wings hockey squad, pitched city officials on a new ballpark for his Tigers. No problem, right? I mean, the guy's a billionaire. Let him do what he wants with his own money. The problem is, Ilitch wasn't just tapping his own piggy bank. He was tapping taxpayers.

Ilitch got the city to issue $80 million in municipal bonds toward the construction of the new stadium, built in downtown Detroit.[7] That's $80 million he didn't have to spend himself—or

40 percent of the total cost of the stadium's construction. Because of interest, taxpayers are estimated to be on the hook for up to $120 million when the bonds are paid off. All so the pizza pimp wouldn't have to pay full price for his new stadium.

Ilitch is hardly alone when it comes to getting tax money to pay for new stadiums. Hell, he isn't even the only guy in his own city getting money for it. As in the Ford family, yes that Ford family, that owns the Detroit Lions. They got money for the construction of the Lions' new stadium, located next to Comerica Park, the tax-subsidized home of the Detroit Tigers. So next to each other, in the heart of Detroit, are two memorials to titans of industry. And both of them milked a bankrupt city's depleted tax coffers to build them.

To be fair, studies have shown that taxpayer-financed stadiums can sometimes be a good investment. They just aren't a good investment for the cities paying for them. People do end up spending money at the new ballpark, but it inevitably comes at the expense of other local recreational opportunities. So the wealthy team owner's gain is someone else's loss. Unsurprisingly, new stadiums are sort of like performance-enhancing drugs for the owners' bottom line. They maximize revenue from the luxury boxes and seat licenses, and minimize their costs by letting you and me chip in via tax hikes. Allen Sanderson, an economist at the University of Chicago, suggested a more effective method: "If you want to inject money into a local economy, it would be better to drop it from a helicopter than invest it into a new ballpark."[8]

Detroit isn't the only city doing this. Bloomberg estimates that, across the country, taxpayers have lost more than $4 billion in subsidies to bondholders.[9] Turns out, crony capitalists across the country are getting pliable politicians to raise a tax here or issue a bond there to make taxpayers pick up their tab. And what happens when new stadiums get built? Ticket prices go up, meaning average sports fans like you and me end up getting priced out of the very thing we got taxed to build.

I would point out, as a native New Yorker, that the new stadium for the Jets and Giants is one of the few new stadiums to be built entirely without tax dollars. Which is good, because as bad a season as they have both had recently, I can't stomach the thought that taxpayers would have ponied up cash to pay for them.

But even if the Jets and Giants had been given tax dollars for MetLife Stadium, it wouldn't be as bad as what Detroit did. Because, you know, Detroit is the largest city in U.S. history to enter into bankruptcy. How a busted and broke city can force taxpayers to pay for stadiums is mind-boggling.

Turns out, the Red Wings need a new arena, too. At least according to Ilitch. So, being the resourceful man he is, and having already secured a boatload of cash to help him build his baseball stadium, Ilitch called a familiar play. He got his cronies in the state legislature to tap the state coffers—to the tune of about $285 million, 60 percent of the arena's projected cost.[10] But the money wouldn't just go to build a new home for the Red Wings. It would build an entirely new "arena district" complete with new construction and renovations of older, classic structures. Care to guess who owns some of those vintage buildings?[11] No, it isn't Eminem. Guess again.

That's right—Ilitch. He already owns buildings like the Fox Theatre and the Detroit Life Building, central pieces in Detroit's urban renewal. And over the last several years the pizza pimp has gone on a buying spree, gobbling up abandoned property that just happens to be located smack-dab in what will be this entertainment district.[12] So that money Ilitch helped secure won't just build a new stadium for him to cash in on; it's also going to renovate his dilapidated ones, too. Talk about Cash for Clunkers!

Keep in mind, the whole thing was projected to cost $650 million. So he has more than one-third of the costs covered, just from his boys in Lansing. Pretty nice move, huh? Surely that would be enough of a boost to get this project that helps his private business off the ground. But when it comes to Detroit, nothing makes sense. Remember, we're talking about a guy who made millions by doubling up on a crappy product and convincing folks it was a deal.

So Mike, not sated by his main course from the state legislature, went for dessert from Detroit. He asked the city, a bankrupt city, to kick in another $45 million for the effort. The balls on that one, huh? But here is the crazy part—they actually considered it!

Literally, at the same time a judge was deciding if Detroit can file Chapter 9 bankruptcy, the city council was contemplating giving Ilitch another $45 million for a new arena complex that would, among other things, host the Red Wings.[13]

Really.

Go back and read that sentence again. That they even considered it is stupefying. Detroit is so broke that almost half the streetlights don't work.[14] Why not spend the money on that? Instead, the city is going to give taxpayer dollars to a billionaire so his company can build a new venue for a private enterprise he already owns.

The good news is that the city council didn't shell out an additional $45 million. The bad news is that Ilitch got them instead to sell the city's thirty-nine parcels of land located within the development to his comanager for . . . $1.

One freaking dollar.[15] The assessed value of the land was $3 million.

In what has to be the understatement of the century, city

councilwoman Mary Sheffield asked, "Why are we transferring over this (public) property for a dollar when the value of the land is worth way more than that?"[16]

Good question.

Yet this is exactly the kind of behavior, and decision making, that has Detroit asking for a bailout. And has hundreds of millions of our tax dollars headed its way.[17]

You'd think city officials or business owners in the city would be embarrassed by what Detroit has become. You'd think they'd be embarrassed to be associated with the municipal equivalent of a black hole. But with Ilitch, you'd be wrong. Turns out, in addition to having his hand out for tax dollars, not paying a debt is also fairly familiar terrain.

Much like the octopi that get thrown onto the ice in celebration of a Red Wings goal, Ilitch has his tentacles in many parts of the city. Having your hand in the till in so many different parts of the city has to be confusing for the family Ilitch. Undoubtedly, they lose track, from time to time, of when they are collecting tax money and when they have to actually pay it. How else to explain the fact that, while the negotiations were ongoing about how much money Mike and Marian would get for their new arena, the Ilitches owed the city more than $1.5 million in back property taxes?[18] It's true. Apparently, Mike loves to take from the city, but when it comes time to actually paying out, he stiffs Joe Taxpayer on the bill.

One of Ilitch's companies, Olympia Entertainment, reportedly was negligent in following the terms of its city lease. According to the *Detroit News*, part of the Red Wings lease said they would pay the city 25 percent of any cable TV rights for live broadcasts. Well, believe it or not given its financial situation, the city performed an audit and found that, hey what do you know, Ilitch's company never really got around to cutting that check. The audit found that Olympia, and Ilitch, owed the city more than $70 million.[19] I guess we figured out why Detroit is going bankrupt. I take it back about spending money on streetlights. Let's just create an Accounts Receivable division—and have them set up shop on Mikey Millions's front door. There you go, Detroit—problem solved!

5 Chris Dodd

No lobbying, no lobbying!

—Chris Dodd

There are sharks flooding the streets! And now there is one swimming in your pool.

—*Sharknado*

There's an old saying that goes, "Politics is Hollywood for ugly people." The implication is that people who lack the looks to be actors instead seek fame and fortune by playing roles on the other side of the country. They go to Washington to pretend they are serving the people. Even though it doesn't pay as well as its California counterpart, it's great work if you can get it. You don't have to have plastic surgery nearly as often, and you can get steady work well past your physical prime without having to play someone's grandparent. And you don't have to get STDs from sleeping your way to the top.

Maybe.

Perhaps no one better typifies the Hollywood/Washington comparisons than former Connecticut senator Chris Dodd. First elected to Congress in 1974, Dodd worked in Washington until 2010, retiring after thirty years in the Senate. As a senator, you get a fair amount of limelight, even if you represent an area that bills itself as the Nutmeg State. But Dodd wasn't content in a supporting role. He wanted to be a leading man.

You probably don't remember, but Chris Dodd actually ran for president in 2008. Well, technically he ran in 2007, because he dropped out three days into the 2008 calendar year. But a guy who finished behind Dennis Kucinich and something called Mike Gravel in a national election somehow still managed to carve himself out a large role in the future.

Dodd returned to the Senate, where he played a major role in the federal bailout. He also helped craft the self-titled Dodd-Frank bill, which was meant to reform Wall Street and protect against a future economic collapse. Both, as we'll learn, benefited some of Chris's favorite "constituents."

But Connecticut Chris's true genius would be proven after he left office. Like many former politicians, Dodd sent the revolving door whirling by cashing in on his access and connections and becoming a lobbyist. But he didn't become the traditional D.C. type. This wasn't Trent Lott or Dick Gephardt setting up shop and renting out his Rolodex by the hour. Dodd finally got himself a leading part. And it pays quite well.

Chris Dodd lobbies for Hollywood now. That he pledged, repeatedly, in his last year in office that he would absolutely, under any circumstances, NOT take a lobbying job, or that the Senate has an official ban on members lobbying their former colleagues for two years after leaving office, didn't seem to prevent him from, as they say on the street, taking a lobbying job.[1] Two months after he left office. And with a nice $2.4 million annual salary.

Talk about a plot twist.

As the head of the Motion Picture Association of America, Dodd leads the organization that "serves as the voice and advocate of the U.S. motion picture, home video and television industries around the world," according to their website.[2] Or, in real-world speak, he bags taxpayer-funded goodies for his corporate cronies.

In *Hollywood Hypocrites* (available wherever books are sold if you haven't read it!), I detailed the welfare scheme Hollywood has lined up for itself, getting tax credits and other perks because they do us the honor of making their crap movies in our country, or states. Critics note that film and television tax credits are ineffective because they "just shift production from one sector to another without producing a net increase in economic activity or employment."[3] Moreover, such crony carve-outs divert funding from long-term state projects, including ones involving education and infrastructure.[4] But since the book came out, unfortunately more states and the federal government, under Dodd's MPAA leadership, have expanded tax subsidies for film production. The MPAA is claiming that film productions are a big boost to the economy. Of course, these are the same people who said having Sylvester Stallone, sixty-eight, and Robert De Niro, seventy-one, star in a boxing movie in 2013 would be a good idea. In reality, film tax credits, like the aging film stars, don't pack much of an economic punch.

Currently, about $1.5 billion of our tax dollars go into Hollywood's pocket through federal and state tax breaks for making movies and TV shows.[5] Dodd loves to brag about how that's money well spent, because the movie business employs over two million people. But that number got a terrible review from the Congressional Research Office, which said in actuality, Hollywood employs about 374,000 people.[6]

Sadly, states are now clambering to offer more money to lure movie productions to their state. Of the twelve "blockbusters" that came out in 2013, eleven were filmed in states like New Mexico, Louisiana, and others that have ramped up their Hollywood handouts in recent years. Of course, Dodd used this to now try to get California to up the $100 million they already set aside for films and TV shows in order to compete with New York's $420 million giveaway.[7] It's a nuclear arms race of tax dollar handouts. And the states are like extras from *The Walking Dead*, staggering along, drawn by the glitz of the Hollywood sign and the glamour of Tom Cruise's new haircut, and gnawing on our tax dollars. It's Crapitalism at its finest. Or worst, depending on your affinity for being eaten by zombies.

Now Dodd gets paid to keep the freebies flowing. During the "fiscal cliff" negotiations at the end of 2012, Dodd called in enough crony chits to score extensions of federal tax and film credits inserted into the final deal, costing taxpayers $430 million.[8]

But as a U.S. senator, he also worked to protect the powers that be (read: the guys who sign his check) by warding off a measure that some claimed would have injected more competition and transparency into the film industry. The Dodd-Frank legislation he coauthored barred a predictions market for films, which would've allowed movie buffs and professional investors to bet on the success or failure of a movie before it hit the big screen.[9] Opening up a "futures market," supporters argued, could've helped smaller production companies get distribution and financing early on if there was significant buzz (and trading) in their favor.[10] Most of the big boys in Hollywood, however, were apoplectic at the proposal and had it crushed.

That there was even a line in the bill meant to save America from another financial catastrophe is an indictment of the way our government screws us over works today. But even worse is that Dodd moved to protect his Hollywood homeboys WHILE HE WAS STILL A SENATOR, and allegedly trying to save the U.S. economy. How did that work?

"Hey, Chris, you've got Tim Geithner on line one to talk about what he thinks the next round of financial reforms need to look like to prevent another Great Depression. And on line two you've got Warner Brothers, who said they'll let you meet Christian Bale and ride in the Batmobile if you can get rid of that thing in the bill."

"Oh sweet, patch me through to Batman, yo."

Taken on its face, Dodd's protection of Hollywood can be seen as just another example of Crapitalism: Dodd looking out for or providing special assistance to an industry that had donated over $150,000 during his last Senate term.[11]

But when you consider the fact that Dodd would bolt the Beltway and cash in with the Tinseltown titans, his actions come off as the worst our country's power structures have to offer—using one position of authority to grease the skids for the next one. Maybe it shouldn't shock anyone that a guy with Dodd's poofy hairdo would be guilty of feathering his nest. But I think we all want to believe that at some level, the people we send to Washington at least *think* about putting our interests above their own. Ironically, we get that idea from the very industry Dodd forsakes his constituents for. Movies like *Mr. Smith Goes to Washington* depict Capra's belief that good people exist and battle the evil special interests on our behalf. It just sucks that in real life, the Mr. Smiths, and Dodds, fight against, not for, us.

Just look at how Mr. Dodd dealt with some of the key players in our country's economic collapse.

As the country's economy was melting down in 2008, Dodd was the chairman of the powerful Senate Banking Committee. Powerless to do anything of actual consequence, the Senate did what it does best: hold hearings. Short on solutions but big on bluster, senators took turns skewering top CEOs about what had gone wrong. But as the *Wall Street Journal* noted, maybe the guy asking the questions should have been the one getting grilled:

> The Connecticut Senator has been out front denouncing the "companies that form the foundation of our financial markets," for "their insatiable appetite for risk." He has also decried "reckless, careless and sometimes unscrupulous actors in the mortgage lending industry" and he has proclaimed that "American taxpayers deserve to know how we arrived at this moment." To that end, we propose he take the stand—under oath.[12]

Turns out, one of the most unscrupulous members of the mortgage lending industry was the leader of a company called Countrywide Financial. Countrywide's CEO was a real peach of a guy named Angelo Mozilo. Angelo was friendly with all the right people. Including Dodd. Mozilo would give sweetheart deals to influential people. They actually called it the "Friends of Angelo" program. And Dodd was right in the thick of it.

Dodd used the program to refinance two of his properties, saving thousands of dollars in the process.[13] And according to Robert Feinberg, Countrywide's loan officer, Dodd knew exactly what kind of special treatment he was getting. But that's not all Dodd knew.

The whole financial collapse happened in large part because of aggressive lending practices and questionable qualification standards. Then unload the loans to government-backed groups like Fannie Mae and Freddie Mac. That was Countrywide's playbook to a tee. And as Senate banking chairman, Dodd oversaw all of it. As the *Wall Street Journal* opined: "Mr. Feinberg's department was charged with making sure those who could influence Fannie and Freddie's appetite for risk were sufficiently buttered up. As a Banking Committee big shot, Mr. Dodd was perfectly placed to be buttered."

What's surprising is how sloppy Dodd was at covering up his corrupt Countrywide dealings, since it was the second time in under a decade that he used his position of power to land a favorable real estate transaction. In 1994 Dodd and a guy named William Kessinger purchased a cottage in a posh part of Ireland. At first, Dodd chipped in only around $12,000, but then a few years later decided to buy out Kessinger for the rest of the land. It turns out that Kessinger was in quite the generous mood. In the midst of Ireland's real estate boom, he accepted Dodd's offer of a meager $122,000. Dodd's Senate disclosure forms would later value that same property near $700,000.[14]

Luck of the Irish, you say? Not exactly. You see, Kessinger had a business associate, Edward Downe Jr., who got convicted of securities fraud. Dodd knew Downe as well. In fact, they were boys. They owned a condo together at one point, Downe contributed to Dodd's campaign, and Dodd even attended Downe's sentencing hearing. As the crony tale goes, during the waning days of the Clinton administration, Dodd lobbied Bill to issue Downe a full pardon. The president obliged.[15] A year later William Kessinger, who, remember, had been Downe's business partner, sold all ten acres of Irish land to Dodd below the market rate.[16] If you believe that was all just one big coincidence, there's a leprechaun I want to introduce you to.

It probably shouldn't surprise us that Dodd was involved with people like Mozilo and Downe. They speak the same language. If you were a friend to Chris, he could be a friend right back. Financial services giant AIG and Chris Dodd go way back. In 2006, AIG exec Joseph Cassano—the man called "patient zero" for the financial collapse—solicited donations for Dodd from his employees over email in an effort to help Dodd bag the Senate Banking Committee chairmanship.[17] AIG employees ended up contributing over $280,000 to Dodd during his time as a senator.[18] Dodd's wife, Jackie Clegg, also worked for a company controlled by AIG. So when AIG needed bailing out, they knew whom they could call on. Chris came through, in a big way. Not only did AIG get their $170 billion in taxpayer-funded bailout bucks, but Dodd inserted a loophole that allowed uncapped bonuses for execs to remain in place.[19] At first, Dodd tried to pretend he didn't know how that got in there. Only after being confronted by mountains of evidence did he fess up. And blame it on members of the Obama administration. Stand-up guy, that Dodd.

As one of the coauthors of Dodd-Frank, obviously Double-Dipping Dodd's fingerprints are all over the "reforms" that have been enacted post-collapse. But it isn't too hard to see the role he played in the collapse, either. In addition to encouraging the risky lending practices of companies like Countrywide and securing big bonuses for his buddies at AIG, Dodd also backed the way Freddie and Fannie would be left holding the bag of practically worthless mortgages.

While outside observers questioned Fannie and Freddie's leadership, Dodd was their staunchest defender. Dodd repeatedly went on record touting the leadership of both institutions. While the mortgage lenders were helping cause the global economic meltdown, Dodd said both were "in sound situation" and "good shape."[20] It's one thing to fiddle while Rome burns. Dodd was actively selling downtown real estate.

Oh, by the way—Dodd was the single largest recipient of Fannie and Freddie campaign donations.[21] So, yeah. Scumbag alert pegged to the max.

As head of the Senate Banking Committee, Dodd collected more than $2 million in donations from the securities and banking industries.[22] And even though he wasn't running for reelection, he was crafting the most influential financial legislation in half a century. For the financial industry, that investment has paid off. While Dodd is now cashing in on other crony connections as the head of MPAA, the industries he helped oversee have "come back from the brink."

> As a group, the six [largest U.S. banks] earned $76 billion in 2013. That is $6 billion shy of the collective all-time high achieved in 2006, a year U.S. housing prices peaked amid a torrid economic expansion. "The industry is back," said Gerard Cassidy, an analyst at RBC Capital Markets. Banks "should break all records" for earnings in 2014, he said.[23]

As a thirty-year milker of the taxpayer teat, Dodd had one of the most important positions in the country. Had he been semicompetent, it's possible the fiscal collapse wouldn't have happened. Instead, he was too busy defending campaign contributors and calling his cronies to compare interest rates. Even though he was cleared by the feckless Senate Ethics Committee for the Countrywide fiasco, Dodd knew this time he had crossed the line. He didn't run for reelection, choosing instead to mooch off movie executives. Dodd essentially left the Senate in shame, only to turn up two months later with "the most prestigious job on K street."[24] Dodd has done such a good job as a crony puppet, he made almost a million dollars more than his lucrative deal was supposed to be worth.[25]

It's an all-too-familiar tale. Politician leaves D.C., cashes in on his connections to pad his clients' profits with your hard-earned tax dollars, then sucks in millions of dollars through the revolving door. The MPAA has the script down pat. Of their 30 lobbyists, 25 of them have previously worked in government.[26] Dodd has a team of former bureaucrats at his disposal who know all the best ways to screw us taxpayers over legislatively. It's like *Sharknado*. One features an endless supply of savage creatures devouring everything in their path to sustain their own existence. The other is a story about sharks flying through the air. Both are catastrophes. But unfortunately for us, one of them is all too real. I can't believe I'm saying this, but where's Ian Ziering when you need him?

6 Chuck Swoboda

We will make electricity so cheap that only the rich will burn candles.

—Thomas Edison[1]

Our goal is to get rid of every single incandescent. . . . Getting consumers' help to do this is essential.

—Chuck Swoboda

One of the most common templates for a joke is "How many (name an ethnicity, gender, religious affiliation) does it take to change a lightbulb?" The implication is that there is nothing simpler than unscrewing one bulb and screwing in another. But, the theory goes, when you get the designated subgroup in place, hilarity ensues.

The funny thing is, a group of people actually went and changed *all* the lightbulbs, not just one of them. But it wasn't blondes or Catholics or Poles. It was Crapitalists. And the joke, it turns out, is on us.

While we used to be able to light our homes and offices with bulbs that cost about forty cents apiece, we will now be forced to buy more expensive bulbs that our tax dollars helped pay for. One of the biggest influences behind the change, and beneficiaries from it, was Cree CEO Chuck Swoboda.

Cree makes lightbulbs. Specifically, lightbulbs that feature light-emitting diode technology, which are known as LEDs. You've seen LED bulbs. They can look different from the traditional bulb, happen to be more expensive, and are toxic if they break (more on that later). But the appeal of the bulb is that they use much less energy than the incandescent bulb, and supposedly last longer, too. So companies like Cree and other LED manufacturers bet that consumers are willing to pay more for a lightbulb now if it saves them money later. And that bet is paying off, as more LED bulbs make their way to the shelves of stores across America, replacing the older, less efficient incandescents.

Of course, they've had a little help.

The Energy Independence and Security Act of 2007 did a few different things, but the one that benefited companies like Cree the most was to place restrictions on the sale of incandescent bulbs in the United States starting in 2012, and eventually phasing them out altogether.[2] That over two-thirds of Americans oppose the forced phaseout doesn't matter.[3] Cree dropped $100,000 lobbying on that bill alone.[4] But Swoboda and company weren't done turning political donations into personal profit.

Swoboda and Cree backed Obama and his green energy agenda in 2008.[5] Since Obama has taken office, Cree's energy has produced a lot more green.

Obama threw Cree nearly $40 million in stimulus cash, and another $18 million through Department of Energy research investments and grants.[6] The same brain trust that rewarded campaign cronies by investing in failed green energy businesses like Solyndra picked out Cree as a winner, too.

For the 2012–13 fiscal year, Swoboda's company bagged $86.9 million in profits. But is that because Cree was a better investment than Solyndra? Is the technology more evolved, or the business plan more skillfully crafted? Or is it because Solyndra wasn't savvy enough to get the government to shut down its competitors?

Swoboda and Cree CFO Mike McDevitt expected a fortune in the first quarter of 2014, nearing $400 million.[7] And why wouldn't they? As the availability of its competition continues to diminish, Cree should only see its future get brighter.

Of course, none of this is a certainty. Cree reluctantly admits as much in a bizarre disclaimer on its own press release:

This press release contains forward-looking statements involving risks and uncertainties, both known and unknown, that may cause actual results to differ materially from those indicated. Actual results may differ materially due to a number of factors, including the risk that we may be unable to manufacture these new products with sufficiently low cost to offer them with acceptable margins; the risk we may encounter delays or other difficulties in ramping up production of our new products; the risk that actual savings will vary from expectations; customer acceptance of LED products; the rapid development of new technology and competing products that may impair demand or render Cree's products obsolete.

Huh?

Kind of funny to see a company that lobbied to make its competition obsolete warning against the same thing happening to them. Then again, maybe it makes sense. Of course they know it can happen. They've done it themselves.

Cree was able to help shape policies that essentially delivered them a government-mandated market share. That's a hell of a business model, thanks to a helping hand from Uncle Sam. It's also an affront to the prosperity-producing engine that is free and unfettered markets.

But Cree has long relied on taxpayer treats.

Since 2001, Cree has vacuumed up $78 million in federal grants.[8] And that doesn't count the millions in state and local tax incentives.[9] You'd think grabbing all those handouts would be tiring. But Swoboda has managed to somehow find the time and energy to get in line for taxpayer-funded projects, too.

Over the years, Swoboda and his legion of LED lobbyists have grabbed nearly $100 million in federal contracts. In 2010 they got then–Speaker of the House Nancy Pelosi to sign off on a $140,000 deal to light the Rayburn House Office Building's cafeteria.[10] It's a great investment, she said, though it will take over ten years for the "investment" to reap actual savings. Think members of Congress won't replace the bulbs before then if it gives them an opportunity to squeeze campaign donations from other potential suppliers?

Me neither.

One of the big advocates of the cafeteria contract was North Carolina senator Kay Hagan.[11] Cree is based in Durham, North Carolina, so Hagan's advocacy makes sense. But she didn't just get Cree money to light the lunchroom where Pelosi and her pals plot more ways to destroy the country. No, she also snagged $500,000 for

Swoboda to make North Carolina's capital the country's first "LED City."[12]

At an appearance at the Cree plant, touting the success of the stimulus money, Vice President Joe Biden said, "I don't think I've ever seen a success story quite like the one here at Cree. . . . It ties so much, so much with what President Obama and I are trying to do: job creation, innovation, environmental impact, domestic manufacturing, exporting American ingenuity around the world. It's all in one package here at Cree."[13]

It really is remarkable: lightbulbs people can't afford or wouldn't buy if they had a choice, funded by a government that uses tax money to prop up a business model and then force it on the people who are paying for it, all in one tidy package.

An LED bulb, by the way, usually costs anywhere from $10 to $20 per unit, while your standard incandescent bulb rings up at the cash register for easily under a buck.[14] That's a substantial price increase up front with the promise of lower energy costs sometime down the road.

To his credit, though, Swoboda is at least up front about the role that our money plays in his business. The Cree SEC filings all but scream their dependence on the government's role in propping it up:

If governments, their agencies or utilities reduce their demand for our products or discontinue or curtail their funding our business may suffer. . . . Changes in governmental budget priorities could adversely affect our business and results of operations. U.S. and foreign government agencies have purchased products directly from us, and products from our customers, and U.S. government agencies have historically funded a portion of our research and development activities. When the government changes budget priorities . . . our research and development funding and our product sales to government entities and government-funded customers are at risk. . . . If government or utility funding is discontinued or significantly reduced, our business and results of operations could be adversely affected.[15]

Here, let me translate that for those of you who skipped past the block quote of corporate speak: "If the tax dollars go away, so do we."

The good news: even if the U.S. government comes to its senses and decides to stop buying ten-dollar lightbulbs (don't hold your breath), Swoboda has another government in his pocket, too. A neat little start-up company. A neat little start-up *country*.

China. Maybe you've heard of them.

Yep, Cree actually has a plant and more than half of its employees in China. So all that tax money Cree has grabbed? It's gone to a company that outsources more than half its jobs. Joe Biden's quote about how Cree "ties so much" into what he and Obama are about? China. *LED Magazine* (yes, there's seriously a publication with that name) wrote about Cree's expansive Chinese footprint, noting, "While Huizhou is Cree's operational headquarters in China, the company has also set up sales and engineering service centers in Shenzhen and Shanghai. Swoboda said that Cree's development strategy is 'Cree Chip, China Heart.' "[16]

China Heart. Funded by American cash. It's enough to make you want to go back to lanterns.

The Left's embrace of LEDs is somewhat surprising, given all the heat they generate over environmental issues.

According to safety guides, if an LED bulb breaks, your cleanup strategy involves rubber gloves, a protective mask, opening the windows, evacuating the room for fifteen minutes, and contacting the local waste management facility for tips on how to get rid of your cleaning supplies "contaminated with lead and arsenic."[17] Don't be shocked if you're instructed to drop off the contaminants at a nearby hazardous waste center because, well, lead and arsenic aren't exactly Play-Doh.

You know what happens if a regular lightbulb breaks? You throw it away, then get another one that you bought for like forty cents and keep it moving. No airing out the house. No hazmat trips. Amazing what the power of the free market can do for you, huh?

Thomas Edison, though commonly thought to have invented the lightbulb, was actually just the most successful at making the technology practical and affordable. He is said to have failed hundreds of times before finally perfecting the incandescent bulb. In fact, Edison's perseverance and its result are often held up as a testament to the virtue and benefit of hard work and determination. Everyone knows about Edison and the lightbulb now. And the longevity of the incandescent technology draws tourists every year to Livermore, California, where a bulb designed by Adolphe Chaillet, one of Edison's contemporaries, has been burning in a fire station for more than 110 years.[18]

Edison's efforts didn't just pad his pockets. He changed the country. Amazingly, Edison was able to achieve this without lobbying Congress or the president to ban candles or lanterns. He didn't need to destroy someone else's creation or livelihood to further his own. He just figured his invention would stand on its own merits, and the power of the marketplace would determine whether society was ready to abandon its waxy ways and, if you'll pardon the expression, head into the light.

What a simp.

That's why Crapitalism is so bad. It isn't just that people pervert the marketplace to maximize their own profits. It's that they demean and defeat the efforts of others to do it. Chuck Swoboda has a business that makes fancy-looking lightbulbs that use less energy and therefore save customers money over the long haul? Sweet. There's probably a market for those. And if you want to play the whole "building more power plants will cost all of us more money in the long run" card and use it to rationalize some government subsidies to hand out some bulbs, I don't love it but could at least understand the logic. But that wasn't good enough for Swoboda. He couldn't just push for a little help, a little taxpayer-funded incentive to give his product a shot. He had to get the other players out of the game.

Writer Tim Carney said, "Cree embodies Obama-era capitalism: profiting from government grants, political connections, revolving-door lobbyists and regulations that force people to buy your product." I mean, why else would Home Depot carry a bulb that costs more than forty dollars? [19]

A lot of business owners like the idea of putting their competition out of business. But they usually look to do it as a result of the overwhelming success of their business. Chuck and the other Crapitalists like him want to do it the other way around. Put the competitors out of business first, then open up shop. It's a brilliant strategy. It's just destroying our country, one overpriced and taxpayer-subsidized lightbulb at a time.

7 Vinod Khosla

Look, we have to take risks. And risks mean the risk of losing money. So let me ask you a question. We've been looking
for a cure for cancer for a long time. How much money has
the U.S. government spent? Billions and billions of dollars.
Should we stop looking for a cure for cancer because we
haven't found a cure?

—Vinod Khosla to *60 Minutes*

One theme that's emerging as we move throughout this book is
the role the financial collapse and subsequent stimulus played in
padding so many of these corrupt Crapitalists' wallets. Some of
this is not new—we knew about how, while the rest of the country are losing their 401(k)s and seeing the price of their gas and
food skyrocket, companies like AIG grabbed more than $170 bil-

lion in bailout money, yet still paid out big bonuses to their fat-cat execs.[1]

We didn't know it at the time, but this would be our crash-course introduction to the Obama economy. After the bailout came the stimulus, then the GM takeover, then Obamacare. Hundreds of billions of our tax dollars flew out the window at a record-breaking pace, but we were told it was all necessary, part of Dear Leader's grand plan to overhaul our broken country and fix us up good for the challenges of the twenty-first century. We needed to get ready for the future. And the future was green.

Obama promised to heal the earth, stop the rising oceans, com-bat climate change, and maybe even produce a fourth season of HBO's *Deadwood*. The man, we were told by his minions in the me-dia, could do it all. And all it would take from us would be a few hundred billion in stimulus bucks. Because that's what it took. No more coal and gas. In Obama's America, we would live in homes heated by windmills, and drive Priuses that ran on kelp. We would lead the world again in innovation and production of the new green economy, and benefit from the five million "green collar jobs" he promised.[2] Obama carried the mantle of Lincoln, but by the time he was done, we'd all be living like a Jetson.

Of course, in reality, six years later and we're still much closer to living like Fred and Wilma than George and Jane.

But while the rest of us were watching our country's economic reality be reset to the Stone Age, Obama's cronies, many of whom came from the green energy sector, were cashing in.

Author Peter Schweizer looked at just how lucrative the Obama stimulus payments were to his campaign cronies. Calling it the "Obama recycling program," Schweizer calculated that for every dollar Obama's campaign bundler contributed to the campaign, they got back more than $21,000 on average in government-backed loans and grants.[3] Crony capitalism is "welfare for the well-off," Schweizer was quoted as saying. The American people, still clinging to the utopian vision painted for them by Obama biofuel Kool-Aid-guzzling media, thought that the money was handed out by scientists, engineers, or at least people who watched *Mr. Wizard* growing up. But as Schweizer documented, the "reality is that the political appointees are making these decisions with our money . . . to their benefit."[4]

So the Green Giveaway went to the well connected, rather than the well suited. And few used their connections to cash in as well as Vinod Khosla.

Khosla hit it big as one of the cofounders of Sun Microsystems in the 1980s, and used his personal wealth to join and form venture capital firms. Hey, God bless him. We wouldn't be anywhere in this country if not for people's willingness to take risks, then reap the reward. And no one knows risk like venture capital firms. They say the average firm will invest in ten start-ups, knowing that nine of them will probably fail, but the money they make on the tenth is enough to make it all work out.

But Khosla, who has graduate degrees from Carnegie Mellon and Stanford, appears to have figured out a better equation.

Khosla no doubt realized the benefits that being pals with politicians could provide for his growing interest in clean energy companies. And he seems to have made lots of pals. Since 2001, Khosla has donated over $4 million just to California candidates and campaigns, with over half of that going to the losing side of the eventual election.[5] Remember that lackluster winning percentage. It portends poor things for our future.

Vinod got involved at the federal level, too. Since 1986, Khosla has donated nearly $500,000 to national candidates, with 86 percent going to Democrats.[6] He also gave $1 million to the

George Soros–backed PAC Priorities USA.[7] But Khosla is an equal-opportunity palm greaser. Khosla also showered Republicans like Orrin Hatch, Dick Lugar, and John Sununu with cash, not to mention the Republican National Committee.[8] Khosla doesn't care about red or blue. He cares about green, as in *your* green.

During the 2008 election, Khosla spread it around, donating to the presidential campaigns of both John McCain and Hillary Clinton. Ultimately Khosla chose Obama, leading his India Policy Team and giving more than $66,000 to Democratic victories. And Barack's backers, as we've seen, banked big taxpayer bucks.

Companies backed by Khosla have already bagged hundreds of millions of our tax dollars, both at the national and state level, for a laundry list of loser companies that promised a green future, but all ended up in the red. And we haven't gotten so much as a thank-you note for the trouble.

CBS's *60 Minutes* did an exposé on the $100 billion catastrophe of wasted cash by so-called clean-tech companies, and our boy was their proverbial poster child. For his part, Vinod doesn't see what the big deal is:

> Look, we have to take risks. And risks mean the risk of losing money. So let me ask you a question. We've been looking for a cure for cancer for a long time. How much money has the U.S. government spent? Billions and billions of dollars. Should we stop looking for a cure for cancer because we haven't found a cure?[9]

Khosla is technically right about cancer. To date, there is no "cure," though scientific breakthroughs continue to happen every day. Meanwhile, Vinod's failed investments continue to kill our economy.

What happens to our tax dollars once Khosla-backed companies get ahold of them? As Bob Dylan sang, "The answer is blowin' in the wind." Literally.

Nordic Windpower manufactured wind turbines. The privately owned company started out as a Swedish research project in the 1970s. Think Volvos with sideburns. They eventually relocated to California. Berkeley, to be precise.

Again, think Volvos and sideburns.

But as a U.S. entity, they caught the eye of our boy. Khosla Ventures took them on, and went about the business of trying to make them profitable—which, we know by now, means hitting up Uncle Sam. In Obama's stimulus green giveaway, Nordic bagged $3 million in tax credits for their facility in Idaho and was approved for an additional $16 million in loan guarantees.[10]

So what happened to Nordic? If you go to Idaho now and are in the market for a wind turbine, can you pick one up? Not exactly. Nordic, like so many of Vinod's visions, went bankrupt. One of Khosla's business partners, Pierre Lamond, joined Nordic's board but bolted after about six months. "They were running out of cash and thinking about shutting the company down," the *Kansas City Business Journal* quoted Lamond as saying. "They were counting too much on having subsidies from the U.S. government, and that doesn't always work."[11]

This theme of relying too much on government funding is repeated, often, when one takes a postmortem look at another of Khosla's failures.

In the summer of 2012, the U.S. Navy put on a "green fleet" demonstration to prove it was possible to operate a carrier group on biofuels for a day. Think "Ride Your Bike to Work Day," only much more expensive. The navy actually spent $12 million on the biofuels to operate their ships for the day as part of the exercise

The navy purchased the fuels from a company called Gevo that just happened to be partially owned by—wait for it—Vinod Khosla. But Gevo wasn't just selling to the navy.

As part of the president's green goal, the U.S. Air Force also purchased fuel from Gevo, spending $630,000 on 11,000 gallons. That worked out to about $59 a gallon, or roughly $55 more than regular gas was costing at the time.[12] Who in the hell pays close to $60 per gallon? Even if you drive a German car, that's pushing it. But this wasn't the first time we had grossly overpaid for Khosla's crap.

Range Fuels, another Khosla investment, was supposed to be the country's first cellulosic ethanol plant.[13] Instead it became a $64 million debt the American taxpayer had to eat. That's not exactly what they meant when they set out to find new uses for wood chips. Khosla's company actually got that guaranteed loan during the Bush administration, which you would think would've made the new administration all the more wary when it came time to play Santa Claus with taxpayer treats.

Not so much, apparently.

In fact, the alliances now run even deeper. Former Obama campaign manager Jim Messina was added to a Khosla-backed company's board in 2013, after Messina gave a speech at Khosla's firm.[14] So if you think the green faucet is going to shut off anytime soon, I've got a windmill farm to sell you.

Coskata was another biofuels company Khosla backed. Coskata bagged a $250 million loan guarantee from the federal government. Peter Schweizer explained in his brutal takedown of Congress's corrupt stock-trading practices, "Company executives have been quite clear that one important measure of corporate success is the amount of 'government money we attract.'" Why do they need so much government money? Because they fail. A lot.

Coskata originally planned a $100 million initial public offering of its stock but changed its mind in July 2012 because of "unfavorable market conditions," according to CEO Bill Roe. Instead, what Coskata decided to do was become a company that converted natural gas to ethanol. Okay, no problem. Still green. Still clean. Still . . . what's a word that rhymes with *green* that means "doesn't work"?

Coskata pulled out of a second IPO the following year because, say it with me, the private market wasn't there.[15] Coskata was one of several green energy plants to decide not to offer IPOs. After all, who needs private-sector money when you've got Uncle Sam (funded by tax dollars) backing your play? Can't get the product to work? Who cares! You've got a loan guarantee. No big deal. We're only $17 trillion in debt. It's all going on China's tab anyway. What's another couple billion? We haven't cured cancer yet, either, remember?

Khosla, for his part, is undeterred. In the *60 Minutes* special, when confronted by Lesley Stahl about myriad failures, plus the fact that his current operation, another biofuels company called KiOr, is still in the red, he had this to say:

> In fact you need dreamers to stretch. I probably have failed more times in my life than almost anybody I know. But that's because I've tried more things. And I'm not afraid to fail because the consequences of avoiding failure are doing nothing.[16]

Failure's fine. Abraham Lincoln failed, both as a politician and as a businessman. Thomas Edison failed repeatedly. Thomas Jefferson failed as a farmer and an inventor, yet we regard him as one of the greatest minds in the history of our nation.[17] But Lincoln,

Edison, and Jefferson paid their own way. And when they profited as the eventual result of their labors, the country still benefited.

The story of our country is the story of successful business enterprises. Names like Ford, Carnegie, Rockefeller, Hilton, Gates. They made their fortunes and, in the process, made our country greater. Vinod Khosla in his green period has precisely nothing in common with these people. Yeah, he's rich. But he's not the same kind of rich. America was forged by self-made men and women, who lifted the country up by the force of their will and the quality of their ideas. Today, we're drowning in a sea of false promises and failed dreams. Because unlike the accomplishments of those titans of industry, Vinod's "clean-tech" dreams won't work unless they're subsidized. Vinod defends his failures. And even worse, in what sounds almost like an ominous threat, he said to *60 Minutes*, "We've done lots of things that failed in energy. But every time we've learned, picked ourselves up and tried something new."[18]

Oh how I pray to the sweet Lord above that he would stop trying something new. You know what happens every time he does? We get broker. Khosla's ideas won't work in a competitive environment. The failures keep mounting, outpaced only by the escalating costs we have to cover. But because he backed Barack, he keeps getting a check. It truly is a green recycling program. They take our tax dollars and turn them into profits for campaign cronies, and even more debt for future Americans. It's some kind of alchemy. And the result is poisoning our future. It has to stop.

8 Neil Bluhm

There is clearly a saturation point, and as you add additional competition, everybody's total win will be going down.

—Neil Bluhm

There's a scene in *Ocean's Eleven* when George Clooney and Brad Pitt are talking about robbing a Vegas casino (spoiler alert—they do it). Clooney's character is trying to convince Pitt's that beating the casino is, despite the odds, doable. "The house always wins," Clooney says. "Play long enough, you never change the stakes. The house takes you. Unless, when that perfect hand comes along, you bet and you bet big, then you take the house."

I always liked the idea of knowing you were up against the odds, but if you were smart, and timed your play right, you could win and cash in. In some ways that's exactly what makes America so great. We allow people to take risks, bet big on themselves and their dreams. With hard work and some luck, a lot of those bets pay off. It's the American way.

What is not the American way are the guys who engage in the deck stacking. They play a different game altogether. Their wins come from our losses. By inside deals and crony connections, they become the house. That's Crapitalism. And it's destroying the country.

Neil Bluhm is one of those Crapitalists. There are lots of ways to describe the depths of his free-market-crushing depravity, but we can start with this: he's a Democrat from Chicago. I mean right there, that's two strikes.

While the rest of country's net worth has crapped out during the reign of that *other* Chicago Democrat, Bluhm's real estate and investment business has been booming.

In March 2009, just months after Obama was sworn in, Bluhm was estimated to be worth around $1.5 billion. Not too bad.

By September 2013, Bluhm's net worth had gone up by a billion dollars.[1]

Jackpot!

Bluhm, a casino magnate, had bet the right way again. And much like many other creatures from Chicago's crony lagoon, among his bets was some serious campaign cash.

Bluhm likes to throw money around—he recently gave $25 million to Northwestern University.[2] For that gift he gets his name on a few buildings. For the campaign contributions, he gets some important BFFs. The names of people Neil Bluhm has contributed to reads like a Who's Who for shyster pols: Rahm Emanuel, Rod Blagojevich, Hillary Clinton.[3] It could, coincidentally enough, also read like the worst season of *The Apprentice* ever.

Since 1994, Bluhm has donated at least $860,000 to that litany of Lefties, among others. All that cash buys a lot of clout. *Chicago* magazine named him to its list of the hundred most influential Chicagoans in 2012.[4] But the $860,000 is chump change compared to what he's given Obama.

In 2008, Bluhm gave the maximum individual contribution to, and bundled over $200,000 for, the Obama campaign.[5] He would go above and beyond four years later, bundling over $500,000 for Obama's reelection bid.[6]

In between, in 2010, when Obama turned forty-nine, Bluhm hosted a presidential birthday dinner at his Illinois mansion, which cost only $30,400 to get into. You think that comes with free cake?

This was just a continuation of long-standing benevolence and brotherhood between Barack and Bluhm. Back in 2004, when Obama was just an Illinois state senator voting "present" and giving good speeches, Bluhm was already playing the long game and laying down his marker by helping him get to Washington with fundraisers and donations. He even got Bill Clinton to come to town as part of the effort.[7] One wonders what the incentive package for that appearance looked like.

And how have things been working out for Bluhm?

Like many senior citizens, Bluhm liked casinos. Only instead of wheeling his oxygen tank to a slot machine and settling down for the night, he settled for a seat at the Illinois gaming license table.

As luck would have it, Illinois had one unused gaming license, and after having been mired in "legal and administrative disputes for a decade" it was now suddenly available. Just weeks after Obama won election in 2008, Bluhm's company, Midwest Gaming & Entertainment LLC, submitted their final bid. Two other companies also submitted applications for the license. One put up $300 million more than Bluhm's bid, and the other was located in an economically blighted area, which Illinois's statutes describe as a criteria for the granting of the license. (In fairness, the gaming board apparently had questions about the associations of the other bidders. I'm guessing they weren't Dem pols!)

In any event, weeks after Bluhm's boy won the White House, Midwest Gaming's horse came in.

But not everyone was thrilled.

One of the concerns raised about Midwest's proposal was that it would be located in Des Plaines, much closer to an existing casino site than the other two bids, and therefore more likely to drain customers, jobs, and other economic benefits from other parts of the state. Eglin, Illinois, is located near Des Plaines and already had gaming. Its then mayor, who now stood to see his blighted town's resurgence muted by Bluhm's bullying, was none too pleased. "It's not a question of sour grapes; it just doesn't make sense, from any point of view," Mayor Ed Schock said.[8]

And he wasn't alone.

The gaming commission member who voted against all the applications, Eugene Winkler, agreed that Midwest was the "least tainted," but also marveled at Bluhm the Baller's conceit. "The arrogance of Midwest Gaming is palpable," Winkler said. "Mr. Bluhm is a smart businessman, but he also wants everything done his way."[9]

Bluhm also got his way into Pennsylvania gaming.

In 2006, the state's Gaming Control Board awarded its Pittsburgh license to a Detroit businessman named Don Barden. You may have heard of Detroit—it went bankrupt. Would you be shocked to learn that Barden's casino proposal would fare no better?

Like a shark smelling blood, Neil Bluhm swam in. Or maybe was called in, by good friend, former Democratic National Committee chairman and then Pennsylvania governor Ed Rendell. Can't help but remember all that money Bluhm had thrown around to Democrats over the years, including $60,000 to Rendell himself?

When the global credit market collapsed, Barden was unable to secure the financing for his project. Luckily for him, Neil Bluhm stood ready with cash. Of course, this wasn't Bluhm being benevolent. Not only would he be able to scratch that casino itch he had developed, but he could avoid the competitive bidding process, and he and his investment team could obtain 75 percent control in the project by handing over a $2.5 million transfer fee for the gaming license that Barden had paid $50 million for.[10]

Hit me?

After a flurry of phone calls involving Governor Rendell, key legislators, and members of the Pennsylvania Gaming Control Board, the deal was closed.

To some outside observers, the whole deal stunk.

They saw it as Crapitalism at its worst.

"This is making a mockery of this issue. . . . I'm completely perplexed as to why public officials are somehow negotiating—involved in any way—in this matter," said Democrat state senator Jim Ferlo. "I'm somewhat incredulous that there are these secret conversations taking place between unknown parties on these [license] transfers. . . . Talk about back-room deal-making."[11]

In both Chicago and Pennsylvania, Bluhm backed the right guys and walked away with the casino license on the cheap. He denies that his contributions have anything to do with the treatment he has received, though. When asked specifically about the Pennsylvania deal, he responded that he had been a supporter of Democrats "long before there was gambling in Pennsylvania."[12]

Nothing to see here; everyone move along.

At least we can expect that Bluhm, as a long-standing supporter of Democrat causes, will run his businesses in line with the vision being cast by our income-equality-loving president and his platform, right? Bluhm, who has supported Obama's pro-labor campaigns at every step of the way, surely runs his business the way his president wants to run the country, right?

Absolutely . . . unless you interpret his efforts of trying to block employees from unionizing to be inconsistent with a pro-labor message.

Turns out employees at Bluhm's Chicago casino wanted to unionize. Seems like the Chicago thing to do, right? I mean, if you own a business in the city that produced our first community organizer president, maybe it shouldn't shock you when the word *union* gets thrown around. To be fair, Bluhm wasn't shocked. But his company reportedly responded to the efforts "with an aggressive anti-union campaign that includes threats, surveillance, and other intimidation."[13]

Doesn't sound like a good Obama Zombie to me.

But that's the thing about Bluhm. He isn't a zombie. He's a Crapitalist. It's an entirely different species. Crapitalists will think for themselves if it's in their financial interests.

They aren't motivated by ideology. They're motivated by crony-fueled profit. A Crapitalist turns around and complains about his tax bill until it gets lowered. That's what Bluhm did. He complained about his property tax bill in Illinois.[14] And Pittsburgh, too.[15]

At least he's consistent.

But it's funny, you know. Bluhm fights so hard to keep from having to pay taxes like you and me. But one of his most famous tenants wouldn't exist without them.

You remember the GSA? The General Services Administration is responsible for the acquisition and maintenance of the properties that house the U.S. government. You and I pay the bill. Details of a

GSA conference in Las Vegas leaked out that included examples of government excess you'd think were made up.[16] The lavish gathering of GSA officials included mind readers, clowns, commemorative coin sets, and other creative ways corrupt bureaucrats cooked up to blow our money. My favorite was the rap video about how much money they were wasting.

Really.

Well, the GSA, like most federal agencies, has its headquarters in Washington, D.C. Ironically, the agency in charge of acquiring land for the government leases its building. Any guesses who the landlord is?

Bluhm's investment firm, Walton Street Capital, in partnership with another real estate investment firm called StonebridgeCarras, leased office space to the GSA starting in 2010. The lease was extended lucratively to include all 329,000 square feet.[17] According to government records, the contract is worth over $35 million.[18]

The "development" is part of the "NoMa Business Improvement District (BID)," which "was created by the District of Columbia City Council and approved by the [DC] Mayor in March 2007."

NoMa itself operates as a PR wing for both StonebridgeCarras and Walton Street Capital. Any new "investment" or government contract in that part of D.C. is touted by the nonprofit NoMa as being hugely beneficial for the district.[19]

The chair of NoMa BID board of directors is Doug Firstenberg, who is the comanager of StonebridgeCarras, the real estate and development firm that partners with Bluhm's Walton Street Capital. The other comanager of StonebridgeCarras is George A. Carras. Both Carras and Firstenberg have given generously to Democrats over the years, including to D.C. congresswoman Eleanor Holmes Norton.

The 1.6-million-square-foot development that houses the GSA also contains the Department of Justice, though the lease was done through the GSA. Because of the long-term security of having taxpayer-funded tenants, Bluhm's group was able to sell the DOJ-occupied part of the facility for over $300 million.[20]

That Bluhm is in bed with the agency that has been known to both blow tax dollars and take kickbacks for awarding contracts doesn't seem surprising. Even though it's headquartered in D.C., there's a lot of Chicago in the GSA's DNA.

And Bluhm, like always, got the deal. Just like with gaming licenses, real estate deals, or tax rates, Bluhm loves to play the game. And like the proverbial house in the same Vegas where the infamous GSA conference took place, Bluhm always wins.

And the rest of us end up Crapping out.

9 Jay-Z

Made my money quick then back to the streets but
Still sittin on blades . . . sippin that ray . . . hustling

—Jay-Z, "Big Pimpin' "[1]

Shawn Carter is a self-described former drug dealer. It's important to remember this, because it helps explain the motives and actions of Carter's eventual rap persona Jay-Z. Raised by a single mother in Brooklyn's Marcy projects, Carter attended the same high school as future rappers Notorious B.I.G. and Busta Rhymes.[2] Must've been a pretty cool music class.

Carter dropped out, though, and like a lot of hustlers from the way, started slinging rock and writing lyrics. He claims he was shot at three times growing up. So he eventually stopped pushing dope and started selling records. It turned out to be a good career move.

After twelve albums, nineteen Grammys, a fashion line, restaurants, and even skin care products, Jay-Z has built a cultural and institutional empire. As he raps, he isn't just a businessman. He's "a business, man."

Forbes estimates his net worth at nearly $500 million. I have no problem with that. Jay-Z built his empire through talent, drive, and white teenagers' desire to alienate their parents by listening to rap music. Good for him. He is also married to actress/pop star and absolute knockout Beyoncé Knowles.

I definitely have no problem with that.

But he retained one thing from his drug-dealing past: making money above all. In their world, amassing your personal fortune happens to come at the expense of the health and even life of your customers, and the quality of life for the people living in the neighborhood you're working in. So what? Drug dealers suck in profit and leave empty lives, destroyed families, and shattered communities in their wake. They satisfy a demand, but they aren't making anything better except their bank accounts. This has been the Shawn Carter way.

As part of his empire, Jay-Z purchased a minority share of the NBA franchise New Jersey Nets. As part of the plan of the majority owner, developer Bruce Ratner, to move the Nets to Brooklyn and build them a new state-of-the-art arena, Jay-Z became the unofficial mascot. He was the front man for the project, appearing at groundbreakings, posing for pictures with kids, and helping to design the new Nets logo. His fingerprints are all over everything. Jay-Z even owned part of the new arena itself, called the Barclays Center, after a lucrative deal secured the naming rights. In some ways, Ratner and his team delivered on their promise to Brooklyn. But the arena, and the overall development surrounding it, stand as a monument to the power and peril of Crapitalism. The project, like Jay-Z's early earnings as a drug dealer, profited only a select few. And Jay-Z sold out his roots to do it.

The story of the Barclays Center, and the Atlantic Yards Project it spearheaded, is perhaps one of the great criminal capers of the past century. Only it was all done legally. And New York tax dollars paid for it.

Ratner, the developer, fell in love with a piece of property located above a railway yard, with trains depositing Long Islanders stopping there, and also serving as the hub for numerous subway lines. But as author Malcolm Gladwell points out, Ratner had a problem.[3] Half of the property Ratner wanted to buy and turn into luxury apartments wasn't empty. Or for sale.

Ratner knew that, under certain conditions, the government could actually seize private land in the name of economic development under the eminent domain statutes. The most famous example of this gave us the Supreme Court ruling *Kelo v. New London*, where the seizure of private property was actually upheld in a 5–4 decision.[4] And part of the decision, written by then-justice Sandra Day O'Connor, suggested that one scenario that would allow for the "sovereign" to transfer the land it seized to a private party was if the entities "make the property available for the public's use— such as with a railroad, a public utility, or a stadium."[5]

So Ratner bought the New Jersey Nets, and decided to build an arena in Brooklyn.

But how could Ratner convince New Yorkers to seize other people's land, move a middling basketball franchise across the New York Bay, and give the rest to a wealthy developer? Enter Jay-Z.

Ratner sold a minority share of both the Nets and the new arena to the rapper. In return, Jay-Z became the head Brooklyn booster. The *New York Times* hailed him as the "unofficial ambassador" of the Barclays Center. The *Daily News* called Jay-Z an "NBA franchise figurehead." And National Public Radio labeled it "Jay-Z's Brooklyn." Again, more power to him. I don't have a problem with him getting credit for bringing the Nets to town. I have a problem with you and me getting the bill.

Then-mayor Michael Bloomberg was so enamored with the idea of returning a professional sports team to Brooklyn (they haven't had one since Jackie Robinson and the Dodgers bolted to Los Angeles) that, with Jay-Z rallying the public's support, he helped push the project through. Ratner and his cronies secured $761 million in taxpayer subsidies and conned the government to snatch up the buildings and land whose owners had the misfortune to be located on property that Ratner and Jay-Z wanted.

It seems, however, that Jigga be Big Pimpin' best when Uncle Sam writes checks. But when tax dollars don't pad the bottom line, not so much. His 40/40 Club is foundering—the Chicago location never opened, and the "80,000 square-foot Las Vegas club complete with 80 plasma TV's totally flopped," shutting its doors eight months after the grand opening.[6] His one in Atlantic City closed down as well.[7] Jay-Z also lost "$50 million in bad hotel development projects" in New York and "defaulted on a $24 million dollar mortgage" when two other real estate deals went sour.[8]

Hey, maybe Hova's not a "business, man" after all. Just a Crapitalist. He, like the developer Bruce Ratner, gorges taxpayers to finance his grand projects. But paying taxes on those projects is something different entirely.

After bamboozling the borough for money and land, what did Ratner do? He sued New York City to try to lower his tax bill. He later withdrew the lawsuit, claiming it was filed "inadvertently."[9] Someone in accounting must've reminded Ratner that part of the deal he struck with the city was that his tax bill for the next decade is one dollar a year.[10]

Really.

Ratner also turned around and, several years later, sold the controlling interest of the team to Mikhail Prokhorov, a Russian oil tycoon.

After all, as Malcolm Gladwell noted, Ratner didn't care about basketball in the first place. Only money:

> Once he won his eminent domain case, the team had served its purpose. He's not a basketball fan. He's a real estate developer. The asset he wanted to hang on to was the arena, and with good reason. According to Ratner, the Barclays Center (the naming right of which, by the way, earned him a cool $400 million) is going to bring in somewhere around $120 million in revenue a year. Operating costs will be $30 million. The mortgage comes to $50 million. That leaves $35 million in profit on Ratner's $350 million up-front investment, for an annual return of 10 percent.

Not to be outdone, Jay-Z rapped about his involvement and motivation in the project, lyrics that drip with civic pride and community responsibility. Or none of that:

> *Would've brought the Nets to Brooklyn for free*
> *Except I made millions off it, you fuckin' dweeb* [11]

Classy.

This is the same guy who goes on Bill Maher's show and acts concerned about the widening gap between the "have[s] and have not[s] . . . it's going to be a problem that no amount of police can solve." [12]

Sort of humorous to hear talk about widening economic dispar-

ities from a guy who raps about his money, fame, use of high-end goods and jewelry, and mansions. But that's nothing new for Jay-Z. His lyrics say one thing. His lifestyle says another. His biggest hit, quiet as it's kept, is hypocrisy. And his iPod's got it on repeat.

This is the same guy whom Al Sharpton (who is supported by Ratner, the project's developer) compared to Jackie Robinson, because of Jay-Z's involvement in the whole Nets project. Sharpton said that "we've gone from Jackie [Robinson, who integrated baseball as a Brooklyn Dodger] to Jay-Z, where we can not only play the game but we can own a piece of the game."[13]

But Jay-Z sold out his homeboys through and through.

Ratner admitted he designed the mall across the street from the Barclays Center in such a way so as to keep "tough kids from the neighborhood" out of it.[14] Anyone who's spent any time in the area knows what Ratner meant: black youth.

This is the project Jay-Z helped bring back to his hometown. Designed intentionally to keep the kids he rolled with as a teenager away. But it makes sense.

While Jay-Z brags about texting with Obama and even released a remix song called "My President Is Black," it turns out that Hova is into black empowerment only when it's good for him. Sure, he is a proud black man. But all you have to do is look at the arena he helped build to see that the color he really cares about is green.

The new Barclays Center features several amenities for the well-to-do. In fact, the arena's website touts one of the most aristocratic touches, "inspired by Jay-Z himself." The Vault is an exclusive level that features only eleven suites, lounge seating, and flat-screen TVs. That it doesn't offer an actual view of the court hasn't stopped anyone from shelling out the $550,000 a year it costs to own a suite.[15] But while Jay-Z may be living the high life, schmoozing with tycoon developers and Russian oligarchs, and getting the en-

dorsement of bought-and-paid-for civil rights advocates like Sharpton, his business affiliations haven't exactly kept hope alive.

Three luxury box owners who are black have sued the arena for $4 million because of repeated discriminatory practices. The plaintiffs say the House That Jay-Z Built ignored any orders they tried to place and accused the plaintiffs of skipping out on tabs. The suit even alleges the suite was investigated by law enforcement, the owners say, "because they are black." The rest of the luxury suite owners, per the complaint, are "treated like royalty."[16]

It honestly isn't that shocking. Like the mall across the street built to keep the "tough" kids out, Hova likes to have it both ways.

One of Jay-Z's big moneymakers is his RocaWear fashion line. You probably see it all over the country in malls and stand-alone big-box stores. Nothing wrong with that. But you might not know or expect a guy who sells Occupy Wall Street shirts to also have a deal to sell $58,000 crocodile-skin jackets at Barneys—a store designed for the one-percenters. When Barneys had a little dustup over a couple of incidents of racial profiling at its store, many called on Jay-Z to pull his line from the retailer in a show of racial solidarity. The line stayed, and Jay-Z's "New York Holiday Collection" brought in over $1 million in proceeds. To be fair, the sale was an effort to raise money for the Shawn Carter Foundation, which purportedly will use the money to send inner-city youth to college. But then again, they also said the real estate deal would bring jobs.

The Barclays Center was one piece of a larger development plan known as the Atlantic Yards. Part of the reason Ratner secured the go-ahead and millions in taxpayer freebies to proceed with the plan was that, in addition to the new arena, other aspects of the Atlantic Yards project would include affordable housing, retail, and more. Most important, though, Ratner said the project would bring jobs. In fact, the official slogan for the redevelopment campaign was "Jobs, Housing, Hoops."[17]

Jay-Z, who reportedly designed the Nets logo himself, was quoted as saying the project had already brought "thousands and thousands of jobs" to the area.[18]

I know Jay dropped out of high school, but you expect a former drug dealer to be able to count. Actual estimates at the time had the total number of jobs somewhere near five hundred. Moreover, many of the jobs offered, subsidized by over three-quarters of a billion dollars in tax breaks and benefits, are part-time only.[19] To make matters worse, an analysis by the New York City Independent Budget Office said the project would cost $40 million more than it would generate in revenue.[20]

Oh, and that affordable housing that was promised? Snatched up by the borough's burgeoning hipster population. With rent around $2,000 a month, it ain't exactly for the average hustler, yo.[21]

This wasn't the first time Jay-Z's been pimped out in an effort to hustle taxpayers. You may recall from the chapter on Crapitalist Greg Meeks that New York's inspector general blasted the bidding process for a contract to operate a racetrack and casino, in the Ozone Park neighborhood of Queens. Aqueduct Entertainment Group, the investment consortium that won the lucrative deal, offered a lower up-front licensing fee—$100 million lower—but they had Team Meeks on their side, which meant insider dealing, a shady selection process, and a contract worth billions. The contract was eventually rescinded and the disgraced governor who helped AEG land the deal, David Paterson, dropped his election bid.

But there was Jay-Z, in the mix of this mess, too. While the inspector general's report revealed that Jay-Z had "scant knowledge" of the proposal, AEG's main financial backers may have been trying to use Jay-Z as a one-man PR machine to curry favor with the governor's office.[22] He and Governor Paterson were hanging out in the Hamptons and becoming buds right around the same time Jay-Z was being wooed to join AEG as a minority investor.[23]

While the self-appointed "best rapper alive" eventually jumped ship because of the state investigation, his being used as a "hype man"[24] to barrel over taxpayers is familiar. Where have we seen that movie before? Oh yeah, I remember. And it's hard to miss in downtown Brooklyn: the Barclays Center. Or as the eyesore's been nicknamed, the Rusty Turtle. Thanks, playa. Appreciate that.

That Jay-Z would voluntarily get in bed with corrupt people shouldn't surprise us. Jay-Z's investment firm is called Gain Global Investments. His partner at Gain is a dude named David Rosenberg. Rosenberg is exactly the type of guy you want to be around, that is, if you're into lawsuits and being the subject of numerous state and federal investigations. Rosenberg's Ohio-based collection agency, Unifund CCR Partners, has been accused of fraudulent tactics, including "going after people who've paid, implying they're lawyers and suing years after the last payment notice was sent." And there's probably something to the avalanche of lawsuits because Rosenberg's company has settled dozens of them. Like the case involving Queens man Jose Luis Muniz. Unifund harassed him to pay off a credit card debt that Muniz had resolved a decade earlier.[25] Muniz sued and Unifund settled.

Not exactly a person you'd want to invest with, right? But Jay-Z does. And that's just another track on the same hypocritical album for Carter. A guy who made $63 million one year but donated only $6,000 to his own charity.[26] Because that's not what thugs, pimps, or drug dealers do. They don't give back. They take. Jay-Z is a taker. They say pimpin' ain't easy. But for former drug dealer turned Crapitalist Shawn Carter, taking sure seems to be.

10 George Kaiser

There's never been more money shoved out of the government's door in world history, and probably never will be again than in the past few months and in the next 18 months. And our selfish parochial goal is to try and get as much of it for Tulsa and Oklahoma as we can.[1]

—George Kaiser

You've heard of Solyndra. The next big thing in solar technology, Solyndra made solar panel tubing. Unlike the traditional flat panels that needed to be adjusted as the sun made its daily trip around the globe, the tubes, because of their rounded surface area, were always positioned to catch at least some of the sun's direct light. When installed on white rooftops—racist—the tubes were supposed to be more efficient, and therefore more desirable.[2] President

Obama touted Solyndra as an example of what the new American economy would look like. And he was right.

Just for the wrong reasons.

Solyndra now stands as a textbook case of Crapitalism 101. A flawed product. Taxpayer-screwing businessmen. "Incentivized" politicians. Tax-dollar giveaways, which turn into taxpayer-assumed debt when the bottom drops out. And the connected cronies coming out ahead, on our backs.

Pencils ready?

The warning signs were there. After Solyndra went bankrupt, and people started asking simple questions like "Hey, so . . . how come we gave all that money to a company that shut down so abruptly?" emails began to surface. Emails that showed how Office of Management and Budget (OMB) employees, aka people whose job it was to evaluate possible recipients of stimulus funds, declared Solyndra "not ready for prime time."

But like Magic Johnson's late-night talk show, it got the green light anyway.

George Kaiser made sure of it.

Kaiser is an Oklahoma billionaire who struck it rich in the oil industry.

During the 2008 campaign, Kaiser threw a lot of energy, and resources, behind Barack Obama. When Obama was trailing in the polls to Hillary Clinton during the Democratic primary, Kaiser hosted an Obama fundraiser at his home that hauled in a reported $250,000 in campaign cash.[3] When Obama advanced to the general election, Kaiser was there for him again, helping him raise between $50,000 and $100,000.

Kaiser was also the largest shareholder in Solyndra.

So once candidate Obama became President Obama, Kaiser came

calling to collect on his investment. Records show he visited the White House repeatedly while the stimulus funds were being divvied out. But don't take the White House's word for it. Let George tell you himself.

At a speech to the Tulsa Rotary Club in July 2009, Kaiser laid out his agenda for the president's first term:

> There's never been more money shoved out of the government's door in world history, and probably never will be again than in the past few months and in the next 18 months. And our selfish parochial goal is to try and get as much of it for Tulsa and Oklahoma as we can.[4]

Mission accomplished.

Despite protestations from the OMB guys, Kaiser's visits paid off. Literally.

Solyndra bagged a $535 million Energy Department loan guarantee.

President Obama, touring the country to promote the good work his $800 billion boondoggle of a "stimulus" was allegedly doing, stopped by Solyndra's Fremont, California, headquarters. Obama's remarks that fine May 26, 2010, day read like a commercial for Beta Max VCRs or New Coke. Even the guy who wrote the "Dewey Defeats Truman" headline would have been embarrassed by this:

> Every day that you build this expanded facility, as you fill orders for solar panels to ship around the world, you're demonstrating that the promise of clean energy isn't just an article of faith—not anymore.
>
> It's not some abstract possibility for science fiction

movies or a distant future—10 years down the road or 20 years down the road. It's happening right now. The future is here. We're poised to transform the ways we power our homes and our cars and our businesses. And we're poised to lead our competitors in the development of new technologies and products and businesses. And we are poised to generate countless new jobs, good-paying middle-class jobs, right here in the United States of America.[5]

Bahahaha!

Solyndra declared bankruptcy the following year, leaving its 1,100 employees in the proverbial dark. But not before modifying the loan it received so that it could pay back $75 million in private loans before letting taxpayers off their $535 million hook. Because of the nature of the loan, it's unlikely that we will get much, if any, of our money back. The U.S. government allowed Solyndra to restructure its loan so that its private creditors would be paid first. That means, as Bloomberg noted, "the government will probably get nothing for its $528 million claim from the loan guarantee because creditors ranking ahead of the U.S. won't be fully repaid."[6]

But Kaiser didn't just get free taxpayer money for a failing company. Like every good rich liberal hypocrite, he used the bankruptcy to dodge paying taxes—even as his main man Obama raised yours.

Kaiser is a study in contradictions. He's an oilman who invests heavily in green technology. And he's a man who decries the unfair advantages his industry gets in the U.S. tax code, then turns around and uses every accounting trick in the book to avoid paying those same taxes.

In 2007, *Forbes* magazine asked George Kaiser what he thought about America's tax rates. Kaiser replied that he thought there was no doubt that America's tax structure was "insufficiently progressive."[7]

So King George thinks the tariffs should be higher on billionaires like him. Fine.

So why did Kaiser keep his books in such a way that it looks like he lives in an outhouse, not a penthouse?

A watchdog group, the Sunlight Foundation, investigated Kaiser's taxable income. Remember, this is a guy on the Forbes 400 list. A billionaire. An oil tycoon. And someone who, per the Sunlight report, made less than minimum wage according to his own tax filings.

"In one six year period, during which he increased his net worth enough to land him on the Forbes list of the 400 wealthiest Americans," the report reads, "Kaiser reported taxable income to the Internal Revenue Service just once, totaling $11,699—equivalent to a full-time hourly wage of $5.62."[8]

You catch that? So while George's income was shooting his name up the list of our country's elite, his taxable income apparently didn't rate reporting.

It wasn't the first time Kaiser skated out of our country's "insufficiently progressive" tax system, either. The Sunlight Foundation says he has a long history of tax avoidance:

In 1997, the Internal Revenue Service sent Kaiser and his companies tax bills for more than $72 million in back taxes, interest and penalties, covering individual and corporate returns filed from 1986 to 1992. Kaiser filed returns showing his personal income averaging *negative* $860,000 between 1986 and 1991; his holding company, GBK Corp., and its subsidiaries reported an aggregate loss from 1989 to 1992 of

$507,000—some years it made money and paid taxes, others it claimed losses and paid none.[9]

So how does a man listed as one of the richest in the country get away with not paying taxes? The same way any Crapitalist amasses his fortune. Legally.

The U.S. tax code contains around four million words.[10] That's more than five times as long as the Bible.[11] So it takes government about five times as long as God to organize mankind. Nice.

And on the eighth day, they created loopholes.

Those four million words contain several provisions that Kaiser knows well.

Provisions like if your company buys or owns a business that loses money, the losses of that business help offset any other income gains you might have had. That's how billionaires like Kaiser make money. And that's how he cashed in on Solyndra, even while the company, and the taxpayers, got flushed down the crapper.

Like all good Crapitalists, Kaiser had the gig wired from the get-go. When the OMB guys had concerns about Solyndra's viability, Kaiser used his inside connections to get then–Obama chief of staff Rahm Emanuel and Biden chief of staff Ron Klain to help grease the loan. Of all the stimulus money that Obama doled out to his own campaign contributors, Solyndra's loan was the first one out the door.[12]

And when Solyndra declared bankruptcy? The Obama White House was there for them once again.

Solyndra was also able to restructure in such a way as to maximize the tax benefits for private investors like Kaiser. So while taxpayers like us are waving good-bye to the hundreds of millions we sent to green energy fantasy camp, billionaires like Kaiser can look forward to as much as $975 million in tax carryovers to use against future income earnings.[13]

That's how guys like Kaiser get to be on the *Forbes* list while declaring no income. They profit from other companies' failures. And in this case, he profited from the failure of a business we financed—and used his political connections to do it.

Many game the system. But few do so with such intellectual dishonesty as King George. Remember that *Forbes* interview where he said he thought the tax rate should be higher for fat cats like him? That wasn't all he said.

"I also agree that the estate tax at levels above $10 million should be retained," Kaiser said. "Higher tax rates for higher levels of income [up to at least 50 percent, maybe higher] not only are socially responsible but also would encourage more charitable giving."[14]

Charitable giving. George knows all about charitable giving.

"Philanthropist" George Kaiser has a foundation called the George Kaiser Family Foundation. But the foundation is set up a little differently than most. Instead of being labeled a "private foundation," Kaiser set his up as a "public charity" that allows it to donate *less* money every year, per IRS laws, in exchange for giving up some control over its investments.[15] Turns out, Kaiser isn't that altruistic after all. Bloomberg studied the foundation's tax returns and found that of the $3.4 billion that Kaiser's foundation held in assets, more than a third was invested to help one cause in particular: his own.

That's right—at least $1.25 billion in "charitable expenditures" went toward helping Kaiser.[16] A Bloomberg analysis of the foundation's tax returns found that "the charity invests alongside the billionaire's stakes in some companies. In other instances, it directs funds in ways that support his for-profit businesses."[17]

You'd think charitable foundations existed to, you know, be charitable. Just like you'd think green energy companies would exist to produce energy, not tax breaks for the rich and tax obligations for the rest of us. But that's what this new breed of Crapitalists looks like. Intellectual honesty isn't a phrase these guys are familiar with, unless it's the name of a hedge fund they invest our siphoned tax dollars in. No, these guys aren't interested in honesty. Hypocrisy is their game. Just look at our president, the Hypocrite-in-Chief. The guy who declared himself "a warrior for the middle class" in 2008 and who won reelection in part by demonizing Mitt Romney and the rest of the "one-percenters" wants you to think he's looking out for you.[18] In fact, the nation's rich have amassed a greater share of our country's wealth during Obama's administration than at any other point in history.[19]

For those who earned it through competition, good on you. For those like Kaiser who made their dough by poaching your dollars using their crony Obama connections—screw you.

The reporters who cover stories like Solyndra think they are covering checkers. They see a politically connected company that gets government goodies and they jump on it. Then it goes bankrupt, and that's another story. But no one connects the dots between incompetent policies and big cash payouts for the guys who lined the politician's pockets to push for them.

Guys like George Kaiser are playing an entirely different game. They're playing Crapitalism chess. And they've put you and me, the taxpayers, in checkmate.

11 Sally Susman

Pharma is a long-trend business. . . . I've been here four
years and I definitely feel the tides shifting.

—Sally Susman

Some phrases cement a president's legacy. George H. W. Bush said,
"Read my lips: No new taxes." Bill Clinton said, "I did not have
sexual relations with that woman, Ms. Lewinsky." The defining line
for Barack Obama will be "If you like your plan, you can keep it."

We may not have a true grasp for some time of how the moun-
tain of medical malpractice known as Obamacare will fundamentally
destroy our country's health care. But here's what we do know: the
country's pharmaceutical companies came out ahead. Way ahead.

And Sally Susman is a big reason why.

Susman is the executive vice president for policy, external

affairs, and communications for Pfizer, one of America's largest pharmaceutical companies.[1] Her bio says she "plays a key role in shaping policy initiatives." "Shaping policy initiatives" in this case is Crapitalist-speak for "screwing over America."

In truth, I am sort of glad to have Sally to list among our collection of Crapitalists. We were getting heavy on old white men, so I wanted to mix it up a bit—you know, in the spirit of diversity. We already had Jay-Z and Maxine Waters in there. Heck, Waters is black and a woman: a twofer! So our quota may have been satisfied with her alone. But, considering how often liberals accuse the GOP of being the party of "old white men," it's ironic how many old white guys are embraced by the Democrats' political machine. These crusty Crapitalists are about as white as you get, but are celebrated and enabled rather than shunned. I guess if you're a Crapitalist, it's okay to be pasty.

In fact, a white dude helped Sally get her start. Her father.

Yep, Sally Susman is a second-generation Crapitalist. Sally's dad is Louis Susman, an investment banker who raised over half a million dollars for Obama's 2008 campaign. As the *Hill* put it, his proficiency at collecting campaign checks for his liberal buddies earned him high praise, and an unusual nickname:

> Susman Sr. was so good, over many decades, at sucking up money for politicians that he was nicknamed the Vacuum Cleaner or the Hoover. Obama rewarded him in 2009 with the plum appointment of Ambassador Extraordinary and Plenipotentiary to the Court of St. James's.[2]

So Sally's dad backs Barack, and as a reward gets a taxpayer-subsidized vacation in England. Pretty sweet gig if you can poach it.

But when it comes to our tax dollars, Sally sucks just as bad.

Here's a quick rule of thumb for Crapitalism detection: anytime you see a new, large government program, assume big businesses are making out like bandits with your tax dollars.

And few are making out better than Pfizer.

You've heard of Pfizer—they tout themselves as the world's largest research-based pharmaceutical company. But you probably know them as the makers of Viagra.

It's fitting that the company responsible for an erectile dysfunction treatment got in bed with the government to bone the American taxpayer by forcing us to buy overpriced health-care plans we don't want or need. But unlike the guys who need to consult a doctor after experiencing an unfortunate side (or in some cases front) effect for more than four hours, consulting a doctor won't help us get rid of the government hard-on that is bending us over. Because of the efforts of Sally Susman and her Pfizer fiends, we have new taxes and regulations to funnel profits to Pfizer. You'd think the never-ending libido of the rapidly aging baby boomer population would have been enough!

Instead, because of Obamacare, Pfizer now gets all the guys from that generation who have less boom than they used to, plus everyone else suffering from any other malady that requires a prescription. How? They helped write the law.

The drug industry has spent almost a billion dollars more than any other industry on lobbying over the last fifteen years.[3] Those investments in politicians have paid off in a few major ways for companies like Pfizer. The Medicare prescription drug benefit passed under George W. Bush in 2006 was certainly a boon to bottom lines across the drug industry. But for Obamacare, they upped the dosage.

The pharmaceutical industry hasn't spent less than $100 million annually on lobbying since 2001. So dropping big bucks to grease the wheels of democracy is nothing new. But they outdid themselves in 2009, with $273 million flowing through the halls of power in D.C.[4] Not coincidentally, this is the same year Obamacare passed the House and Senate.

Big Drug's fingerprints are all over this thing—with Susman helping to lead the charge. As Pfizer's top lobbyist and an Obama bundler to boot, Susman had the kind of access Crapitalists crave. As in thirteen visits to the White House since 2009 kind of access.[5]

The *Wall Street Journal* noted the influence. After reviewing thousands of emails between trade groups and the White House, one name stood out more than others:

> The business refrain in those days was that if you're not at the table, you're on the menu. But it turns out Big Pharma was also serving as head chef, maître d'hotel and dishwasher. Though some parts of the story have been reported before, the emails make clear that ObamaCare might never have passed without the drug companies. Thank you, Pfizer.[6]

As a result, independent analysis shows that Obamacare "represents a dramatic transformation in the fortunes of pharmaceutical companies in what is the world's largest market for prescription drugs." Estimates now suggest that, thanks to the mandate that everyone get covered, pharmacy companies like Pfizer can expect up to "$115 billion of new business over the next 10 years."[7]

Prior to Obamacare, Pfizer's fate looked dour. Generic drugs comprised more than 60 percent of the market, as consumers were purchasing inexpensive drugs over the pricier name-brand ones. And while this was an industry-wide problem for pharmaceutical companies, Pfizer would be hit the hardest. Their patent on Lipitor was set to expire. The popular cholesterol drug represented a huge chunk of their revenue, "bringing in a staggering $12 billion a year" by 2005. As CNNMoney noted, "Once a Wall Street darling and corporate icon, Pfizer has tumbled into disarray."[8] Analysts questioned whether Pfizer could ever find another Golden Goose like Lipitor again. But thanks to Obamacare, the company wouldn't have to.

Susman, who didn't technically have to register as a lobbyist because of what the *New York Times* called "byzantine rules," used her access to help shape the law to her industry's favor.[9] Initially, the Department of Health and Human Services (HHS) agency that was tasked with actually implementing the law proposed a rule to require all insurance policies to pay for a minimum of one drug in every class. (Drugs are classified by the types of diseases they help treat.) But Susman and company helped push for additional coverage that would benefit their bottom line. As Tim Carney detailed:

Led by the lobby group Pharmaceutical Research and Manufacturers of America [PhRMA], the industry argued that HHS should require all insurers to not only cover one drug per class, but also to match the benchmark plan in their state.

And Big Pharma won. HHS's final rule, issued in late November 2012, required all plans to cover "the greater of" one drug per class or whatever the state's benchmark plan covers.

So if your insurance plan met state mandates and covered one or more drug per class, it still might be illegal if it didn't cover as much as the "benchmark" insurance plan. PhRMA and its member companies like Eli Lilly and Pfizer care about this in part because more bare-bones prescription drug plans may cover only generic drugs and not the more costly name brand drugs covered by the benchmark plans.[10]

By forcing insurance policies to meet the "benchmark" policies of each state, Obamacare essentially raised the floor of what policies would provide. It also raised the bottom line of the drug industry. And that is one of the major reasons why the president's whole "If you like your plan, you can keep it" promise turned out to be the national enema it was.

The reality was, you'd be able to keep your plan only if it covered enough of the things a special interest like Pfizer wanted it to cover, whether you need them or not.

Another provision in Obamacare that fattened Pfizer's fortunes was the contraception mandate. Every policy now would require birth control pills to be covered. It didn't matter if you were the Catholic Church, which sort of has a problem with birth control, if you hadn't heard. Or did you think your good friends the O'Malleys with the eight kids were just really affectionate?

The Obama administration would eventually cave and offer an exemption for religious organizations and the Supreme Court would strike down the mandate for family-owned corporations. The rest of us weren't so lucky. Which is great news for the Sandra Flukes of the world. And for the Sally Susmans.[11]

So while Sandra Fluke got her fifteen minutes of fame whining that it was her "right" to get the government to force her employer to supply her and her fembot friends with "free" birth control, her embarrassing display of stupidity wasn't the real story. Nor, as the media would like you to believe, was it Rush Limbaugh calling her a "slut." The *real* story was that Pfizer and others in the medical community were hiding those pills under the fallacious rhetoric of "rights" to mandate new customers. Pfizer already sold nearly $8 million worth of name-brand birth control pills a year, not to mention what they rake in from their generic version. Having most every policy now cover the full cost of all FDA-approved contraception means more people will choose the expensive ones. Which means Pfizer, thanks to Susman, gets paid more.

In addition to birth control, Pfizer and other drug peddlers lobbied to ensure the new essential health benefit packages covered all types of prescription drugs, including drugs for cholesterol and hepatitis C. If you don't lather your pancakes with slabs of butter every morning and if you're not having sleepovers with Pamela Anderson, too bad, you must still buy a health-care plan covering those drugs.

So what does this mean for Pfizer? Money. A lot of it.

According to *Forbes,* 2014 looked much brighter for the drug companies, thanks to Obamacare:

> Projected spending is forecast to grow 5.2 percent next year, compared with 0.6 percent growth in 2013, thanks to greater use among Americans who are newly insured or those [who] sign up for accessible insurance plans, at least according to the US Center for Medicare & Medicaid Services.
>
> Specifically, the projected growth in prescription drug spending would be 2.9 percent lower in 2014 without the oomph from healthcare reform, which suggests a clear benefit.[12]

You think?

And with Pfizer's prospects looking up, Susman's income is, too: She cashed in $4 million worth of stock options in February 2014.[13]

To their credit, Pfizer is spinning the health-care law not as extra money for them, but as extra care for us. Really. Their website brags how "[e]xpanded access to health insurance coverage will help ensure that patients with underdiagnosed and undertreated conditions are able to address them."[14]

Of course! It isn't that the drug companies and the government are making us pay for things that we don't need. It's that we have been walking around *underdiagnosed*. We didn't even know we were sick.

I'm glad we cleared that up.

No, contrary to Pfizer's claims, we aren't sick—at least by any medical definition. But when I read about how the Obama White House gave the drug companies profitable provisions so Susman and her ilk would spend money helping to sell the program to the country, it makes me want to throw up.

In exchange for special provisions like the mandates and the continued illegalization of bringing in cheaper drugs from other countries, Susman used some of her communications expertise on behalf of Obamacare. Pfizer and the other companies that are part of PhRMA agreed to spend $150 million[15] on advertisements convincing Americans that the Crapitalism sandwich that is Obamacare is good for us.[16]

Ultimately, as the details of the law and its destructive impact on the health of the American economy evidence themselves, the rest of the country will realize we have a major problem on our hands. But unlike with the guy who took too much Viagra, Obamacare's side effects will last more than four hours. But Sally Susman doesn't care about that. Rather than fight the heavy-handed tactics of government price controls in the marketplace, Susman used her access and influence to collude with the government, ensuring maximum profits for her, and maximum misery for us.

Sally Susman didn't care about the impact of the bill on you and me. Her job was just to bring Obamacare home for a landing, as long as it had the right prescription for the drug companies. For Susman, Pfizer, and others, Obamacare was a win, no matter the cost.

12

Steven Spielberg

I'm not really interested in making money.

—Steven Spielberg

I like Steven Spielberg. Anyone who grew up watching movies in the 1980s or '90s has to have a place in their heart for the stories and sense of childlike wonder he helped infuse into the American consciousness. The guy brought us *Jaws*, *E.T.*, the Indiana Jones series, and *Jurassic Park*—all out-of-this-world adventure stories that inspired imaginations across the country. As an adult, I can appreciate his ability to tell important stories about history, too. Movies like *Lincoln*, *Amistad*, and *Saving Private Ryan* capture significant periods in our country's history and remind us about the people and ideas that have made this country great.

Sadly, like most *Hollywood Hypocrites* (again, wherever books are sold), Spielberg combines his talent for business with a greed for taxpayer-funded government goodies. He may wax patriotic about American heroes, but he gobbles up our tax dollars and other benefits like one of his animatronic sharks at a beach or dinosaurs at a Brontosaurus buffet.

One of Spielberg's latest films, *Lincoln*, will undoubtedly go down in the canon of great films about American history. Daniel Day-Lewis was amazing as our sixteenth president, and the film as a whole masterfully explored and depicted how Republicans fought against Democrat-led slavery.

Lincoln grossed over $180 million worldwide.[1] Given its estimated budget of $65 million, that's doing pretty well for Spielberg's DreamWorks studio, the company that helped produce the film.

Of course, like most liberals, Hollywood will take all the tax money it can get. During the announcement touting the fact that the movie would be shot in Virginia, Spielberg talked up all the natural advantages for filming in the "Old Dominion" state: "Virginia's rich historic legacy, coupled with the remarkable period architecture found in Richmond and Petersburg, make Central Virginia the ideal location for this production," Spielberg said.[2]

I guess the architecture is nice. But so is the cash.

So while Daniel Day-Lewis took home the Oscar for Best Actor, Spielberg and his production company took home millions in tax breaks, credits, and incentives for filming the movie in Virginia. Between disgraced Virginia governor Bob McDonnell's Motion Picture Opportunity Fund and the state's Motion Picture Tax Credit Program, Spielberg milked $3.5 million from the Virginia taxpayer teat. And that's not counting the "in-kind contributions" estimated to be worth another million more.[3]

I can see how you might not want to blame Spielberg for taking advantage of Virginia's existing tax credit program. After all, if

Spielberg doesn't take advantage of it, someone else will, right? But here's the thing about Crapitalists—they don't just take advantage of programs that benefit them and stiff taxpayers. They help create them in the first place.

And Spielberg is no different.

In Hollywood, movies take a long time to get made. (Probably because, as we're learning, it takes a while to squeeze as many tax dollars as you can before a project gets a green light.) Virginia Film Commission director Andy Edmunds admitted that Spielberg had been thinking about *Lincoln* and eyeing Virginia as a setting for a long time.

"As far back as 2003, he [Spielberg] began scouting and planning here in Virginia, so he was interested in us from the start," said Edmunds.[4]

But there was a problem: in 2003 Virginia didn't have a tax credit program. No worries: enter newly elected Governor Bob McDonnell. You may have heard McDonnell's name in the news recently—he and his wife have taken a lot of heat for cozying up to rich people and allegedly offering them special treatment from the governor's office in exchange for personal items they wouldn't be able to afford.[5] So he's what Crapitalists might call "easy to work with." Takes one to know one.

Shortly after his 2009 election, McDonnell signed Virginia's first movie tax credits into law.[6] He then called Spielberg, selling the filmmaker on filming in his state.[7]

The rest, as they say, is history.

At the beginning of May 2011, McDonnell announced that *Lincoln* was headed back to the D.C. area.[8]

Was Steven Spielberg personally responsible for the creation of Virginia's new tax credit program? Spielberg has been checking out Virginia for years, then decides to film there within months of the creation of the film tax credit program. There is no evidence to prove that Spielberg was personally responsible for McDonnell's efforts to create the tax credit program. But coincidences like that normally happen only in the movies.

In the real world, they happen because of planning. And collusion. And Crapitalism.

For his part, McDonnell was upset afterward that the project didn't bring more of an impact to his state.

"This film alone will be somewhere in the neighborhood of $35 million, and I was really disappointed," McDonnell was quoted as saying during the filming. "I talked to [Kathleen Kelly, producer for *Lincoln*] today, and she said they're under budget. This is one area I actually hoped they'd be over budget, because that means more investment in Virginia."[9]

So how did the taxpayers make out in the deal?

Not so great.

"From my point of view, the state giving $5 million to a billionaire to make his movie in Virginia is a luxury our state can't afford right now when we are cutting education, Medicaid and the rest of our safety net," said one state delegate.[10]

Well, at least in exchange for sharing some of their tax dollars, Virginians got to see the movie for free. Oh, it doesn't work like that?

Sadly, as we detailed in the chapter about Chris Dodd, tax credits for the movie industry almost never give the people forking over the cash a return on their investment. You know, the taxpayers.

Sure, movies bring some temporary jobs to the area. But they are considered "fly by night" jobs—as in, one night, they fly away. So the long-term impact those jobs can have on an economy is really difficult to measure. The real impact tax dollar giveaways have is that politicians like McDonnell get to hobnob and have their pictures taken with the fancy celebrities. That's what McDonnell did—he bragged on his radio show that he had even *spoken* to Spielberg about filming *Lincoln* in Virginia. Then he hosted him in the Governor's Mansion while filming was taken place. That's Crapitalism at its finest. Spielberg gets the tax money. The politician gets the photo op. And the taxpayers, at a time when other programs were being slashed, get stuck with the tab.

It isn't like Spielberg, reportedly worth over $3 billion, needs the money, either. But that doesn't stop him from grabbing our tax dollars at every turn.

In fact, as a huge supporter of Democratic policies, Spielberg is the first in line to laud liberal redistribution.

One of Spielberg's TV companies, Amblin Television, is making a television show in North Carolina and taking advantage of the refundable tax credit it offers. Spielberg and his projects have grabbed tax dollars because of work in New York, Michigan, and Florida as well. And as bad as Spielberg's regrettable *Indiana Jones and the Crystal Skull* was, that he got tax money from Connecticut makes it all the worse. (No—great idea, Spielberg. Let's take a guy known for fighting Nazis and this time let him fight . . . aliens.)

Shockingly, Connecticut eliminated its film subsidies a few years after Spielberg grabbed some for his movie.[11] Apparently they weren't seeing enough return on the investment. Maybe all the aliens weren't eating at enough restaurants.

Spielberg's love of using other people's money to make some for himself even extends beyond America's borders. Ireland recently extended and revised its tax credit program to "attract in the big boys." The program, which Ireland is calling the "Tom Cruise clause," was inspired by one of America's top directors.

"I had the opportunity and privilege to speak to Mr. Steven Spielberg about this," said Enda Kenny, one of Ireland's top politicians.[12] This is the Spielberg way. Where there are tax dollars to be had, Spielberg is there to help grab them. All it costs him is a phone call and a photo op. And maybe an invite to the Golden Globes or some other liberal schmooze-fest. All it costs the citizens of the states that host him are their hard-earned tax dollars. Plus fifteen bucks a pop if they actually want to go see the film.

It's a formula, like a buddy cop movie script, that Spielberg has followed all the way to the bank. He made more than $100 million between 2012 and 2013, more than anyone else in Hollywood except Madonna. (Don't ask me. I have no idea, either.)

Spielberg has used his wealth and cachet to become a go-to for politicians looking to milk the Hollywood Left for cash. He and Bill Clinton are best buds, with Stevie helping to arrange Bill Clinton's "secret" appearance at the Golden Globes to introduce *Lincoln*. (How appropriate. A film about one of the greatest presidents ever introduced by one of only two to be impeached. Who's in charge of casting around here?)

Spielberg is also good friends with our current president Barack Obama. Back when Obama was an underdog in the Democratic primary, Spielberg teamed with his DreamWorks cofounders, Jeffrey Katzenberg and David Geffen, to throw a $1.3 million fundraiser.[13]

And when Obama was running for reelection, Spielberg, also a big donor to the George Soros–backed Priorities USA PAC, helped with some creative visioning.

As *Businessweek* reported:

Steven Spielberg spent three hours explaining how to capture an audience's attention and offered a number of ideas that will be rolled out before Election Day. An early example of Spielberg's influence is RomneyEconomics.com, a website designed by the Obama team to tell the story—a horror story, by their reckoning—of Mitt Romney's career at Bain Capital.[14]

As you may remember from the 2012 campaign, the idea of Romney being a "one-percenter" venture capitalist who liked to fire people was a central theme of the Obama attack. And who can blame Obama for using it. Not only was it effective, but it was given to him by one of the great storytellers in America today. The guy who sold America on a man-eating shark and genetically engineered dinosaurs was now selling us a new monster.

And like sharks and dinosaurs, the venture capitalist was a monster Spielberg was very familiar with. He had been bailed out by one a few years earlier.

Anil Ambani is one of India's richest businessmen. He owns the Reliance Group, a mega-conglomerate that handles everything from life insurance to telecommunications.[15] In 2008, Spielberg's DreamWorks Studios was struggling financially. Apparently not everyone liked the idea of big-budget flop *Cowboys and Aliens*. Luckily for Spielberg and fans of movies that continue to force aliens into places they don't belong, Ambani's group came to the rescue.

Reliance now has a 50 percent stake in DreamWorks, thanks to a $1.2 billion partnership that's already infused $325 million worth of equity.

So just to be clear: If you're running for president, experience with private equity is a bad thing. If you're making movies about presidents, no problem.

And Ambani has made other U.S. deals since.

Ambani's Reliance company had been trying to get $600 million worth of loan guarantees to buy equipment from a Wisconsin coal equipment manufacturer.[16] Though the application had been rejected by the Export-Import Bank of the United States, a government agency, in 2012 Democratic pols stepped in to push it through.

It could all be a coincidence. Or perhaps a friend of Spielberg's is a friend to all capital-D Democrats?

The idea of evil forces conspiring to harm us has long been one of the most popular plots in movies. Villains like sharks, dinosaurs, and artifact-obsessed Nazis have helped Spielberg tell great stories of good versus evil, with the good guys always coming out on top (albeit maybe minus a limb or two). Sadly, in real life, the good guys don't always win. In fact, this book is filled with horror stories of how Crapitalists are winning every day. Unlike the movies, we can't just wait for the hero to free himself and the entrance of the upbeat music to tell us it's all going to be okay. We have to be the ones to save the day. Because Crapitalists like Spielberg are eating our tax dollars faster than a shark or dinosaur could ever dream.

13 Jeffrey Katzenberg

> I want to thank Jeffrey [Katzenberg] not just for this evening, but for his tenacious support and advocacy since we started back in 2007. He has consistently been there for me, through thick and through thin.
>
> —Barack Obama

While less known than his business partner and Crapitalist crony Steven Spielberg, Jeffrey Katzenberg is one of the most influential people in America. As one of the cofounders of DreamWorks Studios, Katzenberg is a leading figure in Hollywood. But because of his bromance with Barack, his reach extends far beyond the big screen.

Katzenberg is now poised, through his new partnership with the Chinese government, to rake in huge profits for his company.

And as we'll see, he was able to cash in on his crony connections to help make it happen.

In 2004, a candidate for U.S. Senate from Illinois gave a keynote address at the Democratic National Convention. The event would ultimately conclude by nominating John Kerry for president that year, but it also laid the groundwork for Barack Obama's ascension to the White House four years later. Jeffrey Katzenberg is a big reason why.

The longtime movie producer was awed by Obama's speech in Boston and set about working to help cast Barack as the country's next leading man. In 2006, Katzenberg's political consultant, a former DreamWorks executive named Andy Spahn, brought Obama by to see Katzenberg and the Hollywood titan pledged his full support if Obama decided to run for president.[1]

That proved to be a promise Obama could literally take to the bank.

Because Hollywood had supported and forgiven (and maybe even cheered) Bill Clinton during his time in office, many assumed Hillary would garner the same support from the reliably lucrative Leftists. But Katzenberg's early support of Obama helped establish the junior senator from Illinois as a legitimate contender. Well, Katzenberg's support, and all the cash that came with it.

Katzenberg became a bundler for Obama's 2008 campaign, helping raise at least $500,000. Obama later praised Katzenberg for his "tenacious support." When talking about how people would, on occasion, romanticize his 2008 campaign, Obama said he sometimes has to remind them it was actually more uneven than some remember—with one exception: "The only person I don't have to remind is Jeffrey because he was there, through all the ups and downs," Obama said of Katzenberg. "Occasionally he would call, and he would say, 'Barack, I don't think that things are working the way they're supposed to.' "[2]

Luckily for Katzenberg, things would work out just fine.

After Obama's election, Katzenberg became a sort of informal adviser to the president. The White House was allegedly impressed that Katzenberg, despite all his financial support, never came to Obama with an "ask."[3]

Instead, he used his relationship to Obama to raise his own profile.

The two spoke regularly, with Katzenberg and his consultant Spahn visiting the White House more than fifty times between the two of them. Spahn has other clients besides Katzenberg, so not all those visits may have been on Katzenberg's behalf.[4] But the fact remains: because of his early and continued support (Katzenberg was one of the first to agree to give $2 million to the PAC supporting Obama's reelection), Katzenberg has access. And because of his access, he has influence.

It's frustrating to think about now, but back in 2012 there was a real sense Obama was vulnerable. The Obama campaign was in danger of losing the money race, partly because of Mitt Romney's bank account and partly because so many on the Left had become disillusioned with the president. As hard as it is to believe, apparently some of the Hollywood types didn't think Obama had done nearly enough to fundamentally transform our country in the first four years.

As bad as Obamacare was, they wanted a single-payer system. Even with the millions in tax dollars he had thrown to his green energy cronies, Obama had yet to actually slow down the rising of the oceans. And during the wailing and gnashing of teeth over online piracy, Obama basically sat on the sidelines of the Stop Online Piracy Act (SOPA) debate and let the bill die in Congress despite the urgent pleadings of the Hollywood Left. It all added up to some of Barack's biggest backers keeping their checkbooks in their wallets four years later. Katzenberg's business partner David Geffen, for example, a $500,000 donor in 2008, gave just $5,000 this time around. Luckily, Katzenberg came to the rescue. With a little help from Batman.

Katzenberg organized a fundraiser at the house of actor George Clooney. And while Clooney may hold the record for being the worst Caped Crusader of all time, he would play a part in helping Obama set a record of a different sort. But only if the president would heed Katzenberg's request.

At fundraisers, President Obama normally slides in after the event has started, gives a speech, then jets away shortly thereafter. But Katzenberg wanted to rewrite the script for the Clooney fundraiser. If you can believe it, Katzenberg had the gall to ask that Obama actually spend time talking at each of the fourteen tables at the event. Shocking, I know.

The *Wall Street Journal* reported that Obama campaign officials "weren't happy about it." After all, the president would have just traveled across the entire country before the dinner, and would have just been at a different fundraiser in Seattle. Sure, he would be flying on the nicest jet taxpayers can buy. That's still a long flight. Plus, collecting checks is tiring work.

Still, when "King Katzenberg" speaks, even the president listens.[5]

Obama ended up staying at Clooney's house for over three hours, which is practically unheard-of in presidential fundraising circles. But then, his take-home of $15 million for the night was unprecedented, too. The event had set a record for the most money raised in a single night, a huge success for the campaign. Katzenberg had come through again. But he was no doubt all too happy to help. And soon all that happier.

In February 2012, Xi Jinping, the vice president of China, came to the United States to meet key dignitaries. Xi was virtually assured of becoming China's next president and thought it wise to know just who was in charge of the country he and his cohorts were systematically trouncing in the global marketplace. For his part, Vice President Joe Biden hosted a luncheon in his honor.

Katzenberg wasn't there by accident. He had been laying the groundwork for months.

The United States had seen a slowdown at the box office lately—2011 was the slowest year for films since 1993.[6] And that was bad for Hollywood's bottom line. China, on the other hand, was doing more than $2 billion a year in movie releases, and was on pace to become the top market in the world, with an estimated $5 billion in ticket sales by 2015.[7] But China, being China, wasn't exactly an open door in terms of permitting things from overseas. All China's film-related companies were state run, and they had a quota of twenty foreign films per year that were allowed into the country. Katzenberg had figured out a way to get past the Great Wall and into the pockets of China's moviegoing public, but he would need some help. Luckily, he had a ton of Crapitalist credit he could cash in.

In early February, just days before Xi would arrive in the States, Katzenberg's political consultant Andy Spahn told the *Financial Times* he was arranging a fundraiser for Obama's reelection at Katzenberg's home. This is the same Spahn who, together with Katzenberg, had visited the White House nearly fifty times during Obama's first administration and whose website touts his services as "government relations."

But, like so many of the people in this book who buy their way into the corridors of power, Spahn doesn't have to register as a lobbyist.

Two weeks after the fundraiser, Biden hosted his lunch. Katzenberg needed Xi not only to help ease access to Chinese theaters for American movies, but also for something bigger. Katzenberg had been working on a deal to partner DreamWorks Animation with three of the state-owned Chinese studios. The partnership would mean that, unlike other companies that were restricted by China's quota system, which caps the number of films it lets in from other countries, such as the United States, Katzenberg's crew could operate with no cap—on the films, or the profits.

A few days after Biden's lunch, Katzenberg attended another lunch with Xi in Los Angeles. Later that day, a deal with Vice President Xi to ease restrictions on the importation of American films was announced.[8] The quota system was still in place, but China would graciously now allow another fourteen films into the country, provided they were "special technology" like 3-D or IMAX.[9]

Hollywood was thrilled. Sure, fourteen movies wasn't a ton, but it was something. After the Obama administration had failed to clamp down on Internet piracy during the SOPA bill debate, movie execs finally had something to cheer about.

But Katzenberg was cheering louder than most.

Shortly after the quota deal was announced, Katzenberg made news of his own. He announced an agreement to create "Oriental DreamWorks," a $350 million studio to be housed in China. In addition to access to China's rapidly growing moviegoing population, the deal also includes plans to build a commercial district in Shanghai. The area, to be known as a "Dream Center," which includes restaurants, hotels, and theaters, is hoped to "rival New York's Broadway and London's West End" when it opens in 2016.[10]

And to make Katzenberg and his DreamWorks company even wealthier.

In an interview after the deal was announced, Katzenberg rattled off the numbers. "There are right now, today, over 14,500 movie theaters in China. They added 4,500 of them last year alone," Katzenberg gloated. "The movie box office this year—well, last year was about 17 billion RMB [Chinese currency]. This year it will grow almost another third to 22 billion. And by the way, 17 was a third up from the previous year."[11]

But then, in discussing the way he went about working the deal in China, he also hinted at something very telling:

> This is the opposite of what we do everywhere else in the world. . . . Because what I was saying to them, "Listen, you know, you have great brands that you bring here from around the world. But the thing that you have done in every industry is you have created your own." And that is the thing that I consider the "Chinese Way."[12]

Oh, the Chinese have a "Way" all right. They have a "Way" of not letting couples have more than one kid. They have a "Way" of selectively enforcing laws like copyright infringements. They have a "Way" of handing out business permits based on bribes and kickbacks. Hell, the quota on movies was only an issue in the first place because China had refused, twice, to enforce an agreement by the World Trade Organization.[13]

China's reputation is so bad, in fact, that because DreamWorks and other Hollywood execs were able to strike a deal, the Securities and Exchange Commission opened an investigation into whether Katzenberg and others had bribed Chinese officials to help push the quota increase through.[14] It seems the SEC, too, had heard about the Chinese Way.

There's one other thing China is known for. Like the fact that, if this book was written there, this chapter wouldn't be in it.

China has an insecurity problem. They don't like negative things being written or said about them. Luckily, their arcane censorship practices haven't stopped businesses from working with them. Google, for example, abides by China's censorship filters. Amazing what a few billion customers will do to your corporate value structure.

But surely, Hollywood would be different, right? The industry known for creative expression and a rigid adherence to free speech and artistic sovereignty?

Not so much.

As the *New Yorker* detailed, Hollywood actually proved to be quite flexible when it came to selling out its own values:

> The latest Bond picture, "Skyfall," was shot partly in Shanghai and Macau, but when it reached Chinese screens, the filmmakers had agreed to cut a scene in which Daniel Craig killed a Chinese security guard and to nix a plotline in which Javier Bardem explains that he became a villain after MI-6 left him in Chinese custody. In another case, Chinese investors put more than ten million dollars into "Cloud Atlas"— the largest Chinese investment yet in a foreign film—but then censors required the removal of no less than thirty-eight minutes of the movie, mostly love scenes.[15]

Katzenberg, the man who helped launch a studio that's given us movies like *The Help* and *Munich*, two critically acclaimed stories about the horrors of prejudice and oppression, was now in business with a totalitarian regime. And they're really excited about the release of one of Oriental DreamWorks' first projects: *Kung Fu Panda 3*.

So how did his Hollywood buddies react to his Chinese expeditions? Did they criticize or rebuke him for working in a country that so regularly violates the most basic of human rights? Close.

They gave him a Humanitarian Award at the Oscars.

State ownership and censorship might be the Chinese way. But hypocrisy and a pursuit of profit above principle are the Crapitalist Way. Get in bed with whomever, as long as you get paid. Jeffrey Katzenberg has made it his business to know all the right people. And it doesn't matter how many of the plotlines in his business narrative seemingly conflict. It only matters that he keeps selling tickets.

14 Ronald Perelman

The reality is that I surround myself with very smart, very strong people—including my ex-wives.

—Ronald Perelman

In the 1980s, Hollywood cranked out a series of films portraying the Wall Street culture as one of excess and avarice. Some, like Oliver Stone's *Wall Street*, were more serious. Others, like *The Secret of My Success* with Michael J. Fox, used the meme as a backdrop for that other eighties specialty—the romantic comedy.

Ronald Perelman may not be a name you know offhand. But if you watched any of those eighties movies, then you know his story. A king of corporate takeovers, Perelman could easily have served as the inspiration for characters like *Wall Street*'s Gordon Gekko. And as someone married a handful of times, including once to a Hollywood actress, he also had the romantic part down, if it wasn't always comical in nature. But Perelman gets a chapter here not because of his behavior while Reagan was in office, but because his maneuvers have morphed. He doesn't just take over companies anymore. He's moved on to easier targets. Now he gobbles up government contracts. Now he's screwing over you and me.

Perelman is your typical everyman. If, that is, your definition of "everyman" is someone who rings in the New Year by hosting lavish parties on a yacht in St. Bart's in what is called "one of the most exclusive social events" of the year.[1] In years past, celebrities like Owen Wilson, Russell Simmons, George Lucas, and Jerry Bruckheimer have all attended the party on *Ultima III*, Perelman's 188-foot yacht. The bash also serves as a birthday party for Perelman, who was born on New Year's Day. When Ronny the Raider turned sixty, he was serenaded by Barry Manilow. (See what I mean about being stuck in the eighties? Apparently Huey Lewis was unavailable.) Perelman is so highbrow, in fact, he calls posh New York restaurant Le Cirque his "cafeteria" because he eats there so often.

Perelman made his money by being what's known as a "corporate raider," someone who takes over companies, wrings them out, then sells them for a profit.

Perelman is so well known for it that when you type in "Ronald Perelman" and "C" into a search engine, Google actually finishes the phrase with "Corporate Raider." Not that he probably cares. With a net worth somewhere near $14 billion, he could probably afford to modify a search engine if he wanted to.

Perelman wasn't the only guy involved in corporate takeovers. He was just one of the best. In describing his status and stature during the eighties, *Crain's New York Business* said Perelman was "a magnate on the make who had mastered the art of financing hostile takeovers with junk bonds, stripping down companies and selling them for big profits."[2]

For people who follow corporate mergers, Perelman's track record, alongside business partner Donald Drapkin, reads like a greatest hits album:

> In 1988, they sold Technicolor for an estimated $650 million profit just five years after Mr. Perelman bought it. They assembled a group of TV stations called New World Communications Group for about $1.2 billion during the early '90s and sold it to Rupert Murdoch a few years later for $3 billion. They bought a California bank in 1998 for $1.2 billion and sold the operation four years later to Citigroup for $5.8 billion.[3]

Perelman also bought the cosmetics company Revlon with $1.8 billion worth of junk bonds. *New York* magazine called it "one of the nastiest takeovers in corporate history."

One of Perelman's favorite tactics is something called "greenmail." It's like blackmail, but for rich people. And it's legal. Basically, greenmail entails the purchase of a portion of a company's stock, then either implicitly or explicitly threatening a hostile takeover if the company whose stock you just purchased doesn't buy its stock back, at a much higher price. (What is it with these Crapitalists . . . they can't just play Candy Crush like the rest of us?)

That's not to say Perelman is all business. Turns out he likes to merge with women, too—and it can get just as nasty.

This is a guy who pushed for a divorce from actress Ellen Barkin—his fourth wife—because of a clause in the prenuptial that would have escalated his alimony payment if he had waited much longer. As part of the settlement, Perelman had to invest in a production company for Barkin and her brother. He would eventually sue Barkin when he wasn't happy with how that was turning out. While his suit with Barkin was ongoing, he was also engaged in a suit and countersuit with his longtime business partner. Guys like Perelman exchange lawsuits the way the rest of us exchange emails.

Perelman has been married five times, each, according to an extensive *New York* magazine profile, allowing access to differing social strata:

> First he married into the Jewish money, then he married the Jewish princess and got to know the New York money contingent, then he met the Hollywood people through Patricia Duff. Ellen was really a continuation of that. Now, if he marries again, it will have to be European royalty. . . . Then he would have had one of everything.[4]

As distasteful as the way he went about his business (professional and personal) may be, at least it didn't involve my money. Unfortunately, that would all change.

In addition to corporate mergers and women, Perelman was also interested in politics. At least, he was interested in giving politicians his money. Perelman was the sole owner of an investment company called MacAndrews & Forbes. Over the past twenty-five years, MacAndrews & Forbes has doled out over $6 million in campaign donations, and more than twice that amount in lobbying expenditures.[5] Though Perelman gives primarily to Democrats, including a $50,000 donation to Obama's inauguration in 2008, a third of MacAndrews & Forbes's donations have gone to Republicans as well.[6]

But like with most things in his life, Perelman, the guy with the star-studded birthday parties on yachts, takes things to extremes. He doesn't just contribute to politicians. He employs them.

Perelman's companies have employed the likes of Henry Kissinger and Nancy Reagan, along with former Service Employees International Union (SEIU) president Andy Stern. Recently, Revlon Cosmetics, one of Perelman's companies, added Diana Cantor to its board. If that name sounds familiar, it should. She's former House Majority Leader Eric Cantor's wife.

My favorite Perelman associate, however, is Vernon Jordan, former adviser to President Bill Clinton. Though he worked with Clinton in a variety of ways during his administration, Jordan is remembered primarily for his involvement in the Monica Lewinsky scandal. After Lewinsky left the White House, but before news had broken of her relationship with Clinton, Jordan had actively sought to assist Lewinsky in landing on her ~~knees~~ feet. One of the people Jordan called to try to get Lewinsky a job was Ronald Perelman.

Lewinsky interviewed with Perelman's MacAndrews & Forbes. After she told Jordan it didn't go particularly well, Jordan called Perelman to arrange a second interview. With Perelman, at Jordan and Clinton's urging, the second time was the charm. Lewinsky "informally" accepted a job with Revlon, owned by Perelman.

A *Washington Post* piece on Perelman's role in the Lewinsky scandal summed it up well: "So the billionaire writes checks, a hundred thousand dollars to Democrats here, a hundred thousand to Republicans there. He chairs presidential fundraisers and hires— 'acquires' is the verb of choice—some former politicians and their friends."

Christine Taylor, a spokesperson for Perelman's MacAndrews & Forbes, defended the practice, saying, "Just like any intelligent business person, Mr. Perelman looks to work with, employ, and promote the best people available. In this regard, thoughtful professionals with prior public service experience are considered a positive addition."[7]

As we've seen, whatever partisan loyalties Crapitalists may have take a backseat to their true ideological pursuits: profit. So the point for crafty Crapitalists like Perelman isn't to have Democrats or Republicans on the payroll. It's to have anyone who can help him further his pursuit of the almighty dollar. *Your* dollar. Those "positive additions," as his spokesperson called them, would help Perelman bag a boatload of tax dollars.

After the terrorist attacks of September 11, 2001, the George W. Bush administration ordered an examination into the varying types of threats our country might face, and asked for guidance on how to best prepare for those threats. In 2004, the Bush administration found that smallpox, though it had been eradicated as a disease since 1978 and existed only in the secure labs of Russian and American facilities, could be weaponized as a biological agent against the United States and therefore posed a "material threat."

The Obama administration, not one to take threats of diseases that have been dormant for three decades lightly, decided to fund the creation of a drug to combat smallpox. Any guesses on who they gave the contract to?

Maybe it shouldn't shock us that a guy with this checkered a romantic history would be so into vaccines. But it's okay to be a little surprised that a guy who pledged that all federal contracts worth more than $25,000 would be competitively bid, as Obama did, would then turn around and hand one for $433 million to Perelman.[8]

Siga Technologies, in which Perelman owns the controlling share, would be awarded the contract to develop a smallpox antiviral drug through a "sole-source" procurement, meaning there wasn't an open solicitation for other companies to compete.

Oops.

At the time, the excuse given to award Siga the "sole-source" contract was that there was an urgent and immediate biodefense need to obtain a smallpox treatment, and Siga could deliver the goods.[9] More on that in a bit.

So being the only company bidding, Perelman's group did the country a solid and lowballed the price, right? I mean, this is national security we are talking about here.

Not exactly.

Siga's contract called for the company to be paid approximately $255 per dose, or what the *Los Angeles Times* said was "well above what the government's specialists had determined was reasonable."[10] I don't know why. Regular smallpox vaccines, which the government already had in significant amounts, cost us only three dollars a dose.

What a bunch of tightwads, huh?

Government specialists, known on the street as "scientists," had a few other concerns about Siga as well. The drug Siga was developing, known as ST-246, was designed to treat people infected with smallpox who could no longer be administered the more than $1 billion worth of vaccine the government already had on hand. But, because of ethical constraints, Siga's drug couldn't be tested to know if it, um, actually worked.

So you can imagine why Dr. Richard Hatchett, the chief medical officer for the Department of Health and Human Services biomedical defense preparedness unit, balked at Siga's 180 percent profit margin, which he termed "outrageous," when negotiating the contract. Internal emails showed that negotiations, even though there was only one company, had stalled because of it.[11]

That's where those "positive additions" of Perelman's came into play. Andy Stern, the former SEIU chief and, you know, a biotech expert, is on Perelman's payroll. The unions backed Obama big in 2008 and would come through again in 2012. The SEIU's $70 million—$16 million more than the George Soros–backed Priorities USA PAC—made the union "the top financial backer working directly for Democratic candidates in the 2012 election."[12] So if one of Stern's and Perelman's companies was having an issue with some high-minded bureaucrat actually trying to do his or her job and save us taxpayers some money, it could be dealt with.

And it was.

After Siga complained about Hatchett's "approach to profit," Hatchett was replaced in negotiations. One month later, the deal was done.

There would be plenty of howling from both Republicans and Democrats over the appearance—and result—of the negotiations. Senator Claire McCaskill (D-MO) even called for an investigation. Of course, congressional investigations are where stories and scandals go to die.

Perelman ended up with the contract. And there's a good chance the United States will end up with a drug about as effective in combating smallpox in humans as Flintstone vitamins are. Oh, and remember how the Department of Health and Human Services had no choice but to award Siga the procurement contract because they were the only company that could rapidly deliver the treatment? Good times, good times. HHS noted in March 2014 that the expected date for Food and Drug Administration approval of the ST-246 drug is—wait for it—2019.[13]

But Crapitalists like Perelman don't care about things like that. They just care that the medicine makes their bank accounts bigger. Even if it's bankrupting the rest of the country.

15   Al Gore

Big money is having a corrupting influence and it is degrad-
ing the quality of our democracy.

—Al Gore

On December 13, 2000, Al Gore stopped dragging America through
the mud that was his crybaby temper tantrum. After more than a
month of lawsuits, recounts, and debate over the value of the Elec-
toral College, the 2000 presidential election was finally over.

Lots of things come to mind when thinking about Albert Ar-
nold Gore. From the unexpectedly passionate make-out session
he shared with his wife, Tipper, when accepting the nomination,
to his appropriately mocked sighing and grandstanding in the
debates during the 2000 campaign, to his recent chakra-rubbing
escapades.

While he never would seek public office again, it isn't entirely fair to say that our former vice president has stayed away from the public spotlight. He also hasn't stopped cashing in on our tax dollars, and is "poised to become the first 'carbon billionaire,'" according to the *New York Times*.[1]

Today, Gore is a fearmongering Crapitalist, who pushes a cause purely to put the profits in his pockets. And it's worked.

Everyone knows Al Gore has been sounding the global warming alarm for some time. But his global warming hucksterism isn't the first time he has foisted regulations on us.

Along with his wife, Tipper, Gore pushed for the forced labeling of CDs (google it if you've never heard of one, kids) if the albums were deemed to contain offensive lyrics. It was a controversial move at the time, with many musicians protesting. That bad boy of rock and roll John Denver testified before a Senate committee that he was "strongly opposed to censorship of any kind in our society or anywhere else in the world."[2]

Al Gore, then a senator from Tennessee, also testified at the Senate hearing, offering his full support for the proposal. The hearings ended with the record industry agreeing to "voluntarily" put Parental Advisory labels on CDs and cassettes (again, google it) that contained potentially offensive material.

I mention it here only because, had the Gores been invested in a company that made Parental Advisory labels and stood to benefit from the new regulation, everyone would have cried foul at an obvious abuse of power that would have indexed into the Gores' own self-interests.

And while he didn't financially benefit from the Parental Advisory labels, Gore has raked in millions pushing global warming hysteria.

When Al Gore left office in 2001, he had an estimated net worth of $2 million.

Today? He's worth $200 million.[3]

And even though he never got to be president, he used Barack Obama for much of his largesse. (Financial largesse, that is. The extra weight is on him. Try some cardio, Al!)

Essentially, Gore travels the country scaring people about the dangers of global warming, hawking so-called green prescriptions he has invested in.

In 2004, Gore teamed up with Goldman Sachs executive David Blood to form Generation Investment Management (GIM). GIM is primarily invested in so-called green-tech companies—or businesses that claim to operate with a smaller carbon footprint. But business didn't really pick up until Obama took office.

While Gore was giving speeches and winning Oscars and Nobel Prizes for his movie *An Inconvenient Truth,* Gore's business partner and fellow Crapitalist John Doerr (more on him in another chapter) was setting up a business infrastructure of a different sort. Doerr was a lifelong friend of Gore's, and was a partner at another investment firm, Kleiner Perkins. Thanks to his Silicon Valley connections, Doerr raised $800,000 for Democrats in the 2008 cycle, much of which went toward electing Obama.

From the beginning, as noted by the *Washington Post,* it seemed clear that Gore's investments would pay off.

As Obama was preparing to take office, it was clear his public agenda supporting clean energy aligned with Gore's personal agenda. Obama held a highly publicized meeting with Gore at transition headquarters in Chicago to talk about energy policy. Later, Obama closely echoed several of Gore's talking points and his plan for public investment in clean energy. Obama even adopted Gore's campaign catchphrase for the effort, "Repower America."[4]

With roots in campaign contributions and a shared ideology, Gore's tree of influence would now branch out into a new presidential administration. His former chief of staff, Ron Klain, would grab the same post with the new vice president, Joe Biden. Another former Gore political adviser, Carol Browner, became Obama's climate change czar.

And it didn't take long for the branches to bear fruit.

In October 2009, Jonathan Silver, a candidate to lead Obama's clean-energy loan program, emailed the Department of Energy's chief financial officer to let him know he would be hosting a fundraiser for Al Gore's advocacy group, the Alliance for Climate Protection.

Silver would eventually get the job. And Gore would get plenty of loans.[5]

Fourteen of the companies Gore invested in have bagged a staggering $2.5 billion in subsidies from the Obama administration.[6] Not coincidentally, Gore is now worth $200 million.

At least *someone* is doing okay in this Obama economy!

One of the first moves Obama made once he took office was to dump $831 billion worth of our tax dollars, known as "stimulus money," into the economy.

At the announcement of the stimulus program, Obama assured the country that "[d]ecisions about how Recovery money will be spent will be based on the merits. They will not be made as a way of doing favors for lobbyists."[7]

As part of the stimulus scheme, the Department of Energy released $20.5 billion in loans, many of which were guaranteed by the government. An astounding 80 percent of our money went to companies backed by people who helped raise money for Obama in 2008. So, technically, the president was right about not helping lobbyists. He helped out his campaign contributors instead.

And Al Gore benefited as much as anyone.

One of Gore's investments that received a DOE loan was Fisker Automotive, the electric car company mentioned earlier. Fisker, thanks to Gore and Doerr, bagged over half a billion dollars in tax money from the Department of Energy.

Fisker's top model was the Karma—a luxury car retailing for the bargain price of $107,000. But hey, just because you can't afford it doesn't mean it wasn't worth the investment. I mean, those taxpayer loans were at least helping to create jobs, right?

Absolutely.

In Finland.

Idiots.

Two years after the loans went through, and those first new models were rolling off the rack, the workers who helped make them were undoubtedly praising President Obama's name. They were probably just doing it in Finnish. Two years later, and the cars were still being made overseas.

Henrik Fisker, Fisker's founder, explained the strategy:

"We're not in the business of failing; we're in the business of winning. So we make the right decision for the business," Fisker said. "That's why we went to Finland." Fisker also explained to ABC News that, really, it wasn't a tough choice: "There was no contract manufacturer in the U.S. that could actually produce our vehicle."[8]

They didn't seem to have too much trouble taking our money, though.

And it gets better.

A *Forbes* review of the Fisker Karma found that, when factoring in the amount of energy it takes to charge the car when not driving it, the fuel economy of the company that Gore invested in and helped funnel our money into is actually comparable to another well-known American-made vehicle. From *Forbes*:

> The Fisker Karma electric car, developed mainly with your tax money so that a bunch of rich VC's wouldn't have to risk any real money, has rolled out with a nominal EPA MPGe of 52.
>
> Not bad? Unfortunately, it's a sham. This figure is calculated using the grossly flawed EPA process that substantially underestimates the amount of fossil fuels required to power the electric car. . . .
>
> One needs to multiply the EPA MPGe by .365 to get a number that truly compares fossil fuel use of an electric car with a traditional gasoline engine car on an apples to apples basis. In the case of the Fisker Karma, we get a true MPGe of 19. This makes it worse than even the city rating of a Ford Explorer SUV.[9]

So Mr. Global Warming used our money to help build the fuel economy equivalent of the Ford Explorer. I guess burning fossil fuels to charge a car is okay, as long as the profits end up in his pocket.

Another of Fisker's investors, Ray Lane, touted the work of the Obama administration in "bringing new technologies that have renewable energies to the marketplace." Lane bragged, "For the first time in my memory we can see that the policy, government, private capital cooperation is actually beginning to work."

What was the first example of these tax-funded partnerships that he mentioned?

"Solyndra, which is a new technology that will allow solar cells to be more efficient."[10]

Unfortunately for Lane, and the American taxpayer, Fisker's fate would be the same as that of Solyndra. In November 2013, Fisker, like Solyndra, would declare bankruptcy.[11]

But that mattered only to peons like us, the taxpayers who backed the loans. To the connected Crapitalists like Gore, the check had already cleared.

To be fair, Alarmist Al doesn't just make money off failed green energy policies. He also mooches off failed health-care programs. While the rest of the country struggles to deal with the catastrophic coverage that Obamacare herded us into, Gore is seeing the health of his portfolio continue to improve.

Remember Generation Investment Management, the company founded by Gore and David Blood? While thought of as primarily a green-investment firm, it turns out they were diversified in other areas as well. Specifically, health-care companies. Twenty-six percent of GIM's portfolio included health insurance companies poised to profit off Obamacare.[12] That Blood bundled another $500,000 for Obama's reelection probably didn't hurt the thought process behind those investments.

When Blood and Gore team up, it's the American taxpayer who gets gutted.

At least sometimes Gore will put his money where his mouth is. He became a vegan, a move designed perhaps in part to reduce the greenhouse gases created by the animals grown and kept to feed the American carnivore.[13] In other areas, however, Gore is a complete hypocrite.

In an editorial for the *Wall Street Journal* he coauthored with business partner Blood, Gore argued for an abandonment of investments in fossil fuel energy: "Investors can strand fossil-fuel energy assets today, or absorb the cost of inaction by causing a much larger stranding across industries and asset classes in the future."[14] So being invested in, or doing business with, fossil fuel companies would only exacerbate our current climate change crisis then. Makes sense.

What makes less sense is that, when it came time for Mr. Gore to unload one of his assets, the failed Current TV, Gore chose not to sell to a company that was particularly invested in green energy. No, the company that gave Keith Olbermann a job decided instead to sell to Al Jazeera. You may have heard of them. Al Jazeera is funded by the wealthy nation of Qatar, located on the Arab Peninsula. The Arab Peninsula, in case you're keeping score at home, isn't known for its abundance of windmills. It's one of the biggest oil producers.

The move was so egregious that even liberal talk show hosts like Jon Stewart and Matt Lauer, not exactly scions of conservative media, grilled Gore over the blatant hypocrisy.

"You had an opportunity to make a statement, probably, about your principles, and some people would feel, and for me as well, I thought it was an odd move," Stewart said. "Not because of some of the other things, but because it is backed by fossil fuel money."

"I'm really proud of the transaction," Gore replied with a straight face.[15]

Given that Gore bagged a reported $70 million[16] in the deal, I guess we can understand why.

Gore, once again, had cashed in. By now that shouldn't surprise you. Because Al Gore clearly cares about the environment. He really does. He just doesn't care about it enough to keep from living in a mansion in Nashville with a utility bill twelve times that of the normal household,[17] buying a $9 million oceanfront villa in Montecito, California,[18] or hopscotching around the country in a fossil-fuel-burning jet, or living in a house built on a zinc mine.[19]

No, Gore cares about the environment. *His* environment. And that environment continues to thrive because of his Crapitalist connections, and your money.

16 Zygi Wilf

This code of conduct will establish new rules. It will allow our franchise to operate in the same fashion as my family business, one of high standards, high morals and success.

—Zygi Wilf

From a historical standpoint, Vikings as a culture get a sort of raw deal in this country. Though they are widely recognized as having visited the land that would become North America well before Christopher Columbus, you don't see banks and governments shutting down and going to parades where people wear helmets with horns.

That we sort of consciously forget to honor or recognize the Vikings is ironic, given that if they were standing before us today, I'm pretty sure we would pay them all the attention they wanted.

After all, a people known for pillaging and plundering typically commanded a certain level of respect.

The Minnesota Vikings football franchise is then, in some sense, a perfect metaphor of that legacy. Created as an expansion team in 1960, Minnesota quickly established itself as one of the best teams in the pre-merger National Football League. Feared for its physically intimidating style of play (its defense carried the moniker the Purple People Eaters), the Vikings played in four Super Bowls in the 1970s. But they lost all four of them—making them one of the NFL's most successful losers of all time. And, since losing to Oakland in Super Bowl XI (that's 11 to you hipsters who have moved on to more modern methods of enumeration), the Vikings haven't made it back to the big game. Still, the team remains a proud franchise, with rabid fans and, until recently, one of the more unique home-field advantages in the league.

I say until recently because, in 2005, the team was purchased by a New Jersey land developer named Zygi Wilf. With his European-sounding name, Wilf seemed like the natural successor to lead the Norse-inspired franchise.

After buying the team, Wilf was generally praised for his character and integrity.[1] And, personally, he may deserve such praise. But professionally, Zygi seems to have more in common with those original Vikings than just a goofy name.

In October 2013, Wilf and his family found themselves on the wrong side of an $85 million judgment, for, according to the judge, acting in "'bad faith' and evil motive by cutting partners out of what started as a fifty-fifty business proposition to develop an apartment complex."[2] The Wilfs are appealing the settlement, which came as a result of a twenty-one-year lawsuit over a development in New Jersey. Part of the Wilfs' legal efforts, other than reducing the settlement (which would be more than $100 million including legal fees), is to try to keep their net worth private.[3] For some reason, they thought people would be upset if they knew the size of their private fortune. Maybe it has something to do with all the public money they've gobbled up.

Buying your way into an NFL franchise is like joining one of the most exclusive country clubs in the world. And it comes with some pretty unique benefits. The NFL is by far the most dominant sports league in America. It also, not coincidentally, spends more money on lobbying than all the other professional sports leagues.[4]

Despite the fact that the league and its teams haul in over $9 billion a year in revenue, the league itself is categorized as a nonprofit.[5] That's not to say that the teams, and owners like Wilf, don't pay taxes. But the central office, run by Roger Goodell, himself the son of a former senator, doesn't have to.

Owners like Wilf get special privileges, too.

Thanks to a law passed more than forty years ago, the NFL's teams are allowed to collectively bargain the broadcasting rights with their TV partners. Those contracts, worth an estimated $27 billion by the way, also permit the teams to black out the games from their local markets if the games themselves aren't a sellout.[6]

Not only do the owners make millions off the TV contracts, but the contracts themselves allow for the owners to make even more money by forcing fans to actually go to the games.

So the fans go to the stadiums to watch their favorite teams play. But it's the stadiums themselves that can make the owners' scoreboards light up.

Once Wilf bought his way into one of the most exclusive fraternities in the country, he began working on building a new stadium to replace the Hubert H. Humphrey Metrodome, the home of the Vikings from 1982 until the end of the 2013 season. The Metrodome was the only stadium in America to host the Super Bowl, the NCAA Basketball Final Four, the World Series, and the Major League Baseball All-Star Game.[7] Built with a fabric roof that intensified the noise from the hometown fans, the Metrodome was generally considered to be one of the loudest stadiums in the country. But, like many older stadiums, it lacked the "modern amenities" that were so sought after by current ownership groups. Put simply, it lacked the luxury suites that help billionaire owners cash in even more. As such, the Metrodome, one of the most famous sporting complexes in the country, was demolished in early 2014.

In its place will be the new stadium. It hasn't been named yet, which just means Wilf hasn't figured out which business he can bilk for the most cash yet. But this new modern monument of Crapitalism was largely built on the backs of the same hardworking, tax-paying Minnesotans who will have to fork over big bucks to watch their sorry team play.

I feel for you, Minnesota. I've seen *Little House on the Prairie*. You're good people!

The new stadium is estimated to make its debut in 2016, built on the same site as the Metrodome. Current estimates peg the cost at $975 million. But Wilf, whose worth is a reported $1.3 billion in his own right, won't be picking up the entire tab.[8] Far from it.

Per the agreement, Wilf's wallet will be responsible for less than *half* the total tab. The state, being Vikings fans and all, kicked in $348 million worth of future tax monies. And the city of Minneapolis will contribute $150 million.[9]

Midwesterners are known for their generosity. But they didn't just voluntarily fork over their hard-earned cash to this billionaire. In fact, the last poll done before the state legislature passed the bill to dump the stadium's worth of tax dollars on the billionaire's doorstep showed that 58 percent of Minnesotans wanted the stadium to be financed entirely with private money.

Oops.

That's not to say that Wilf didn't do his part to win the hearts and minds of the public to get this deal done. His definition of public is just different from yours and mine.

Wilf earned his taxpayer money the way any good Crapitalist would: he lobbied for it. The year before Wilf bought the team, he didn't make any campaign contributions to Minnesota politicians or elections. Starting in 2006, however, Zygi suddenly got a whole lot more interested in the local scene. And he got a lot more invested, too.

Wilf started throwing money around like the Vikings throwing passes. But unlike the team's on-field efforts, which led to a 6-10 record in 2006, Wilf would quarterback a much more successful result.

In football, not being able to distinguish the team of the person you are throwing to can lead to a lot of interceptions. But in Crapitalism, it typically leads to a winning record.

Wilf and his family gave $20,000 each to the state Republican and Democrat parties, plus at least another $10,000 to each party's legislative caucus. He also kicked in $5,000 to then-governor Tim Pawlenty, and another $5,000 to his Democrat challenger.[10]

Wilf continued his pattern of campaign contributions and lobbying expenditures. In 2010, he donated to the gubernatorial candidates again, including the winner and current governor Mark Dayton. And he helped Minnesota's other state politicians get through those frigid winters by lining their pockets with cash.

All told, Wilf shelled out $5.5 million.[11] Considering that he received a total of nearly $500 million in tax dollars for his project, I'd say it was worth it.

John Marty, a Minnesota senator who opposed the project, broke down just how generous the state's taxpayers were being with the subsidies:

> Data from the Senate Fiscal Analysis Office shows, under the final legislation, that the taxpayer "investment" in the Vikings stadium breaks down to a $72 public subsidy for every ticket, to every game—including preseason ones—for the next 30 years!
>
> And this calculation doesn't include the granting of a property-tax exemption for the stadium. Counting that, the subsidy climbs to over $110 per ticket.[12]

And while asking for hundreds of millions of dollars from Minnesota taxpayers, Wilf was buying a four-bedroom, four-bath $19 million co-op in New York City.[13] The listing agent described the master bedroom and bathroom for the Park Avenue pad as "a quiet Zen-like retreat," which will come in handy when needing an escape from how awful his football team is. It's also a perfect place to plot other devious ways to soak Minnesota taxpayers for cash, like his threat to forgo hosting Super Bowl LII in 2018. After extorting hundreds of millions in subsidies, the Vikings and the NFL demanded that Minnesota provide "waivers on sales taxes on game tickets and related events during the week leading up to Super Bowl LII" or else they won't get to host the Big Game.[14]

I like this idea of selectively paying my taxes. Where do I sign up?

• • •

Stadium subsidies are wrong for a lot of reasons. Like we talked about in Jay-Z's chapter, they don't actually result in economic benefit for the communities that pay for them. In fact, they usually suck up dollars that would have gone for other recreational expenses. But taxpayers, or, rather, politicians, keep forking over tax dollars out of a fear that the teams will relocate, or because the teams cry poor with outdated stadiums that lack the modern moneymaking amenities.

Except that wasn't happening here.

Ted Mondale, son of Walter Mondale, was appointed by Minnesota's governor Mark Dayton to chair the Metropolitan Sports Facilities Commission. Dayton, remember, was the recipient of thousands of dollars of Wilf's campaign cash, and can expect to collect thousands more when he runs for reelection in 2014. So Mondale, at the behest of Dayton, led the effort to lobby for the construction, and financing, of the new stadium in the state legislature.[15] This was particularly galling for opponents of the deal, as you now had someone being paid with tax dollars lobbying for the expenditure of millions more.

What a country.

Mondale, believe it or not, was at least honest about why he was pushing for the new building. He didn't claim some bogus benefit to the economy. At least, not the public economy. "The whole reason we're doing this is so the team can make money," he said.

The thing is . . . they were already raking it in.

Wilf bought the team in 2005 for $600 million. *Forbes* estimates the current value near a billion.[16] As Senator Marty described, "Homeowners have seen the value of their homes drop by as much as a third from the recession, but Wilf's investment *grew* by a third."[17]

So it isn't like the Vikings' ship was in danger of sinking. But that didn't stop the state officials from giving a billionaire hundreds of millions of tax dollars to improve his personal bottom line.

The worst part is, Minnesota's citizens won't stop being bilked once the stadium gets built. As part of the agreement, the city of Minneapolis is on the hook for $7.5 million in annual operating costs, too. So not only did taxpayers help build the stadium, but they're gonna kick in to help run it.

Midwestern hospitality at its finest.

If it helps, lots of states and teams use public financing for the construction of stadiums. Just like with film credits, there's something about the allure and star power of professional athletes and billionaire owners that help convince states to throw hundreds of millions of dollars their way. Running back Adrian Peterson, one of the best players in the league and one of the Vikings' only real stars, contributed to the lobbying effort by going to the legislature and posing for pictures before one of the key votes. And as he does on fall afternoons, he helped move the ball down the field.

This happens all over the country. Billionaire owners don't just feast on the tax dollars given to them for construction, either. By having the municipalities finance the bonds that pay for the construction, the team owners get tax exemptions on the interest for those bonds. A Bloomberg analysis estimated that sports teams across the country save $146 million a year on these financing schemes. All told, sports teams like the Vikings owned by Crapitalists like Wilf have saved a projected $4 billion in bond tax exemptions since 1986.

Taxpayer-funded touchdown!

Americans love football. The NFL now makes billions of dollars because of it. An average NFL franchise is worth more than double the average baseball team, and more than three times an

NBA team. The owners are raking in cash hand over fist. Crapitalists like Wilf don't need the tax money to make their businesses
viable. They do it just because they can.

The NFL penalizes its players for all sorts of misdeeds on the
field. If the offense is particularly egregious, it can carry a fine as
well. What bothers me is that, as fans, we are getting fined, too.
Not because of our misdeeds, but because of our passion. Because
we like the league and its teams so much, our representatives throw
our money to billionaires like quarterbacks to receivers. Owners
like Wilf may write the checks to the players, but they're using our
money to pad their profits.

17 Tom Steyer

Really, what we're trying to do is to make a point that people who make good decisions on this should be rewarded, and people should be aware that if they do the wrong thing, the American voters are watching and they will be punished.

—Thomas Steyer

In early April 2013, about one hundred guests gathered at the home of hedge fund manager and climate change activist Tom Steyer. Steyer's home, located in San Francisco's wealthy Sea Cliff neighborhood, overlooks the Golden Gate Bridge.[1] The real estate website Zillow.com lists the property as being worth nearly $6 million. Steyer's palace serves as a pep rally of sorts for his fellow activists. It's also hosted an Obama fundraiser.

After Steyer's wife, Kat, entertained everyone with a song (this is how rich people do things; I will write you a check, Mr. President, after you listen to my wife croon), Tom introduced the guest of honor.

"He is doing everything he can on the issues that we care about," Steyer said. "He has political limitations . . . so we really have an obligation to help him. We are like role players in basketball. And we have the great star gunner who has to take the star shot . . . we have the best left-handed shameless gunner in the world."[2]

But the president hadn't been scoring as many points for the climate change activists as the rest of the team would have liked. He tried to explain why, noting "the politics of this are tough":

> Because if you haven't seen a raise in a decade; if your house is still twenty-five thousand, thirty thousand dollars under water; if you're just happy that you've still got that factory job that is powered by cheap energy; if every time you go to fill up your old car because you can't afford to buy a new one, and you certainly can't afford to buy a Prius, you're spending forty bucks that you don't have, which means that you may not be able to save for retirement. . . . You may be concerned about the temperature of the planet, but it's probably not rising to your No. 1 concern.[3]

Obama told the folks in the room they would need to balance their concern for the planet with "a genuine, passionate concern about middle class families" and explain to those few peasants that he is "working just as hard for them as we are for an environmental agenda. And that's going to take some work."[4]

Steyer, however, is committed to doing something about "global warming." But his concern has as much to do with the way that agenda helps his own family as with how it might help the planet. And he is anything but middle class.

Referencing the influential conservative Koch brothers, Steyer said, "I completely disagree, because what they're doing is standing up for ideas that they profit from. We think we're representing the vast bulk of citizens of the United States. We're not representing our pockets."

Like the idea that human activity is causing the temperature of the planets to rise, that's a lie.

Almost three decades ago, Steyer founded Farallon Capital, a global investment firm that manages wealth for institutions and high-net-worth individuals. Essentially, Steyer's shop helps the rich get richer. So much for reducing so-called income inequality.

Indeed, Steyer has amassed an estimated $1.6 billion net worth himself. And while Steyer has been an advocate for efforts he thinks will curb climate change for years, his investments haven't exactly done the same.

In 2008, as part of its efforts to diversify and protect against the global financial collapse, Farallon invested in a company called Adaro.[5] Adaro is Indonesia's second-largest coal company. And just when you thought it couldn't get any less environmentally friendly than the concept of Indonesian coal, Adaro made sure that one of its biggest customers was that environmentally friendly oasis known as China.

Maybe you've heard of them.

Steyer's investment firm has also invested in Sandridge Energy, and Energy Partners Ltd., two fossil-fuel-producing energy companies.[6] Surely Steyer found the whole idea gross.

As in *gross* profit.

Steyer stepped down as head of Farallon in 2012, but he remains one of its largest investors.

And Farallon continues to be invested in "dirty"-energy-related companies. The Keystone Pipeline, for example, is a 1,700-mile pipe that carries oil from Canada to the Gulf of Mexico. The last phase of the pipeline, called Keystone XL, would require permission from the president to be completed. Keystone has become a go-to issue for environmentalists. In fact, urging the president to stop its completion was the goal of those who attended Steyer's Sea Cliff fundraiser. But it was also the goal of protesters who lined the street to Steyer's house, hoping to catch Obama's eye as his carbon-spewing motorcade sped past. The protesters, carrying signs that read STOP THE KEYSTONE PIPELINE with the "O" in "Keystone" written as the signature Obama logo.[7]

The protesters had more than signs, too. A *New Yorker* article on the fundraiser noted a sort of militant vibe:

> "What do we want from our Pre-si-dent?" the protesters yelled. "No pipeline for the one per cent!" One marcher led the crowd in a call and response: "When I say 'pipeline,' you say 'kill'! Pipeline! Kill!"[8]

But whether they knew it or not, the protesters may have been shouting at the wrong one-percenter. In addition to Farallon's investments in fossil fuel companies, it turns out Steyer's company was also backing the Keystone Pipeline's biggest competitor. Another U.S. pipeline company called Kinder Morgan has plans to extend its TransMountain pipeline, which carries tar sands oil from the Edmonton, Alberta, area to British Columbia. Kinder Morgan, if granted its expansion, would be able to carry up to 900,000 barrels a day for eventual export to Asia.[9]

So if Keystone gets blocked, Kinder Morgan, which doesn't require Obama's approval because it travels only through Canada, sees its value goes up. Which makes money for Steyer.

Steyer isn't just opposing Keystone. He's also opposing Northern Gateway. That's another proposed pipeline that would carry Canadian crude to British Columbia for export. Northern Gateway, if prevented from operating, would also benefit Kinder Morgan's and Steyer's bottom lines.

What a coincidence.

This being the information age and all, Steyer's hypocrisy isn't exactly a secret. Steyer, a man who "owes his personal fortune to a lifetime of investments in oil, gas and pipeline companies," has called on Farallon to divest his stake in fossil fuel holdings.[10]

But not everybody's buying it.

"I think it's hypocrisy, quite frankly. Who knows when he's going to divest of these investments," questioned Louisiana senator David Vitter. "Maybe in a few months when his helping kill Keystone will boost them up to top value. . . . Who knows?"[11]

And how is that divestment coming, by the way?

"This divestment has been taking place consistent with the applicable legal requirements," said Steyer spokesman and political adviser Chris Lehane. As of June 2014, Steyer's portfolio showed that "dirty energy" was still part of his investment portfolio.[12]

Lehane, by the way, was also an aide to former vice president and ongoing fellow climate change Crapitalist Al Gore. Which makes sense. Because besides hypocritically bashing fossil fuel companies while profiting from them himself, Steyer, like Gore, has learned how to cash in on feigning green.

In addition to his investments with Farallon, Steyer invests with Greener Capital, a venture firm that supports "clean energy" companies.[13] Those companies, and the investments they hold, will stand to benefit from another of Steyer's recent interests—financing California ballot initiatives. Steyer has shelled out at least $37 million perpetuating the green economy—for California and himself. One, Proposition 39, closed a tax loophole for out-of-state companies and diverted $500 million a year toward projects that foster "energy-efficiency." He also helped defeat Proposition 23, which would have suspended California's edict to lower statewide carbon emissions.[14] Both, according to Steyer, "bolstered the state's environment and economy."[15] They also can bolster Steyer's bottom line.

But don't take my word for it. He's boasted how renewable energy is a "big business opportunity" and a "chance to make a lot of money."[16]

Steyer remains committed to spend whatever it takes to protect and further his own interests. But it's always easier if you can get your government buddies to do it for you.

While Steyer might not ultimately get his way on the Keystone Pipeline, his generosity toward the Obama administration may have already paid dividends.

Steyer made bank after the administration approved the dubious takeover of an energy company.

It started when CNOOC, a Chinese government-backed corporation, attempted to purchase Nexen, a Canadian oil company. The sale required our government's approval because of Nexen's drilling leases in the Gulf of Mexico. Steyer was particularly interested in this, since Farallon had just purchased 8.7 million shares of the company. Some wondered if the deal would even be allowed to go through at all, since the United States "has traditionally been more wary than Canada of Chinese investment" and had previously "thwarted CNOOC's $18.5 billion bid for Unocal due to national security concerns."[17]

But the United States didn't seem to have as many concerns

this time around. Funny how things can change when major Obama donors like Steyer are invested in the company. The United States eventually signed off on the deal, which saw CNOOC pay an almost 60 percent premium on Farallon's investment.[18]

So Steyer, Mr. Green, was cashing in on the export of "dirty" Canadian oil to China, which isn't exactly known for its cutting-edge clean energy technology.

Steyer's apparent ability to compartmentalize and separate his words and his own deeds is breathtaking. I mean, here's a guy swimming in cash exactly because he helped finance the production of fossil fuels now pledging to spend $100 million in 2014 "to help elect Democrats who are committed to fighting global warming."[19] Ironically, while he can schmooze and sell his fellow Crapitalists on his environmental authenticity, the real granola greenies aren't so quick to give him a pass. Farallon has been the subject of student protests across the country because of its track record in investing in companies that would make the Native American guy in the TV commercial cry.

Students at Yale, Steyer's alma mater, targeted the university's investments with Farallon because of a Colorado water development project backed by the company. The students claimed it had become an environmental disaster. They started a website, Unfarallon.info. And the message spread:

> The protests spread beyond Yale as activists on college campuses tried to turn Farallon into the symbol of what they saw as the depredations of unfettered global capital. Last May, Steyer was accosted on Stanford's Palo Alto campus by students complaining about the treatment of workers at an Australian lead and zinc production company in which Farallon held a small stake.[20]

A profile by *Institutional Investor* noted, "The protests hurt on a personal level" because "Steyer sees himself as aligned with student protesters, not capitalist oppressors."[21]

Stunning.

For Crapitalists like Steyer, cognitive dissonance isn't just an art to be honed. It's a way of life. That the way he enriched his life runs in direct conflict with the way he currently tells other people to live theirs doesn't seem to blip the radar. He's too busy manipulating the system to maintain an edge to think about it.

Steyer is also flirting with running for elected office. So if you thought the green giveaways to Obama cronies was bad before, just wait until this guy starts roaming Capitol Hill on the taxpayer dime. Steyer has already proven quite adept at greasing policies to enrich his bottom line. If he isn't exposed soon, we might actually start paying him to do it.

18 James Sinegal

Business needs a president who has covered the backs of businesses, a president who understands what the private sector needs to succeed. A president who takes the long view and makes the tough decisions. And that's why I am here tonight supporting President Obama.

—Jim Sinegal[1]

When you think about progressive businesses, and the liberals who lead them, the guy who runs a big-box store isn't the first name that comes to mind. Places like Costco, liberals claim, are part of the problem, not the solution. Cozy boutiques are going the way of the horse and buggy because of the big, bad diesel-spewing smoke of the chain retailers. So some were undoubtedly surprised to see the cofounder of Costco, the store that allows you to buy milk, jeans, and tires all within a few hundred thousand square feet of one another, speaking at the Democratic National Convention. But there Jim Sinegal was, on the stage in Charlotte, North Carolina, with a prime-time speaking slot, the same day as President Clinton and professional whiner Sandra Fluke.

Of course, unlike the aforementioned Oval Office occupants, he had paid good money to be there.

In both 2008 and 2012, Sinegal had maxed out his contributions to Obama's campaign and donated $100,000 to Obama's Super PAC. Sinegal also hosted a fundraiser at his home that brought in a reported $2 million, plus he donated $43,000 to the Democratic National Committee.

But Sinegal's help with the campaign extended well beyond his checkbook.

Probably Obama's biggest blunder during the 2012 campaign came during a July speech on American businesses.

"If you were successful, somebody along the line gave you some help. Somebody helped to create this unbelievable American system that we have that allowed you to thrive," Obama said. "Somebody invested in roads and bridges. If you've got a business, you didn't build that. Somebody else made that happen."

Americans seized on Obama's comments as evidence of the disconnect between Obama's collectivist mind-set and the self-reliant initiative that entrepreneurial success requires. With the weak Obama economy already a central campaign issue, Obama's rhetorical misstep sent the campaign into damage control mode. So they called on one of America's most successful businessmen for some help.

Sinegal penned a defense of the idea, writing in an email to Obama supporters: "You might be seeing some ads or hearing some folks say that President Obama doesn't support small business owners. But he understands that small businesses grow and prosper because of individual initiative—because entrepreneurs like you and me do the hard work it takes, and we can't do it alone." Sinegal continued, "Thanks to a strong nationwide transportation system and internal infrastructure, we've opened warehouses across the country and around the world."[2]

Sinegal would repeat similar drivel during his speech in Charlotte on the second night of the Democratic National Convention. But Costco wasn't just helped by government-funded roads. Their business model is helped by policies as well.

In March 2013, Iowa senator Tom Harkin introduced the Fair Minimum Wage Act of 2013. The bill would regularly increase the federal minimum wage by almost 40 percent, from $7.25 an hour to $10.10, with automatic cost-of-living increases thereafter. The same day the bill was introduced, Costco's current CEO, Craig Jelinek, was quoted in a press release issued by Business for a Fair Minimum Wage, an advocacy group for, well, you can figure it out.

Costco was already well-known for its high wages. When Labor secretary Thomas Perez was sworn in, he touted the pay scale Sinegal had put in place:

> Costco is one of the nation's most successful retailers. Their longtime CEO Jim Sinegal believed that he could sell good products at competitive prices and pay his workers a living wage and benefits. Costco workers make a minimum of $15 to $20 per hour, plus benefits. Real wage, middle class jobs. If you invested in Costco stock 15 years ago, today your stock's value would have increased 350 percent.[3]

So Costco was already out in front when, during his 2014 State of the Union address, Obama called for the country to raise its minimum wage to $10.10. If the president, and Harkin, got their way, the rest of the country's retailers would then have to up their pay scales. But not Costco, since they were already well above the threshold.

Plus, as *Forbes* pointed out, Costco's business model doesn't exactly make for an apples-to-apples comparison. Costco employs roughly one-fourth the staff per dollar as compared to their competitors.[4] That Costco pays people more by employing fewer of them didn't seem to make the labor secretary's remarks. And I am sure you won't hear that part of their business model cited when Obama Zombies discuss the benefits of an increase in the minimum wage. But Costco doesn't care about that so much. If the president can help push through a massive wage increase to hurt Costco's competitors, so be it.

Costco, led by Sinegal, actually gets quite a bit of government help. In addition to having the president be their cheerleader-in-chief, touting their business model and having Vice President Joe Biden show up for store openings, Costco takes advantage of local governments' generosity.

A new Costco in Wheaton, Maryland, was built thanks in part to a $4 million grant from the local Economic Development Fund, despite projections that show it may take up to nine years to recoup the investment.[5] They also got some sweet perks from the backyard of their best buddy Obama. The Chicago City Council approved $2.5 million worth of tax breaks for a new Costco in previously blighted land.[6] But it isn't just places near where the president hangs out. Costco grabbed $3.5 million from Rochester, New York, too.[7]

But they may have made out in Louisiana best of all.

The Baton Rouge parish/city council approved $7.8 million worth of reimbursements for building a Costco in another blighted neighborhood. Council member C. Denise Marcelle said, "I believe it's a win for the city of Baton Rouge, in terms of the wages, in terms of getting rid of the blight."[8]

Saint Sinegal. Taking care of blight, one multimillion-tax-dollar check at a time.

But Jimmy, being the swell guy that he is, won't just take taxpayers' money. Thanks to the assistance of local governments, he'll also take their land.

Costco cashes all those tax-funded checks because they agree to come in and open up stores in areas that local governments are looking to refurbish. And if the money's right, Sinegal and company are only too happy to offer heavily discounted toilet paper and frozen chicken, all bought in bulk, of course. But what about when the governments aren't offering money to come into a certain space? Or if the space isn't for sale at all?

Like other Crapitalists I've detailed in the book, Sinegal and Costco are well familiar with the eminent domain laws.

Long before the Supreme Court ruling codified the rights of governments to seize private lands for "public good," a Costco shareholder wrote to headquarters with concerns over a pattern she had begun to notice. As the *Weekly Standard* pointed out, Susan Watson's letter to Jim Sinegal noted her affections for the company, but disapproval of its tactics:

> "I recently learned that Costco has been or will be the beneficiary of at least four pending eminent domain actions, where private property was or may be condemned so that Costco could build or expand a warehouse," Watson wrote, ticking off examples in New York, Missouri, and California. "If Costco had benefited from eminent domain once, I might regard it as a lucky break. Twice would be a happy—albeit unlikely—coincidence. But the list is long, and it appears

to be a strategy of Costco Wholesale Corporation to deprive others of their private property rights. To bully small business with the power of eminent domain is wrong." For that matter, she added, "among Costco's most valuable customers are small business owners."[9]

Joel Benoliel, senior vice president and chief legal officer at Costco, answered candidly, admitting that "there are probably dozens of other Costco projects where eminent domain or the threat of it has been involved in acquiring land for redevelopment."[10]

No wonder Sinegal is so quick to admit that they "didn't build that." Of course they didn't. They just took it.

When a Costco store in Lancaster, California, wanted to expand into a space currently occupied by 99 Cents Only, a smaller retailer, they threatened to bolt if they didn't get their way. City officials went with the classic Costco appeasement method of eminent domain to try to force David off Goliath's property.[11]

99 Cents Only would sue and eventually prevail, preventing the condemnation. The court, in ruling in favor of the smaller retailer, noted that Lancaster had acted solely "to appease Costco."

On the one hand, it isn't as if Costco is unilaterally bullying its way into these communities. After all, in most instances, the governments are paying them to be there. Plus, it isn't like they are going into Park Avenue. As one Costco attorney noted about its use of eminent domain in a Kansan neighborhood, "Theirs is not much of a neighborhood, anyway."[12]

On the other hand, grabbing public monies while you take private lands sounds more like the tactics used by the kinds of businesses that Obama, and supporters like Sinegal, demonized during the 2012 campaign. Not that hypocrisy is an altogether unfamiliar concept to Sinegal.

Like most good Crapitalists, Sinegal actively supports President Obama and his policies in public, while working as hard as he can to avoid actually abiding by them.

One of the planks of the president's reelection efforts was the idea that those nasty one-percenters needed to chip in more of their fair share. Sinegal, while supporting Obama's higher tax schemes, played fast and loose with the rules to make sure Costco avoided the penalties a higher tax bracket would entail. By having Costco issue a dividend to stockholders on borrowed money to avoid the higher capital gains taxes that went into effect in 2013, Sinegal and his wife saved millions on taxes. As the *Wall Street Journal* detailed, Sinegal's savvy, while hypocritical, proved extremely profitable:

> The giant retailer announced Wednesday that the company will pay a special dividend of $7 a share this month. That's a $3 billion Christmas gift for shareholders that will let them be taxed at the current dividend rate of 15%, rather than next year's rate of up to 43.4%—an increase to 39.6% as the Bush-era rates expire plus another 3.8% from the new ObamaCare surcharge.
>
> More striking is that Costco also announced that it will *borrow* $3.5 billion to finance the special payout. Dividends are typically paid out of earnings, either current or accumulated. But so eager are the Costco executives to get out ahead of the taxman that they're taking on debt to do so.[13]

Costco's credit rating actually took a hit because of the maneuver, but for some reason that wasn't enough to dissuade Sinegal from going forward. Could it be because those dividend payments netted Sinegal roughly $14 million? And since it was done at the lower rate, he'll keep about $4 million more than he would have the following year. As the *Journal* noted, "This isn't exactly the tone of, er, shared sacrifice that Mr. Sinegal struck on stage in Charlotte."

Of course it wasn't. And not just because of the event's unofficial slogan, "What happens at the DNC stays at the DNC." By now, Crapitalist hypocrisy should be neither unsurprising nor unexpected. But that doesn't mean it can't be disappointing. Because it sure is destructive.

By using their political influence to push for policies that will hurt their competitors, Costco is cashing in on their crony connections. And like most Crapitalist exploits, it doesn't happen in a vacuum. We all suffer when unemployment goes up because Costco gets its way on minimum-wage hikes. And when they gobble up tax dollars to build in a city they wanted to go to anyway, that means fewer dollars for schools, roads, or, you know, the actual taxpayers to keep in their pockets.

19

Warren Buffett

When it comes to paying for our government and making sure the investments are there so that future generations can succeed, everybody's got to do their part. That's why I put forward the Buffett Rule.

—Barack Obama

Early in 2014, during the two week period between the conference championship games and the Super Bowl, Omaha, Nebraska, was mentioned almost as often as Denver and Seattle, the cities whose teams were actually playing in the game. Denver quarterback Peyton Manning, as part of his pre-snap routine, had taken to shouting "Omaha!" at the line of scrimmage before plays. The shouts were so loud, they were picked up by the on-field microphones and broadcast to the millions of fans watching the AFC championship game.

The city of Omaha had a lot of fun with it, and local businesses offered to donate money to charity every time Manning repeated their city's name during the Super Bowl. TV networks descended on the Nebraska capital to do stories on the phenomenon. For football fans, it may have been their first introduction to Omaha. But for political and business observers, Omaha was already well-known. And not because of its trademark steaks.

With a net worth of $63 billion, the "Oracle of Omaha," Warren Buffett, is largely considered to be the most successful investor of the twentieth century. He's fourth on the *Forbes* billionaires list. He is worth more than the GDP of over one hundred countries.[1] He is an almost ubiquitous presence on CNBC's screen and the *Wall Street Journal*'s front page. When Buffett, whose dominant market presence comes via his Berkshire Hathaway firm, speaks on investments, people listen.

Obama included.

Buffett is such a big deal, he donates to campaigns by just showing up. Unlike many of the Crapitalists in this book, he refuses on principle to donate to Super PACs.[2] But that doesn't mean he doesn't get involved politically.

"When [Berkshire Hathaway vice chairman] Charlie [Munger] and I took this job, we did not decide to put our citizenship in a blind trust," Buffett has said.

Unfortunately for the country, while Buffett's eyes may be open when it comes to his political involvement, he's been helping to lead us in the wrong direction.

By backing Barack in 2008, Buffett bolstered Obama's economic credibility, lending economic ethos to a "community organizer" who could barely tie his own shoes. But with one of the world's most successful businessmen in his corner, Obama could at least fake like his economic policies wouldn't destroy the country.

Four years later, Buffett's political heft, more than his actual financial contributions, helped land Obama in the White House again. At Obama fundraisers, people obviously show up to see the president. But they showed up to see Warren Buffett, too. At one event, touted as an "economic forum" and held at the Four Seasons restaurant in New York, Buffett was the headliner. Guests coughed over $10,000 a pop to attend, and $35,800 to host, which got you into a special reception with Buffett.[3]

On the surface, Buffett's support for Obama seems odd. For example, Buffett has spoken out against the idea that man-made climate change is this imminent threat. "The public has the impression that because there's been so much talk about climate that events of the last 10 years from an insured standpoint and climate have been unusual," Buffett told CNBC. "The answer is they haven't."[4] Buffett is also a proponent of the expansion of the Keystone Pipeline, saying it would be good for the country.

But Buffett and the president agree on one key economic point. They both think taxes should be higher. At least, for some people.

A major issue in the 2012 campaign was that Mitt Romney was some corporate raider elitist who paid lower tax rates than regular Americans. Obama would cite Romney's effective tax rate of 14 percent as an example that the rich were getting off too easy, and needed to pay more of their fair share.[5] To support his argument, Obama cited Buffett. A lot.

As part of his effort to help the campaign, Warren Buffett told anyone who would listen that he *wanted* to pay more taxes, but those pesky IRS agents refused to charge him his fair share. Surely someone as smart as Buffett knows that citizens can actually write the IRS a check for more than they owe. And the government will cash it, with the eternal thanks of Uncle Sam. But Buffett didn't write an extra check. Instead, he wrote an op-ed for the *New York*

Times titled "Stop Coddling the Super-Rich," in which Buffett famously claimed that he paid a lower tax rate than his employees.

The letter closed with a compelling call. "My friends and I have been coddled long enough by a billionaire-friendly Congress," Buffett said. "It's time for our government to get serious about shared sacrifice."[6]

Obama would echo that theme repeatedly throughout his campaign for reelection, citing Buffett as an example of a wealthy person who knows they need to pay more, for the good of the country.

The problem is, Buffett isn't as big of a fan of paying more taxes in real life as he is in op-eds.

In reality, Berkshire Hathaway, at Buffett's direction, performs any number of maneuvers to keep from paying "his fair share."

In 2011, less than two weeks after Buffett's op-ed hit newsstands, Berkshire Hathaway announced it would be investing $5 billion in the foundering Bank of America. Like many financial institutions, Bank of America was hit hard by the subprime lending crisis, and lost almost half its value in the previous year.[7] The move was seen as a tremendous boon to the bank, and a show of faith in the relative health of the country's financial institutions overall. But it was also a boon to Buffett's tax bill:

> Berkshire will hold the [BofA] investment in a property-casualty insurance subsidiary. Such corporations can exclude from taxation 59.5% of the dividends they receive from an investment in another corporation. This exclusion is intended to prevent double- or even triple-taxation as money is earned by one company, paid to another company and then ultimately paid out to shareholders. The policy makes sense; we only wonder why the exclusion isn't 100%.

With the exclusion for Mr. Buffett and his fellow share-holders, Berkshire will enjoy an effective tax rate of 14.175% on the $300 million in dividends it will receive each year from Bank of America.[8]

That rate, 14.175, is about on par with Romney's, and still less than what Buffett's secretary pays. But let's not jump on him for being a heartless hypocrite just yet. Maybe he gave her a nice fruit-cake at Christmas.

The Bank of America gambit is only one of the ways Buffett says one thing and then pays another. Like when he admitted to being in the windmill business solely for its tax benefits. "I will do anything that is basically covered by the law to reduce Berkshire's tax rate," he told investors. "For example, on wind energy, we get a tax credit if we build a lot of wind farms. That's the only reason to build them. They don't make sense without the tax credit."[9]

Calling Buffett out for his hypocrisy has almost become passé. In fact, it's been labeled "a cottage industry" for websites trying to get traffic.[10]

Buffett may not contribute to Super PACs, but he will spend money to lobby elected officials. In fact, since Obama took office, Berkshire Hathaway's lobbying bill has skyrocketed. Until 2009, Buffett's company hadn't spent more than $2 million lobbying in a single year. Since Obama was sworn in, Buffett hasn't spent less than $7 million.

And when you see the result of some of their efforts, it's easy to understand why. One of Berkshire's properties is the private jet company NetJets. In 2012, a bill passed that NetJets spent more than $2.5 million lobbying for. The law created a special tax pro-vision that benefits only a few private jet companies. A *Huffing-*

ton Post analysis found that it would "deprive the government of roughly $25 million in annual revenue over the next three years due to a provision that benefits the fractional aviation industry."

But Buffett the Billionaire wouldn't be so bad if he just liked paying lower taxes. Sure, the fact that he encourages the rest of his one-percenter friends to cough over more of their own cash while he turns every trick he can to avoid shelling out any of his own is, um, inconsistent. But what truly pushes Wiggly Warren to the top of Hypocrite Hill is that, in addition to actively trying to lower his taxes, he oftentimes *just doesn't pay them.*

An analysis of Berkshire Hathaway's annual report by Americans for Limited Government revealed that, buried in its own documents, Buffett's business admitted it hadn't exactly been chipping in its fair share.

"We anticipate that we will resolve all adjustments proposed by the US Internal Revenue Service ('IRS') for the 2002 through 2004 tax years . . . within the next 12 months," the report read.[11] Elsewhere, the report indicated that tax issues from 2005 through 2009 remain unresolved as well. Some estimates put Berkshire's back-taxes bill at a billion dollars.[12]

Remember that op-ed Buffett wrote for the *New York Times*? Its title was "Stop Coddling the Super-Rich." Now, maybe I fundamentally misunderstand the nature of the word. But it seems to me that if I owed anywhere near a billion dollars' worth of taxes, I wouldn't be able to brush the issue off with a mention in my company's annual report. I'd have to address it during my one and only court appearance before being hauled off to prison. Ask Wesley Snipes what he thinks about Warren Buffett's tax issues. And whether he picked up any good tats in prison.

So Buffett supports Obama's tax policies, even if he doesn't actually abide by them. And while he expressed an attitude of generosity with his desire to pay more taxes, when it comes to his companies, his actions indicate anything but.

In 2013, Buffett's Berkshire Hathaway, along with a Brazilian investment company, acquired H. J. Heinz Company for $23.3 billion.[13]

Heinz cut six hundred jobs as part of the deal, and accelerated the already-in-progress Obamacare-related restructuring of its health-care plans.[14]

After the acquisition, Heinz cut its contribution to retirees' health-care plans by more than half.

Of course, Heinz wasn't the only company to scale down because of Obamacare. According to a survey conducted jointly by Towers Watson/ISCEBS, 60 percent of employers were "rethinking their role in" providing retirees with medical benefits.[15]

It's weird that Buffett penalized one of his company's acquisitions for the impact of Obamacare, since the law appears to have helped him make so much money in other areas. During the discussion of just how the law would be implemented, the Centers for Medicare & Medicaid Services (CMS) reversed itself on how much it would reduce payments to kidney dialysis providers.

Instead of much deeper cuts previously considered, the CMS announced that it would instead just reduce payments by less than 1 percent over the next two years. That was great news for dialysis providers like DaVita, which saw its stock go up 8.7 percent as a result. And it was good news for Buffett, too, since Berkshire Hathaway held 17 percent of the company's stock.[16]

So no wonder Buffett supports the direction in which Obama has taken the economy. It's been great for his business. To be sure, the stock market has boomed in the age of Obama. The reason: Obama's Treasury Department has borrowed billions from China, charged the tab to future generations, and pumped the economy with easy money. But billionaires like Warren Buffett don't care about that. He's in his eighties! He isn't interested in leaving a leg up to future generations. That's why he favors an inheritance tax—not having one would be like "choosing the 2020 Olympic team by picking the eldest sons of the gold-medal winners in the 2000 Olympics," he said.[17] At least with that position, surprisingly enough, he's consistent. He's said he doesn't plan to leave that much of his money to his own kids, so I guess we can understand why he doesn't mind borrowing from yours and mine.[18]

At least with Buffett, the word is out. Increasingly, people see him for the Crapitalist hypocrite that he is. John Hayward from *Human Events* said it best: "Warren Buffett is no different from the other liars and frauds orbiting Barack Obama. His hypocrisy just runs billions of dollars deeper. When it comes to 'shared sacrifice,' you do the sacrificing, and they do the sharing."[19]

20 Jeffrey Immelt

Does the debt, deficit need to be reduced? Absolutely, right?
Is government too big, in many ways? Absolutely. But does
the country still need to invest in education? Does the country still need to invest in infrastructure? Does the country
still need to invest in—in the types of innovation and R&D
that are going to make this country competitive in the 21st
century? Yes, we do.

—Jeffrey Immelt

I'm just gonna warn you in advance, you may want to pour yourself
a drink for this chapter. At the very least, sit down. If movies are
required to warn about potentially offensive material up front, I
should at least warn you that, in exploring the Crapitalistic catastrophe that is Jeff Immelt and what the company he commands

has wrought on our country, there will be some obscene content. I mean, General Electric (GE) helped lobby for and make money from the federal bailout, green mandates, cap and trade, tax subsidies, and increased energy costs. And if that wasn't bad enough, he also owned the network that brought you Keith Olbermann and Rachel Maddow.

Better make it a double.

I'm not saying that GE and Jeff Immelt are the devil. I'm just saying they have the same legislative agenda and investment portfolio.

It didn't used to be that way.

When you think of GE, you probably think of refrigerators and washer/dryer combos. But GE has actually had its hands in many tills for a long time. Founded by a merger between two energy companies, including Thomas Edison's, GE has been an American institution for over a century. One of the original twelve companies when the Dow Jones index was formed, GE helped expand radio operations by founding RCA and contributed vital technologies to America's twentieth-century war efforts. At one time, they even hired an actor named Ronald Reagan to star in their commercials.

GE is still a huge part of what makes America run today. But their relationship with the country has changed. Thanks to a massive lobbying effort and crony connections, GE now gets as much as it gives. As even leftist *New York Times* columnist Paul Krugman noted, "with fewer than half its workers based in the United States and less than half its revenues coming from U.S. operations, G.E.'s fortunes have very little to do with U.S. prosperity."[1]

GE, thanks to Jeff Immelt, still seems to suck up a ton of it, though.

In 2011, President Obama, looking to bolster a lagging economy that didn't seem as energized as he was hoping for after the billions of bailout and stimulus dollars had been released, created a President's Council on Jobs and Competitiveness. GE's CEO, Jeff Immelt, was selected as its leader.[2]

It seemed an odd choice at the time, for a variety of reasons. One, GE had been actively downsizing jobs here in the United States and sending more overseas. In fact, GE had been creating jobs in India and China that were in part subsidized by U.S. tax dollars. And maybe it shouldn't be a shock for a company that did business with Iran until 2005, but Immelt's praise of China's state-run economy seemed odd for someone in charge of creating jobs here at home.[3]

But despite Immelt's shoddy contributions to U.S. job creation, he leveraged his position on the president's jobs council to full effect. After all, the key to GE's competitiveness seemed to have less to do with innovation, and more to do with Crapitalism.

Immelt visited the Obama White House at least thirty-three times.[4] And even though Immelt swears "[w]e are not receiving special treatment; we compete for business just like every other company," the amount of money that has found its way to GE's pockets begs otherwise.

In many senses, Immelt is the quintessential Crapitalist. A registered Republican, Immelt started cozying up to the taxpayer teat during the previous administration.

The George W. Bush White House passed two energy bills, in 2005 and 2007, that "created a government loan guarantee program for private sector green-energy projects, and effectively outlawed the traditional incandescent light bulb."[5] GE was a beneficiary of both. With their efforts to manufacture more energy-efficient products, including the more expensive LED bulbs, GE benefits from programs that either subsidize their production or give rebates to the customers who buy them. And that track record for innovation for having their hand out would continue well into the Obama era.

GE gets $2 billion in federal loan guarantees for its investments in wind and solar projects. GE lobbied to expand the subsidies for both programs, which will also net Immelt's company a cool $1 billion in Treasury grants.[6] Even when they don't directly receive the subsidies themselves, Immelt cashes in on them. GE has contracts worth hundreds of millions of dollars to sell turbines to wind plants that were built with our tax dollars.[7]

To be fair to Immelt, though, he's paid good money to grab all that government green.

GE makes a variety of products, but perhaps what it does best is lobby. With a total bill of $300 million since 1998, GE is a lobbying behemoth.[8] For that kind of money, you expect to see results. And when you employ the squadron of cronies they do, you count your benefits by the billions.

The names of the folks who lobby on behalf of GE read like a Who's Who of people who used to work in politics. And it spreads across party lines. Republicans like former Oklahoma senator Don Nickles and former Senate majority leader Trent Lott have no problem arguing for a larger government role in GE's financial fortunes. Neither do Democrats like former House majority leader Dick Gephardt or Linda Daschle, wife of former senator and majority leader Tom Daschle.[9]

It's an effort that continues to pay dividends. In late 2013, the U.S. Department of Energy awarded subsidiary GE Global Research two grants worth $6.9 million for programs that "support the development of advanced technologies that will help enable efficient, cost-effective application of carbon capture and storage (CCS) processes for new and existing coal-fired power plants."[10]

If there is government money to be had for green-related production, Immelt's lobbying team has their hand out for it. In fact, pretty much any massive government program you can think of,

GE is, um, plugged into. Even programs you wouldn't think they qualify for.

Remember the bank bailout? The Temporary Asset Relief Program, or TARP, was intended to help stabilize the financial system by authorizing the federal purchase or insurance of "troubled assets." GE's finance arm, GE Capital, owned some of the same bad investments as other financial firms, so Immelt asked for some relief through an accompanying federal bailout package. Oddly, GE didn't qualify for the bank bailout program initially because—oh wait, let me find it—they aren't a bank. But "because of behind-the-scenes appeals from GE," Immelt was able to get regulators to ease the eligibility provisions. According to the *Washington Post*:

> As a result, GE has joined major banks collectively saving billions of dollars by raising money for their operations at lower interest rates. Public records show that GE Capital, the company's massive financing arm, has issued nearly a quarter of the $340 billion in debt backed by the program, which is known as the Temporary Liquidity Guarantee Program, or TLGP. The government's actions have been "powerful and helpful" to the company, GE chief executive Jeffrey Immelt acknowledged in December.[11]

Powerful and helpful, no doubt. Immelt was so grateful to the taxpayers, in fact, that he proceeded to do everything in his power to avoid joining them. See, GE has a philosophy on taxes. It rhymes with "Don't pay them."

In 2010, GE earned $14.2 billion in global profits, with $5.1 billion of that originating inside the U.S. Even with the lower Crapitalist tax bracket, you'd think they'd be looking at somewhere close to a billion in taxes. In actuality, GE's tax bill came to $3.2 billion.

Only they were *collecting*, not writing the check. It's outrageous and shocking. But it wasn't exactly new:

> The assortment of tax breaks G.E. has won in Washington has provided a significant short-term gain for the company's executives and shareholders. While the financial crisis led G.E. to post a loss in the United States in 2009, regulatory filings show that in the last five years, G.E. has accumulated $26 billion in American profits, and received a net tax benefit from the I.R.S. of $4.1 billion.[12]

Reading about GE's exploits is enough to make you throw something out a window. Or at least go hire one of their accountants. For its part, GE defends its actions and says it is acting as a "responsible citizen."

For example, in 2008, when Jeff Immelt announced a $30 million donation to benefit New York City schools, that reeked of responsibility. That $11 million of that donation would go to schools in the district of Charlie Rangel, the disgraced chair of the House Ways and Means Committee, with whom GE's tax chief, John Samuels, met privately a month earlier to ask for an extension of a tax break, well, that made it seem less responsible. Rangel reversed his position, granting the extension, saving companies like GE billions of dollars.[13]

Anne Eisele, a spokesperson for GE, said, "G.E. is committed to acting with integrity in relation to our tax obligations."[14]

At least they have a sense of humor about it.

But not giving up any tax dollars himself clearly hasn't stopped Immelt from grabbing as many as he can.

GE remains poised to capitalize on the so-called green economy, an economy they lobbied to help create. And it doesn't matter if the industries, or the technologies that drive them, aren't ready for prime time. That just means we need to pour more money into them. For example, in 2009 GE invested in lithium battery company A123, with Immelt promising that his company's "capital, resources and technology expertise will help A123 scale up faster and more efficiently."[15] The Obama administration agreed, kicking in another $132 million of your money.[16] Less than three years later, A123 went bankrupt.[17]

But the repeated failure of electric battery technology companies hasn't stopped GE from pushing forward. After all, with Uncle Sam writing the checks from our accounts, anything is possible!

Immelt is also part of the Electrification Coalition, which aims to dramatically increase the number of electric cars on the road today. All on our dime. The members of the coalition tout themselves as "leaders of companies representing the entire value chain of an electrified transportation system."[18] Which just means they are juiced in enough to smash the taxpayer piggy bank.

In 2012, GE helped lobby for the passage of a Senate bill that contained $2 billion in grants to deploy 400,000 electric cars around the country. The bill is stuck in Congress (thank you, Partisan Gridlock!) but if passed would also include $25 million to convert the federal fleet plus another $235 million for "research and development for electric vehicle batteries and infrastructure." It just so happens that GE builds the charging outposts for electric vehicles.[19]

Kind of makes you long for the days when they just sold washing machines, huh?

The reality is, those days are long gone. GE is so intertwined in so many things we pay for, it would be hard to even keep track. There's one GE initiative that gets more attention from conservatives than others, though.

GE no longer owns NBC and its properties, after being bought out completely by Comcast in 2013. But when it did, it instituted Green Week, where most NBC shows highlighted the idea of green energy, or conservation in some way. No wonder their prime-time lineup sucks so bad.

Still, as if having Bob Costas turn off studio lights during an NFL broadcast to promote "environmental issues" wasn't Orwellian enough for you, NBC has also seen the pro-Obama mind-set of its former parent company trickle into other areas. Like the news.

NBC News is regularly cited as having a pro-Obama bias. But it's obviously tame compared to the liberal talking point drivel that comes from the cable news side, MSNBC. GE sold 51 percent of NBC, and its left-leaning cable affiliates, to Comcast in 2009. But it still held 49 percent ownership. And while Comcast's ownership just happened to coincide with liberal douche bag Keith Olbermann's departure, Immelt still held sway over the message coming from NBC properties.

One former CNBC employee, Charlie Gasparino, said Immelt was very sensitive to how one of his networks was treating Immelt's sugar daddy:

> There was this issue where Jeff Immelt, Chairman of GE, called in some of the senior staff [of CNBC] and clearly was worried, according to the people I spoke to, who were in that meeting, about the possibility that we were becoming too "anti-administration."[20]

This is perhaps the most damning thing of all. Immelt used his position of authority to help soften coverage of a news channel he owned to do the bidding of a president that was helping subsidize his empire. No wonder Immelt didn't have a problem with China's state-run economy.

Well, I have a problem with it. And so does Wu Jinglian, a leading economist in China who bashes statism and crony capitalism. In a recent interview, he complained about a Chinese problem Americans can empathize with. "I have two enemies," he said. "The crony capitalists and the Maoists. They will use any means to attack me."[21]

That's where we are today, Chinese dissidents ripping a system that Immelt is praising.

Good Lord.

Some crony connections raise our ire because they are wasteful and unproductive uses of our tax dollars. But GE, thanks to Immelt and Obama, is well past that threshold. The relationship between government and businesses like GE creates incentives that don't just destroy free markets, they damage our country.

Immelt, for his part, thinks we are heading in the right direction:

"In a reset economy, the government will be a regulator; and also an industry policy champion, a financier, and a key partner," Immelt told shareholders. "The interaction between government and business will change forever."[22]

I'm terrified he's right.

21 John Podesta

I'm in this race to tell the lobbyists in Washington that their days of setting the agenda are over. They have not funded my campaign, they will not work in my White House.

—Barack Obama

In late 2008, after the euphoria of Barack Obama's election had set in, and the reality of Hope and Change was upon them, Team Obama turned to a seasoned political hand to guide its transition team. John Podesta, then the head of liberal think tank Center for American Progress, had been Bill Clinton's chief of staff. In fact, he had been Bill Clinton's last chief of staff, which is significant if you remember the kinds of issues Clinton was dealing with toward the end of his term. You know, things like sex scandals, an impeachment, and pardoning billionaire fugitive Marc Rich.

Podesta, known as a fixer of sorts for the Clinton White House, had become known as the "Secretary of Crap" because of his regular responsibility of dealing with political manure. So he was definitely a seasoned hand when it came to navigating political sewage. Five years later, Podesta agreed to return to the White House as a senior adviser to President Obama. After all, considering the number of scandals plaguing Obama's second term, having someone who worked in waste management can come in handy. But Skippy, as he's known, has experience in other things, too.

In 1988, John Podesta left his post as chief counsel of the Senate Agriculture Committee and opened up his own lobbying shop, creatively titled Podesta Associates.[1] It may seem hard to believe now, but back then the revolving door between those in charge of spending our money and those trying to influence them wasn't spinning quite as fast. Podesta was, as one columnist noted, "a bit of an entrepreneur in the access-for-profit game."[2]

It's a game he's mastered.

When John left to start his own lobbying firm, his brother, Tony, also a Democratic staffer, went with him. And while the names of the lobbying business started by the two brothers have marginally changed, the profits have skyrocketed under the Obama administration.

When George W. Bush was in office, the firm that became known as the Podesta Group averaged around $10 million a year in lobbying income. Under Obama, the Podesta Group hasn't made less than $25 million a year.

Meanwhile, John headed up the liberal think tank Center for American Progress (CAP), which saw its influence, and donor list, increase significantly in the new administration as well.

Under Obama, the Podesta brothers have operated as one of those new McDonald's drive-throughs—two lanes for faster service.

Tony ran the traditional lobbying arm, and with the access granted by his family name, has visited the White House over thirty times.

Since CAP is a think tank, it gets to play by different rules than lobbyists. But when John Podesta headed to the White House as Obama's senior adviser, CAP released the names of some of its corporate donors, though it didn't release the amounts given by individual companies. In fact, though names were leaked in various articles, CAP didn't officially release the names of any of its donors until late 2013, when John Podesta announced he was heading back to the White House.

For anyone who has read the chapters before this one, familiar names like GE and the Motion Picture Association of America would stand out. Others, like Toyota, Visa, Microsoft, T-Mobile, Google, Comcast, and defense giant Northrop Grumman should help dispel the myth that big businesses are inherently conservative.[3] Sure, they like to keep their tax bills low. But they also like to do whatever it takes to make sure the game is played by the rules that they help write.

But if you listen to the new CAP president, Neera Tanden, the fact that the corporations that donate to CAP have an agenda that's fairly well aligned with White House policy is a total coincidence. "I don't think he even knows who our corporate supporters are," Tanden said.[4]

Well, I guess that settles it. There's obviously no connection between the companies that hire a firm run by the guy who headed Obama's transition team and any policies enacted by that president's administration. I apologize for bringing it up. Except . . . and this is weird. In 2011, Podesta stepped down as president of CAP, but he remained its chairman. Podesta said the move would allow him more time to teach at Georgetown University, and also to serve as an unpaid adviser to longtime pal Hillary Clinton's State Department. And then there was this—"I intend to use this greater time and latitude to play an instrumental role in planning CAP's strategic growth, increasing our financial support, and drawing new initiatives into the organization," Podesta said.[5]

But come on. The fact that CAP has a "Business Alliance" program for corporate donors, and that those businesses just happen to have interests that overlap with CAP's positions, well, it's just one of those things, right?

If he didn't know much about the companies responsible for funding CAP before, Podesta sure demonstrated an almost supernatural ability to echo their message at an appropriate time.

A month before the car company that became known as "Government Motors" scored $50 billion of taxpayer cash, CAP posted an article with the title "As General Motors goes, so goes the nation."[6] GM was a member of CAP's Business Alliance.

Pharmaceutical company Eli Lilly says they became a donor because of CAP's "advocacy for patients' rights." As the *New York Times* noted, this was happening "just as the debate heated up in Washington over potential cuts to the Medicare program that covers Lilly's most profitable drugs."[7]

Shortly after Pacific Gas and Electric sent in a donation to CAP, Podesta was touting tax-funded incentives for solar energy that Pacific consumed at a rate higher than most other utilities. But come on. Just because the guy backs projects that benefit his donors doesn't mean he's in the bag for the highest buck. He's backed lots of clean energy programs . . . that also coincidentally have contributed to his organization. Even lefty publications like the *Nation* took notice of how CAP's support for taxpayer loan recipients matched its own supporters. Energy company First Solar bagged $3.73 billion from the Department of Energy, some of which will go to its Antelope Valley project in California:

Last year, when First Solar was taking a beating from congressional Republicans and in the press over job layoffs and alleged political cronyism, CAP's Richard Caperton praised Antelope Valley in his testimony to the House Committee on Energy and Commerce, saying it headed up his list of "innovative projects" receiving loan guarantees. Earlier, Caperton and Steve Spinner—a top Obama fundraiser who left his job at the Energy Department monitoring the issuance of loan guarantees and became a CAP senior fellow—had written an article cross-posted on CAP's website and its Think Progress blog, stating that Antelope Valley represented "the cutting edge of the clean energy economy."

Though the think tank didn't disclose it, First Solar belonged to CAP's Business Alliance.[8]

Comcast is another familiar name on CAP's list. Comcast has been throwing huge piles of cash at Democrats for years now, laying the groundwork for their $45.2 billion merger with Time Warner Cable. The company's chief lobbyist, David Cohen, for instance, has bundled over $2 million for Obama since 2007.[9] But under Obama, there are more ways to ensure access and cooperation. Like supporting the think tank that Podesta built, considered the "policy arm" of this administration.[10] Not only did Comcast help fatten Podesta's paycheck by belonging to its Business Alliance, they now have another ally to champion their bid to buy Time Warner Cable. And they'll need those friends in high places, too. Because when the largest cable provider is proposing to merge with the second-largest cable provider, a little something-something called a "monopoly" can form. And there are antitrust laws to prevent just that. But Comcast has their Crapitalist man Podesta literally in the White House. I doubt they're worried. But you can expect your cable bill to go up.

• • •

John's brother, Tony Podesta, also attracted the interest (and checks) of some heavy hitters who just happened to have businesses, or hoped to, with the government. Twelve of CAP's corporate contributors also hired the Podesta Group over a two-year period.[11] And the sibling rivalry cost all of us. Dearly.

Podesta Group client Amgen, a pharmaceutical company, got a $500 million Medicare price control extension.[12] And green energy hopeful SolarReserve paid Podesta Group $100,000 in lobbying fees.[13] And it bagged a $737 million loan guarantee for a solar project in Nevada.

And we all know how well those government-backed solar projects work out.

The SolarReserve project is particularly troubling, though, because another one of its key investors was Oklahoma billionaire George Kaiser, previously associated with the now-defunct green turd known as Solyndra. Basic rule of thumb—when more than one Crapitalist is involved in something, two things seem certain: 1) the project can't compete on its own merits, and 2) you're paying for it.

This is especially worth watching on the Keystone Pipeline project. Fellow Crapitalist Tom Steyer sits on CAP's board of directors. As we discussed in his chapter, Steyer, while being opposed to the Keystone Pipeline's extension for "environmental" reasons, also held investments that would benefit from having the extension denied. Like Steyer, Podesta has long argued against the extension and said he would recuse himself from dealing with the issue in his new official capacity in the White House. But he hasn't recused himself from his seat on the Foreign Affairs Policy Board at the State Department, the same State Department now reviewing the pipeline project.[14]

In a *Politico* editorial published just before he left for the White House, Podesta praised a speech delivered by Obama at the Center for American Progress. In the piece, Podesta declared that they were finally taking some concrete steps to help address income inequality in the United States. "We've established the new Washington Center for Equitable Growth (WCEG), a long-term effort to support serious, sustained inquiry into structural challenges facing our economy. Our aim is to enable rigorous research on the relationship between inequality and growth."[15]

That's cute. Establish a new think tank that can do research and issue reports on just how the rich keep getting richer. Here, let me save you the trouble, and the money: Stop Being Crapitalists! End the special deals to connected insiders. Stop allowing lobbyists who contributed to campaigns to manipulate the process and pick winners and losers with our tax dollars. Allow free markets to create competition, where the best idea beats the best relationship. Do that and you'll see income equality increase. Basically, get Obama to stop being a Crapitalist.

After all, while income inequality has been increasing for decades, the trend has picked up dramatically under Obama. As Podesta admits, "Ninety-five percent of income gains since 2009 have gone to the top 1 percent of earners. In 2012, the top 10 percent took home more than 50 percent of the nation's income—a record high."[16]

The criticism that Obama was looking to radically redistribute the country's wealth was correct—just not in the way we imagined. Instead of being a Marxist or a socialist, he's proven to be a Crapitalist. And with Podesta now in the White House in an official capacity, it's only going to get worse.

It's fitting that Podesta is so open about his belief in the existence of aliens, because in many ways Podesta has modeled his career after them. Aliens, I'm told, move from planet to planet, sucking the resources out of hosts before leaving their desiccated carcasses behind. Podesta's lobbying family and their Crapitalist clients are essentially doing the same thing with our tax dollars. But unlike alien ships that may or may not be hidden in secret government labs somewhere in the desert, Crapitalists like Podesta hide in plain sight. It's sort of like *Men in Black*. Actually, it's a lot like *Men in Black*, since Podesta, in the Obama administration, is now involved in a sequel!

Remember when Barack Obama, then a candidate for president, announced that the era of special interest influence would be over? "The cynics, and the lobbyists, and the special interests who've turned our government into a game only they can afford to play. They write the checks and you get stuck with the bills . . . they think they own this government, but we're here today to take it back," he said. "The time for that politics is over. It's time to turn the page."

That Barack Obama doesn't exist anymore. He found a way to carjack truckloads of cash.

In a foreword to a book about the existence of extraterrestrial life (bizarre, I know), Podesta, who has called on the government to release any classified files about the existence of aliens, wrote, "It's time to find out what the truth really is that's out there. The American people—and people around the world—want to know, and they *can* handle the truth." [17]

I agree. Only I don't think that the existence of aliens is nearly as relevant to the survival of our species as the threat of Crapitalists. That's why I wrote this book. The people can handle the truth. And the truth is, we'd be better off if Podesta and his ilk went away on a spaceship, alien or otherwise.

22 Harry Reid

Getting something done in Nevada usually means giving the Reids a piece of the action. You want to buy a large piece of land and develop it? You will probably have to deal with the Reids.

-Peter Schweizer

Crapitalists, in case you haven't figured it out by now, largely are heads of companies or investment firms that cozy up to government officials and suck up tax dollars for their own personal benefit. Whether it's via government-backed loans that they don't have to pay back, or tax-funded grants, or just changes in policies that benefit the exclusive few, Crapitalists have cracked the code for making government work for them. But Harry Reid, as we learned with Greg Meeks and Maxine Waters, is a different kind of Crapitalist. Not only does he make government work for him, he also *works* in government.

Reid has been in the U.S. Senate since 1987, coming over from spending four years in the U.S. House prior to winning statewide office. So if you're counting at home, Harry Reid has been drawing a check from the American taxpayer for more than three decades now. But he's been on the taxpayer teat for longer than that.

The man Rush Limbaugh calls "Dingy Harry" has actually been bilking taxpayers for a paycheck since the 1960s. Then he was working as a city attorney, before getting elected to Nevada's state assembly. From there he was elected lieutenant governor, before losing in an unsuccessful bid for the U.S. Senate in 1974. Shockingly, Harry Reid went over *two years* without siphoning tax dollars into his pockets.

Luckily for Harry, he was appointed to the Nevada Gaming Commission in 1977. While there, Reid was offered a bribe of $12,000 to sanction new games for the state's casinos. Reid went to the FBI, which set up a sting operation. When Jack Gordon, the man offering the bribe (and future husband of La Toya Jackson), showed up, the FBI moved in. After the agents broke up the transaction, Reid jumped on Jackson, choking him and shouting in his most righteous indignation, "You son of a bitch, you tried to bribe me."[1]

It was, without a doubt, one of the more principled things you could do when assured that your actions were both being watched and protected by the FBI.

Pretty good for a guy who would end up being named to lists of Most Corrupt Members of Congress on multiple occasions.[2]

But it served Gordon right. You don't bribe Harry Reid.

Not for $12,000, anyway. Besides, everyone knows if you want to get to Harry, you hire his kids.

Like many members of the Church of Jesus Christ of Latter-day Saints, Harry Reid has a large family. With his wife, Landra, the Reids have five children, including four sons. And with their daddy's last name, several spawn have found good work following in their father's footsteps.

In 2011, Harry Reid and nine other senators went to China to tour the clean-energy facilities of Chinese energy company ENN. Because when you think of clean energy, you think of China. Reid was accompanied on the trip by Chinese billionaire and ENN founder Wang Yusuo. Reid was clearly a fan of Yusuo, inviting him to be the featured speaker at Reid's Clean Energy Summit in Las Vegas a few months later.

The trip to China would prove to be beneficial, and profitable, for all parties involved. According to Reuters, the Nevada senator saw a project that could potentially not only be located in his home state, but also help his own backyard.

"Reid has been one of the project's most prominent advocates, helping recruit the company" while in China and "applying his political muscle on behalf of the project in Nevada" to help close the deal, Reuters reported.[3]

With ENN on board in principle, the Chinese company needed a local law firm to help give them the lay of the land. They ended up hiring Lionel, Sawyer & Collins, the most prestigious law firm in Nevada, to facilitate the scouting and acquisition of the area needed to build the solar plant. The firm was headed by former Nevada governor and attorney general Richard Bryan. Bryan also served in the U.S. Senate with Harry, and happened to have a partner Harry Reid knew well: Reid's son Rory, a former chairman of the Clark County Commission.

Rory would prove just as valuable as dad Harry, helping ENN locate a nine-thousand-acre plot less than a hundred miles from

Las Vegas, in the same county he helped run. Technically Rory, who stepped down from his position on the county commission in January 2011, couldn't negotiate the acquisition of the land because of the one-year "cooling-off period" Nevada requires of former officials. But ENN seemed to manage to make out okay anyway, bagging the property for laughably below value. The Clark County Commission agreed to sell the land, appraised anywhere from $30 million to $39 million, for just $4.5 million.

Imagine what they could have gotten it for had Rory actually been involved!

Harry, being the doting father that he is, wasn't done, either. He helped push for a package of tax incentives for ENN, too. But there was a problem: for ENN to get the full value of the deal, they had to find a customer. You know, someone to actually buy the energy. Harry wanted NV Energy, Nevada's largest utility company, to step up. Silly NV Energy didn't seem to get it. They kept saying ridiculous things, like how solar energy was too expensive, and how they were already meeting the mandated minimum for alternative energy purchases. Harry wasn't having it.

Papa Reid used an online chat to bring up the issue and try to turn the screws a bit in favor of his son's client. Reid argued that the development "would start tomorrow if NV Energy would purchase the power," adding that the company manages "95 percent of all of the electricity that is produced in Nevada and they should go along with this."[4]

ENN eventually pulled out of the land deal because they couldn't find a ~~sucker~~ buyer for their overpriced solar energy.[5] But the fact that Reid was even involved in the first place was pretty outrageous. After all, in 2003 Reid issued an official ban to prevent relatives from lobbying him or his staff. And shortly after becoming Senate majority leader, Reid, who accepted campaign contributions from disgraced lobbyist Jack Abramoff's clients, helped pass the Honest Leadership and Open Government Act, which was supposed to curtail lobbying by close relatives.

Of course, since Rory isn't officially a registered lobbyist, the law doesn't technically apply to him. Not to worry, though—Rory and Harry both swear that they never discussed the deal. Not once. Promise.

Cross my heart?

Sure, it strains any semblance of credulity to think that a father and son, working on the same project, wouldn't talk to each other about that project at any time. But not in Reid World.

If Harry and Rory didn't talk about the $5 billion energy plant they tried bringing to their home state, it was only because Harry was too busy talking to his other son about all the projects he was throwing his way.

Key Reid, a collegiate soccer player for the national championship-winning University of Virginia, followed in the family footsteps and became a douche bag . . . er . . . an attorney. His counsel has proven quite lucrative. All because of Daddy's access to tax dollars.

According to Government Accountability Institute president and bestselling author Peter Schweizer, Papa Reid has "sponsored at least $47 million in earmarks that directly benefited organizations that one of his sons, Key Reid, either lobbies for or is affiliated with."[6]

Not bad for a soccer player.

Key made headlines in Las Vegas recently because the soccer association he was affiliated with was positioned to get exclusive access to the soccer fields in Las Vegas, even though his group, the

Southern Nevada Soccer Association, had roughly half the member-
ship that the other soccer group, the Nevada Youth Soccer Association, boasts.[7]

Welcome to Las Vegas, where even access to soccer fields requires political juice.

There's also Josh Reid. In 2011, he had his eyes set on the job as
the city of Henderson's attorney, a position his dad held back in the
day. And why wouldn't he. Henderson is Nevada's second-largest
city, and the position came with a fat government paycheck of
$199,000 per year, including other perks. But there was one prob-
lem for the young Reid. He didn't meet the criteria, which included
a minimum of ten years' experience as an attorney and five years
working with a "public agency." Minor roadblock. Papa Reid lobbied
the mayor and other Henderson officials to get his son the job. As
it turned out, the city council amended the job requirements. Guess
who was now qualified? Josh Reid was appointed, and still is, the
city's attorney.[8]

With the Reids, you don't even have to be blood to cash in.
Harry's son-in-law Steve Barringer is affiliated with $6 million
worth of earmarks from Hustling Harry.[9]

Not that Harry is totally selfless. After three decades in Congress, he's taken care of himself plenty, too. Reid is now worth an
estimated $4 million. (His net worth is $3–6 million.) Not bad for
a guy who has been drawing a government paycheck all his life.

When asked about his wealth by a Senate challenger in 2010,
Reid defended his estate, saying he had invested wisely. What he
neglected to mention was his ability to influence the market, especially when it came to some of his land deals.

In 2005, Congress passed a $286 billion federal transportation
bill that contained needed ~~earmarks~~ funding for projects across
the country. Tucked into the bill was $18 million for construction

of a bridge from Laughlin, Nevada, to Bullhead City, Arizona. Reid was pleased to have been able to secure money for his state's infrastructure. But he was also improving his own bank account's stability. Reports the source:

> Reid called funding for construction of a bridge over the Colorado River, among other projects, "incredibly good news for Nevada" in a news release after passage of the 2005 transportation bill. He didn't mention, though, that just across the river in Arizona, he owns 160 acres of land several miles from proposed bridge sites and that the bridge could add value to his real estate investment.[10]

Turns out Reid had paid a total of $160,000 for that land, and, gee, just didn't get around to mentioning that his earmark might improve its value slightly. Since the deal went through, Reid has valued the land anywhere from $250,000 and $500,000 and even as high as $5 million.[11]

It was a galling abuse of power at worst, and an incredibly profitable coincidence at best. But the latter seems pretty unlikely, since it was hardly the first time.

Reid has been linked to shady land deals with business associates multiple times before, and always with a glaring lack of transparency.

Reid helped Nevada real estate developer Harvey Whittemore "secure favored treatment for a $30 billion land development project in Nevada, the future site of a 960-megawatt solar thermal power plant operated by BrightSource Energy, a company whose executives have given thousands to Reid's campaign and hosted fundraisers for the senator."[12]

Whittemore, who employed Reid's other son Leif as his attorney, would later get sentenced to two years in the slammer "for funneling more than $130,000 in illegal campaign funds" to Reid's coffers through family members and employees as a way to circumvent federal campaign finance laws.[13]

Reid's newest trick is to divert attention away from his own corruption by focusing on the Koch brothers. Reid's wife, Landra, is said to have come up with the 2014 campaign season slogan of "Republicans are addicted to Koch." Get it? Like the drug, cocaine. Get it? See, it's like a play on their name. See what that witty Landra did there?

So hip, she is.

Reid loves to attack the Koch brothers on the Senate floor, saying things like "The oil baron Koch brothers are very good at protecting and growing their prodigious future and fortune. There's nothing un-American about that. But what is un-American is when shadowy billionaires pour unlimited money into our democracy to rig the system to benefit themselves and the wealthiest one percent."[14]

That Reid had recently returned from a fundraiser with Tom Steyer, the billionaire hedge fund manager turned green energy zealot who has pledged to do exactly the same things that the Kochs are doing, didn't seem to register. But what really stands out is how he absurdly calls out the libertarian Kochs for rigging a system to benefit themselves and other elites.

What kills me is that his criticism of the Kochs could just as easily be a summary of Harry's senatorial career.

Maybe I'll send him a copy of this book. I'll inscribe it:

"Dear Harry. Thanks for your work on the prostitution issue. Now please just stop screwing us over. Sincerely, The U.S. Taxpayer."

Reid has advocated for the banning of prostitution in his home state of Nevada. In remarks to the state legislature, Reid said that prostitution was regarded as much more negative than gambling, and that Nevada should consider banning it. Reid would later acknowledge that those remarks went over about as well as a "pregnant high jumper."

How ironic that Reid is opposed to people selling themselves for money. Dingy Harry's been pimping himself for decades—and all on your dime.

23 Fred Hochberg

It's time to drop the fantasy that a purely free market exists in the world of global trade. In the real world our private enterprises are pitted against an array of competitors that are often government-owned, government-protected, government-subsidized, government-sponsored or all of the above.

—Fred Hochberg

By now you may be feeling a little overwhelmed. Trust me, I understand. At least all you have to do is read about it. (And pay for it.) How do you think I feel? I'm over here reporting on these douche nozzles.

One of the reasons I wrote this book is to help people understand the way things really work and how it is killing the free market system that made America great. It seems like no matter where you look, no matter which industry you select, you'll find Crapital-ism's tentacles creeping in. Yeah, we've talked a lot about the green energy businesses that are cropping up, paid for by our tax dollars, and the wealthy businessmen who take advantage of the breaks and come out ahead even when the businesses themselves go broke. But there are other ways to benefit as well.

The business owners in this book work in industries ranging from big-box retail to professional football, and virtually every-thing in between. No matter the product, the people behind it are all looking for every tax-funded helping hand they can find. The pursuit of the handout is troubling for several reasons, but the most important is this: not everyone gets them. That's the point of Crapitalism—to subvert genuine free market competition by using your inside connections to squeeze out everyone else. By bellying up to the tax-backed bar, businesses gain an advantage over their competitors not because of innovation, but by political access.

Gone are the days of entrepreneurs developing an idea, then presenting it to a bank that makes the call on whether they'd like to invest in and lend money to fund it. Today, businesses are liter-ally addicted to taxpayer-backed subsidies, loans, or other guaran-tees that minimize the risks inherent in any free market system. And Fred Hochberg is the drug dealer.

Hochberg runs the Export-Import Bank of the United States, or Ex-Im, as it's known. The Ex-Im Bank was founded in 1934 as a way to make it easier for U.S. businesses to export goods to other coun-tries that otherwise wouldn't have been able to afford them. Every four years, its charter needs to be renewed by Congress, and its head is appointed by the president. Hochberg served as an admin-istrator of the Small Business Administration under Bill Clinton, a tenure that surely gave him the business savvy and know-how that caught Barack Obama's eye. Well, that and the fact that Hochberg was a campaign bundler for Obama, helping him raise over $100,000.[1] Now he's on his fifth year enjoying a fat $165,000 salary courtesy of you, the taxpayer.[2] But, as we've seen already, what good is it bundling money for politicians if the perks don't extend to your loved ones as well? Hochberg, who is openly gay, is partners with artist Tom Healy. Healy was appointed by President Obama to the prestigious J. William Fulbright Foreign Scholarship Board in 2011.

As chairman of the Fulbright board, Healy "has traveled extensively to promote Fulbright through the Americas, Europe, Asia, and Africa."[3] As a member of the Fulbright board, Healy is compensated for travel, appearances, and other work done on behalf of the organization at the GS-15 rate, the highest in the government.

A taxpayer-funded hopscotch around the globe. What's the word I'm looking for? Oh yeah, the title of this book: *Crapitalism.*

As head of the Ex-Im, Hochberg now uses his "expertise" to grow businesses around the country. Of course, he does that by lending your money to businesses that aren't in our country. But still, businesses should be grateful to the man. After all, what would small business owners do without the brilliance of Hochberg. If you listen to Hochberg himself, apparently they wouldn't know how to sell their products to potential customers.

"Sometimes small business owners aren't necessarily strategic, you know, and they export to the country they go on vacation to," Hochberg explained. "So I met one small business owner [and] he listed the four countries and I said, 'how did you pick those four?' he says, 'I go there on holiday.' So that's not the best strategic way of doing it."[4]

Those poor, simpleton small business owners. You guys don't

know how to grow your own businesses. Luckily there are government programs, backed by our tax dollars, to help them. If it weren't for Hochberg's help, a Montana business wouldn't have had near the success in exporting pet toys around the world. Yep, your tax dollars helped West Paw Design export their pet toys and apparel to Mexico and Scandinavian countries. As the Ex-Im website brags, "The Bank's credit insurance allowed West Paw Design to offer open account credit to its buyers. Typical terms were 30 to 60 days rather than having their customer pay cash-in-advance."[5]

God bless America.

Our tax dollars, thanks to Hochberg, have helped send everything from lobster and quiche to hair care products and electric motorcycles around the world.

You're welcome.

And under Obama, the help has increased. Big-time. With Hochberg in charge, Ex-Im subsidies have skyrocketed 40 percent, from $100 billion to $140 billion today. That's a lot of help for certain businesses. And it's a lot of exposure for the taxpayer.

Hmm . . . taxpayers being left on the hook for guaranteeing billions of dollars' worth of loans? Where have we seen this movie before? Oh yes, Fannie Mae and Freddie Mac, which are still in a government conservatorship.

Ex-Im shills say there is no risk to taxpayers, that the bank is profitable and contributes to the Treasury. But that claim appears to be misleading. By accounting for "market risk," the Congressional Budget Office projects that the Ex-Im Bank will actually cost taxpayers $2 billion over the next 10 years.[6] And if the Fannie/ Freddie meltdown showed us anything, it's that financial crashes can happen suddenly. The point is that taxpayers should not be exposed at all.

Don't take my word for it, though. Check out what a Government Accountability Office report had to say about it:

Ex-Im faces multiple risks when it extends export credit financing. These risks include (1) credit risk (the risk that an obligor may not have sufficient funds to service its debt or be willing to service its debt), (2) political risk (the risk that expropriation of the obligor's property, war, or inconvertibility of the obligor's currency into U.S. dollars may result in nonrepayment), (3) concentration risk (the risk that events could negatively affect not only one entity or location but also many entities or locations simultaneously), (4) market risk (the risk of loss from declining prices or volatility of prices in the financial markets, which could arise from changing macroeconomic conditions), and (5) operational risk (the risk that loss may result from inadequate or failed internal processes, people, and systems, or from external events).[7]

See, some countries aren't exactly what we'd call "stable." So when you have a billion dollars' worth of exposure to businesses in a country like, say, Russia, people understandably get nervous.[8] To be fair, decisions about whose customers deserve the loans are made only by the most ardent examinations. That and by who has the best lobbyist, or other access to the cash.

The Ex-Im beneficiaries read like the table of contents for this book. We've talked about how Crapitalist George Kaiser bought his way into the Obama giveaways to grab tax money for Solyndra. Well, the Ex-Im provided a $10 million loan guarantee to a Belgium bank that facilitated the purchase of solar panels from Solyndra.[9]

Another politically connected green company, First Solar, a member of the Business Alliance of John Podesta's Center for American Progress, not only got Ex-Im loans[10] but also was allowed to essentially take that money and give it back to itself:[11]

> Some of the Ex-Im money went to a Canadian company named St. Clair Solar, which is a wholly owned subsidiary of First Solar. St. Clair Solar received a total of $192.9 million broken into two loans to buy solar panels from First Solar. In other words, the company received a loan to buy solar panels from itself.[12]

Under Hochberg, Ex-Im has come under fire for even more egregious conflicts of interest.

Former New Mexico governor Bill Richardson, Bill Clinton's energy secretary, served on the Ex-Im Advisory Committee. He also sits on the International Advisory Board for a Spanish company called Abengoa. Would you be shocked to learn that Abengoa bagged $33.6 million from Ex-Im to buy solar fluid from Dow Chemical? Probably just a coincidence, right?

I want to be clear, though. It isn't like Hochberg and his boys are just sitting around taking direction from the connected cronies. Sometimes they have to go out into the field and inspect firsthand the companies they might loan money to. And if those companies want to pay for the trip, no problem.

Exxon flew four Ex-Im employees to London, Tokyo, Australia, and Papua New Guinea, showing them the route a gas project would take. And I'm sure the employees deliberated methodically while being "entertained by costumed villagers."[13] Exxon ended up paying nearly $100,000 for the trip. But when the bank approved $3 billion worth of financing, it probably seemed worth it.

Sometimes the businesses that end up with the money say they don't even need the help! A Mexican satellite company's CEO said that even though his company's project was "fully funded" because of, you know, regular business principles, he was still pursuing an Ex-Im loan for $255.4 million for the purchase of two satellites.[14] When in Rome, right? Or, Mexico.

But it raises the question: why are U.S. taxpayers being put in the position to lend their hard-earned money in support of Mexican businesses that, by their own admission, say they don't need it? At least that money went to a business that actually existed. In 2007, $243 million worth of Ex-Im loans went to fake Mexican companies for equipment "that wasn't even real."[15] A local news station in Dallas investigated and "discovered that some of the people who got the Ex-Im Bank loans may have drug connections. The $243 million worth of bad loans were originally made to help trade with Mexico. The loans have been linked to the Juarez drug cartel, which is known for its brutal murders. The cartel killed one dozen people and buried them in a suburban backyard across the border from El Paso."[16]

Oops.

It's fitting that some of the Ex-Im cash might have ended up with the Mexican cartel, because most of its disbursements end up supporting the powerful interests domestically as well.

The bank tries to mask the loyalty to big business by saying that 90 percent of its "transactions" go to small businesses. That's disingenuous. The vast majority of its authorizations go to huge, profitable businesses, like Boeing and GE. In 2013, for instance, out of $27.3 billion in authorizations, less than a quarter ($5.2 billion) went to small businesses.[17]

While most Ex-Im Bank loans go to subsidize big business, Hochberg and company must put a positive spin on things, so they highlight how they help small businesses, and the fact that risks of default are offset by the fees the bank charges the businesses. And naturally they get business owners who benefit from the programs to help get the bank positive publicity. Organizations like the U.S. Chamber of Commerce love Hochberg, because their members benefit from the program.

But sometimes they can't control the publicity. Like when the competitors of the businesses they help "win" don't play ball. Sometimes, believe it or not, businesses actually stand up for themselves and say, "Hey, all that money you're throwing around to my competition that, you know, comes from my taxes? If you could stop, that'd be great."

That's essentially what Delta said. When over 60 percent of the $12.2 billion in loan guarantees subsidized Boeing sales,[18] Delta politely objected. Turns out they weren't so on board with their government helping their competitor Air India purchase Boeing planes. So Delta sent a Hallmark card, commonly known as a "lawsuit." [19]

I don't know what Delta's problem is. Boeing fought for that money fair and square—Boeing CEO Jim McNerney chaired Obama's exports council.[20] Step up your Crapitalism game, Delta!

The CEO of Whole Foods, libertarian John Mackey, said, "Capitalism is ultimately people cooperating together to create value for other people as well as for themselves."

This is almost exactly the opposite of the idea of the Ex-Im. At least some people are beginning to realize it. When the bank came back up for reauthorization, critics, thanks to the Tea Party, finally came out of the woodwork. They started to call out the practice for what it was.

"The Ex-Im Bank perverts the concept of open market competition by picking winners based off of political standing rather than merit. This is the true definition of crony capitalism," according to a report by Real Clear Policy.[21]

The Ex-Im Bank claims it doesn't technically cost taxpayers money. But as we've seen with Freddie and Fannie, the threat of losses is real. In addition to imperiling our financial future, it rewards the wrong type of behavior and indeed perverts real free market capitalism. Companies now focus less on innovative practices, and more on fostering crony political relationships. And it's weakening our economic base all the same. Even as we're paying Fred Hochberg a fat salary to do it.

Excuse me while I go light myself on fire.

24 George Soros

A lot of the evil in the world is actually not intentional. A lot of people in the financial system did a lot of damage without intending to.

—George Soros

If you think of Crapitalists like planets in the solar system, a certain pecking order begins to emerge. Obama would be the sun, since the energy of his position is what makes life on all the other Crapitalist planets possible. Mercury and Venus would be people like John Podesta and Jeff Immelt, people who draw their identity by virtue of their proximity to the sun.

Terry McAuliffe, clearly, is Uranus.

But while many of the people profiled in this book would be metaphorical planets, George Soros would be the galaxy. The

Hungarian-born billionaire has so many entities that manipulate institutions in this country and around the world that they might as well make up their own universe. And many of those organizations fund, support, advocate, or otherwise influence our government's pursuit of policies that are ruining our country.

Soros funds myriad organizations that, under the guise of philanthropy, promote the Soros—and therefore Obama—agenda. Soros's millions have helped elect Obama twice. In return, Obama has helped Soros.

A *New Yorker* article gives insight into Soros's expectations of the president—the man some call the leader of the free world. Crapitalists like George Soros call him other things. And expect, above all else, access:

> When Soros wanted to meet with Obama in Washington to discuss global economic problems, Obama's staff failed to respond. Eventually, they arranged not a White House interview but, rather, a low-profile, private meeting in New York, when the President was in town for other business. Soros found this back-door treatment confounding. "He feels hurt," a Democratic donor says. "They pissed on him," a confidant says. "He didn't want a (blasted) thing! He didn't want a state dinner, or a White House party—he just wanted to be taken seriously."[1]

Soros undoubtedly got over the snub. It probably helped when Obama, after his reelection, hired the head of Soros's Center for American Progress to be a senior adviser. As we discussed in a previous chapter, Crapitalist John Podesta ran the Soros-backed CAP, which has a great track record of funneling tax dollars to its supporters. Now that Podesta is in the White House, Soros has even more cronies on the federal dole.

That matters to Soros. Because he's already seen how profitable having access to key staff can be.

Shortly after taking office, President Obama dialed up $831 billion in taxpayer-funded treats for connected companies through the stimulus program. One of the key players in that program was Cathy Zoi, who administered the awarding of Department of Energy grants. In 2011, Zoi left the agency and took a job with a green-tech investment fund. A fund that was established by George Soros, whose investments just happened to receive so much of those awards that Zoi oversaw.

Soros, famous for his currency speculation, would now make millions more off Obama's alleged recovery.

Author Peter Schweizer's book *Throw Them All Out* exposed the connected companies that ended up with tax dollars, including myriad Soros investments. Schweizer noted the Hungarian's incredible timing, increasing some holdings and adding others at just the right time. In the first quarter of 2009, Soros "doubled his holdings in medical manufacturer Hologic" and "tripled his holdings in fiber channel and software maker Emulus." Both companies benefited from the Soros-sought stimulus issued just a few months later. Soros also acquired 300,000 shares of Constellation Energy group and 1.5 million shares of American Electric Power. Both power companies ended up generating some of our money for their pockets via the stimulus, with American Electric snagging $1 billion taxpayer-funded Obama bucks.[2]

Soros also bought into companies that would grab those infamous loans from the Department of Energy. Ameren, a utility company, snatched a $540 million Department of Energy loan shortly after joining Soros's portfolio. Ameren was joined in the DOE loan line by NRG Energy, Entergy, Powerspan, and Public Service Enterprise Group. Guess what they all have in common, besides being energy companies that Obama threw our tax dollars toward?

You guessed it! They are all part of Soros's portfolio, though finding themselves there only a short time before President Giveaway came through. Soros wasn't alone in scoring political favors at our expense. According to Schweizer, 80 percent of the green energy loans made their way to Obama's campaign donors. In fact, Obama's bundlers made, on average, a staggering $21,000 in stimulus cash for every dollar they funneled to the campaign.

And Soros donated more than most.

Soros proudly claims to be one of Obama's earliest supporters. In 2008, Soros gave more than $5 million to Obama's election.[3] And in 2012, Soros donated more than $2.7 million to outside groups to help ensure Obama's reelection.[4]

But then, he's benefited quite a bit, too. For all the hype the adoring media heaped on the president's ceremonial dumping of cash to his cronies, by 2012 the adulation was less forthcoming. Something about an elevated unemployment rate and the massive failure of recipients like Solyndra seemed to have dampened enthusiasm somewhat. So Obama had to figure out a different way to hook up his lefty sugar daddy. But stimulus infusions were so passé, not to mention costly, ineffective, and destructive to our country's future financial sovereignty. Other than that, no problem.

So Obama, the king of "clean" energy, started pushing for a different policy. He decided in January 2012 to start pushing for tax incentives for natural gas technology. Not exactly the same thing as solar, but not exactly Styrofoam-coated coal, either. Obama's proposal would enact incentives for companies to purchase trucks that run on natural gas. Analysts noted that a company named Westport Innovations stood to benefit from Obama's proposal. Westport converts diesel engines to run off natural gas, so they would see a nice uptick in business if companies suddenly wanted vehicles with natural gas engines. And you'll never guess who was one of the largest investors in Westport. Yep, Sugar Daddy Soros. His hedge fund held 3,160,063 shares.[5] The proposal, while championed on the Left, never really got moving, though. A year later, Soros dumped it from his portfolio.[6]

Hey, you can't blame the guy for trying.

Soros would have to get over it. Obama had already done quite a bit to help him.

In August 2008, Soros managed to put aside his environmental zealotry long enough to sink $811 million into Petrobras, a Brazilian government-controlled oil company. Bloomberg noted that Soros's investment made the dirty, nasty fossil fuel company the largest holding in his investment fund.[7] The *Wall Street Journal*, among others, observed the curious inconsistency in Soros's investment strategy versus his public declarations:

> It's not only that Petrobras is a fossil fuel company. The more interesting aspect of the Soros investment is that Mr. Soros's Petrobras investment cannot be profitable if the company does not exploit its Tupi oil field, the largest offshore find in the hemisphere. Indeed, Petrobras is rapidly emerging as a world leader in technology to exploit such no-no reserves, while Brazil has thousands of miles of pristine coastline and a large indigenous population. Is Mr. Soros not outraged that he will be funding corporate interests that threaten these? Apparently not as long as there is money to be made that will go into his own pocket.[8]

And there was money to be made. In April 2009 the Ex-Im Bank authorized a "preliminary commitment" of $2 billion in loan guarantees for Petrobras to purchase drilling equipment from American manufacturers. A few months later Soros repositioned his holdings in the Brazilian company, selling common shares in favor of "preferred shares," a move *Bloomberg* noted provided an additional 10 percent dividend.[9] So, if you're keeping score, while Soros funds every left-wing group under the sun determined to restrict domestic oil production, he was capitalizing on oil exploration in a foreign country buoyed by U.S.-backed loans.

That, ladies and gentlemen, is a black-belt Crapitalism ninja move.

With gas prices well above $3 a gallon, I guess you and I can take the bus. Oh wait, that bus is probably running on natural gas because Obama's buddy runs a company that took our money to produce less efficient technology that we will have to subsidize because . . . uh . . . you know . . . "global warming"? Honestly I lose track. Are we doing these things because of the weather, or because of the economy, or because of income inequality? The narrative changes constantly, but the Obama hypocrisy remains constant.

The worst part is how the media let them get away with it.

Of course, Soros helps Obama with that as well. If you ever wonder why you hear so little about Obama's efforts to stoke Soros's stock, even though it contradicts so many of his campaign pledges, just follow the money. Soros has his hands, and money, in organizations that support the media, too.

In early 2014, a commissioner at the Federal Communications Commission (FCC) blew the lid on the agency's plan to begin a "Multi-Market Study of Critical Information Needs." The plan would have put FCC employees, or, as some said, "government agents," into newsrooms across the country to "study" the kinds of stories being reported. The plan was based off a report commissioned by two journalism schools, one at the University of Wisconsin and the other at the University of Southern California. Both programs receive money from George Soros's Open Society Foundation.[10]

The proposal drew outrage from conservative media outlets like talk radio and Fox News. And rightly so. The idea that the government would be coming into newsrooms and "evaluating" whether "critical information" was being disseminated sounds like an idea from China or Russia. But for some reason, you didn't hear "mainstream" news organizations howling about the potential trampling of constitutionally protected rights.

It's amazing what $50 million will get you.

As the Internet age has hit media organizations just like the computer hit the typewriter, newsrooms have seen their staffs, budgets, and profits shrink. Enter Soros. His vast network of left-wing entities has donated $52 million to news organizations over the years.[11] Was that the reason you heard about it mostly from news outlets that were more "fair and balanced"? Maybe. But for media outlets obsessed by the meddling and influence of libertarian billionaires like the Koch brothers, they are historically unconcerned with the actions of Soros. One study showed that, among news outlets like *Politico*, the *New York Times*, and the *Washington Post*, Soros's Tides Foundation was referenced only a fraction as much as the Koch brothers.[12] In fact, *Politico* even has a former Soros-funded employee on staff. The reporter's beat: reporting on the Kochs.

A famous rhetorical question asks, "If a tree falls in the woods, but no one is there, does it make a sound?" The George Soros version of that is "If a tree falls in the woods, but all the reporters are getting money from the person who cut it down, would it make the nightly news?"

As we learned from Maria Shriver, absolutely not.

Shriver made the rounds on a host of national television shows promoting the *Shriver Report*, which looked at the impact that the War on Poverty, enacted in part by her father, Sargent Shriver, was having fifty years later. Shriver went on air with NBC, her former employer, and presented the findings that showed, to her mind, the disproportionate effects the War on Poverty was having on women. The Media Research Center detailed Shriver's appearance:

> Shriver was invited to the White House on Jan. 14 to present her report to President Barack Obama, whom she promoted as being "sympathetic" to working mothers. On NBC "Nightly News" that same night, Shriver contrasted a supportive Obama against a Congress that is supposedly dragging its feet on the matter. "While President Obama has pledged to fix the problem, Congress has been slow to respond," Shriver said.[13]

What NBC didn't note was that the report was done in conjunction with the Center for American Progress, which Soros funds. This is why this matters so much. Soros can use his money to produce infomercials on mainstream television for the guy he helped get elected, and who has paid him back tenfold in Crapitalist crony kickbacks since. By continuing to promote the Obama agenda, Soros promotes his quest for taxpayer-backed goodies.

25 John Doerr

It is the mother of all markets. It's probably the largest economic opportunity of the 21st century.

—John Doerr

In February 2009, recently elected President Obama tapped venture capitalist John Doerr to his Economic Recovery Advisory Board. Doerr, a big Obama backer, seemed a logical choice to advise the president because of the success of his investment firm, Kleiner Perkins Caufield & Byers. Only one month earlier, Doerr had addressed members of the U.S. Senate, complaining that the country was losing the green race. Doerr confessed that two of his investment company's biggest holdings were foreign, because the United States didn't have the best technology.[1] It was a somewhat startling admission for a man who was partners, recall, with the former vice president of the United States Al Gore.

Doerr implored members of the Senate Environment and Works Committee to think of investments in green technology like we thought of other investments a few decades ago. "We won the space race with the Soviet Union," he said. Then, referencing *New York Times* columnist Thomas Friedman, Doerr warned, "we're in an Earth race with other nations to see who can invent the technology so that men and women can stay on Earth. And we are not winning today."

The U.S. Senate, along with the president whom Doerr helped elect, would increase the national investment in so-called green tech. Bankruptcies of companies like Solyndra mean taxpayers have come out as losers. But Crapitalists like Doerr have won big. As part of Obama's economic recovery team, Doerr helped shape the stimulus package in a way he thought would help boost the country's economic recovery. It just so happened that sixteen of the companies Doerr funneled money to were firms in which he was invested.

Basically, it was a taxpayer-financed stimulus selfie. Not overly surprising for a guy whose investment philosophy is "No conflict, no interest."[2]

Even the firms that didn't directly receive stimulus funding were helped by the infusion of taxpayer cash. With money pouring into green tech, the market improves even if the technology sucks. And few were as invested in the market as Doerr. As the *San Francisco Chronicle* noted, Doerr's firm "has invested $600 million in 45 green tech startups, and Doerr said the firm will invest in at least 40 more over the next two years. Venture capitalists poured more than $1.8 billion into clean energy ventures in California (in 2008) and about $5 billion into green tech projects nationwide."[3]

At least with John Doerr, we could see it coming. The push for public money to fund private ventures had been going on well before Obama took office. And Doerr was one of its biggest proponents.

Because of his enthusiasm and advocacy for acquiring our tax dollars, a 2007 *Condé Nast Portfolio* profile on Doerr noted that he was "helping to create the biggest new market the world has seen since the dawn of the oil industry—and asking for taxpayer dollars to do it."[4]

As *Condé Nast Portfolio* also noted, there are some pretty profound differences between the green-tech field and the Web technologies that were emerging from Silicon Valley earlier in the decade:

"None of the alternative energy sources being developed today—solar, wind, geothermal, or biomass—is close to financial sustainability, which means that the supersize returns V.C. funds depend on will require massive government subsidies, regulations, and mandates."[5]

Oh. Remember, this piece was written in 2007, before the economic collapse, and before the massive misuse of tax dollars in the name of so-called economic stimulus. But like other emerging trends, you have to give Doerr credit. He knew a promising opportunity when he saw one, even though, as the *Portfolio* noted, "government interference runs against Silicon Valley's libertarian grain." Still, the publication observed, "money is money, and since venture capital funds typically have a 10-year life span, the clock is already ticking."

What follows should be printed, buried in a time capsule, and dug up one hundred years from now. People need to know that it didn't used to be this way. Ideas and products used to compete on their own viability and merit. But if things are just as bad, if not worse in the following century, future Crapitalists can thank John

Doerr. In 2007, Doerr laid the groundwork for everything our country is dealing with now, and everything I write about in this book:

> Doerr has launched an audacious campaign to invest millions in handpicked political candidates and influential political action committees, to push for subsidies and pro-greentech policies and require the government to purchase the kinds of fuels and technologies his startups will be marketing. Since 2000, Doerr and his wife, Ann, have contributed more than $31 million to political candidates and causes.[6]

And like with most good Crapitalists, those investments yield a healthy return.

The policies Doerr advocated during his Senate committee appearance are, unbelievably, policies that put money in his pocket. Doerr called on the country to modernize the electric grid. Doerr and his partners just happened to have invested $75 million in a company called Silver Spring Networks, a contractor for "smart grid projects." Though they didn't receive any stimulus funds directly, they were hired by companies that did for the modernization Doerr called for. Customers of Silver Spring grabbed more than $560 million of the stimulus funds Doerr helped designate.[7] The stimulus language was even crafted in such a way as to give Silver Spring a leg up on its competitors.[8] I guess the $560 million to their customers just wasn't enough in the down, Obama economy.

Another Doerr investment, Amyris, grabbed $24 million in a Department of Energy grant. After bagging the cash, Amyris went public with an initial public offering (IPO), which saw Kleiner Perkins more than triple its investment. But Doerr wasn't the only one celebrating.

Democratic California senator Dianne Feinstein bought $1 million of equity in Amyris only weeks before the grant was announced. Two years later, Senators Tom Coburn and Ben Cardin introduced legislation that would repeal the ethanol tax credit, which would hurt companies like Amyris, which makes biofuels. Luckily, Senator Feinstein swooped in and introduced a bill that would leave the tax credit in place for companies like Amyris. Feinstein's legislation would actually benefit Amyris even more by penalizing other ethanol makers by repealing the credit they receive for corn-based ethanol.[9]

You know what they say, all's fair in love and war—and in jawboning for bills that benefit your portfolio.

Meanwhile, we still pay more at the pump because of the ethanol mandate, which makes cars less fuel efficient, makes engines wear out faster, and causes global food prices to increase, thereby exacerbating worldwide hunger.

Other than that, though, it's a great idea.

Another policy Doerr advocated for was the creation of a national renewable energy standard. Doerr wanted the government to follow California in mandating that a certain portion of the energy that utility companies generate come from renewable sources, like solar or wind. It may be gratifying to know that at least that hasn't happened yet. We all know how well the ethanol mandate has worked out. And while you may hear some rumbles from the true greenies out there who run their Priuses on vegetable oil, Crapitalists like Doerr and Gore give the president a pass. As they should, because he's taken care of them in other ways.

A solar panel company Doerr was invested in, MiaSolé, got $102 million in manufacturing credits from the Obama stimulus.

MiaSolé is actually one of the success stories, not just for Doerr, but because they are still in business. The company generated its 50 millionth cell by November 2011, and in January 2013, Hanergy

Holding Group purchased MiaSolé.[10] Have you heard of Hanergy? They're a clean energy company—in China. But hey, the Chinese deserve clean energy and innovative solar technology, too. I'm sure that's what attracted their investment. Oh, that and the sale price of $30 million. I guess that's a pretty good deal for a company "attracting more than $550 million in finance," including the tax credits they bagged. The $30 million wasn't all that surprising, according to observers. Turns out, when the government stopped investing, so did everyone else. Venture capital funding for the "clean tech" industry dropped 50 percent in 2012.[11]

To be fair, at least MiaSolé turned out better than Fisker.

I wrote about Fisker Automotive, another Kleiner Perkins investment, in the Al Gore chapter. Fisker bagged a $192 million loan from the Department of Energy to make electric cars. Now, personally, I love the idea of an electric car. I mean, just because I document the repeated failure of these green companies that grabbed our money because of crony connections, it doesn't mean I'm anti-environment. If you can produce a competitive product that beats its competition, and I can drive it for less money, great. But that isn't what happened with Fisker. Fisker went bankrupt, and vaporized 139 million of our dollars.[12] That's the amount DOE ate on the deal when it sold the loan to a Chinese investor.[13]

At least Matt Damon and Leonardo DiCaprio ended up with one. Maybe they can make *The Departed 2*, the story of how a connected Crapitalist took off with our money.

What really kills me is, Doerr knows better. As with most Crapitalists, there's no doubting Doerr's legitimate business acumen. Doerr's firm was among the first to invest in companies like Google and Amazon, giving them their start and profiting from their international success still. What terrifies me is, like with those two Web

companies, what if Doerr's investments in green tech are the wave of the future as well? What if Crapitalists like Doerr have invested too much money in them to see anything else happen?

Unless you're just still in love with the phone book and the card catalog system at the library, you've probably used Google at some point in the last decade. And if you're reading this book, maybe you bought it online at Amazon. (Maybe check out *Obama Zombies* and *Hollywood Hypocrites* while you're there, yo.) Those sites, like my other books, became successes because of the market demand. No one made you use a search engine, and no one made you use a website to buy admittedly fantastic *New York Times* best-sellers. John Doerr has succeeded on the free market before. But apparently, like our planet's temperatures and weather patterns, he's changed. Competing against other companies is for suckers. Getting U.S. taxpayers to fund your start-up, that's the Crapitalist way. After all, we're trying to save the planet over here, people!

Maybe folks would believe those screaming the loudest about global warming if those screamers didn't also happen to be the same ones making the most money. But by and large, the climate change alarmists tend to want to put our money where their mouths are. Don't claim, as Doerr did on Charlie Rose's show, that "[t]he latest fear from scientists at Caltech is not that Greenland will melt but that it's going to slip off the rocks. If we lose Greenland, all the scientists agree that oceans will rise by 20, 30 feet. That puts downtown Manhattan underwater. That means where we are in Silicon Valley will be underwater. We will lose most of Mumbai in India," when your solution only slips more of my money into your pocket.

Crapitalists like Doerr and Gore know their investments can't compete on their own merits. So they scare the public into buying,

and when that doesn't work (apparently people care more about their expenses rising than the seas) they pursue a different type of innovation: the mandate. But despite the millions in taxpayer-funded help he has received, Doerr still thinks of himself as a "raging capitalist." What terrifies me is, what if he actually believes it?

26 Elon Musk

I always invest my own money in the companies that I create. I don't believe in the whole thing of just using other
people's money. I don't think that's right. I'm not going to
ask other people to invest in something if I'm not prepared
to do so myself.

—Elon Musk

Elon Musk was unhappy.

That the forty-two-year-old South Africa–born billionaire
would be unhappy about anything is, in and of itself, unusual.
Worth $2.7 billion in 2013, the PayPal cofounder had seen his net
worth more than triple in the past year. Now worth $8.4 billion,
Musk was seemingly on top of the world. His electric car company
Tesla Motors saw its stock jump 625 percent. The SolarCity company

he chaired enjoyed a stock boom of over 300 percent as well. And he was enjoying the fruits of his labor. The man on whom director Jon Favreau admitted *Iron Man*'s Tony Stark character was based was living up to the eccentric billionaire stereotype. Musk already lived in a 20,000-square-foot home in Bel Air, which featured six bedrooms and nine bathrooms, plus a five-car garage.[1] But you know how cramped those Bel Air neighborhoods can be. So Musk had also just purchased his *neighbor's* home, one that formerly belonged to actor Gene Wilder, of *Charlie and the Chocolate Factory* fame, for another $6.75 million.

I told you, eccentric billionaire.

So why was Musk unhappy? Something wrong with the sound system in his massive home theater? His two-story library's rolling ladder was making too much noise?[2]

No, Musk was upset because New Jersey's Motor Vehicle Commission had unanimously passed a rule that effectively banned Tesla from operating in the state. Tesla's business model involves selling directly to customers, eliminating the need for auto dealers. But the commission voted, with Governor Chris Christie's backing, to ban direct sales to New Jersey customers. Tesla, already operating in the state for a year, would have to close its stores, thus also closing off a lucrative customer base.

So yeah, Musk was mad.

He issued a lengthy statement on his company's website, blaming Christie for being in the pocket of the state's auto dealer lobby, which had spent $150,000 lobbying the issue and had given $60,000 to his recent campaign for governor.[3]

Musk blasted what he viewed as a corrupt process:

> Governor Christie had promised that this would be put to a
> vote of the elected state legislature, which is the appropriate

way to change the law. When it became apparent to the auto
dealer lobby that this approach would not succeed, they cut
a backroom deal with the Governor to circumvent the legislative process and pass a regulation that is fundamentally
contrary to the intent of the law.[4]

Musk continued, comparing Christie's rationale of intervention
for "consumer protection" to another industry New Jerseyans are
familiar with, the Mafia. "When a politician acts in a manner so
radically opposed to the will of the people who elected him, the only
explanation is that there are other factors at play," Musk concluded.

That Musk was complaining about a government entity protecting a function of private enterprise is about as ironic as an
electric car being fueled by an engine burning coal and asbestos.

Obviously electric cars like Tesla don't run on fossil fuels. But
they do run on something other than electricity. It turns out, the
real-life version of Iron Man does have a superpower—he has a supernatural ability to gobble up tax dollars.

Back before Tesla was portrayed as a success, the company was
actually in danger of going the way of so many other green-tech
start-ups due to being over budget and to massive delays in getting
product to market. In 2008, Musk took over as CEO and slashed the
payroll. With the company short of the cash it needed to become
viable, Musk, whose early business ventures in college involved
throwing massive parties, returned to his roots. As the lefty *Mother
Jones* reported, "He threw a kegger."[5] Politicians gathered for beers
in D.C.'s National Building Museum and Musk, ever the showman,
took them for a spin in the new Model S.

The Department of Energy was undoubtedly not convinced or
swayed by the kegger, nor by the dozen trips Musk had taken to
D.C. to lobby for taxpayer-funded loans. And the fact that Obama

bundler Steve Westly, who raised a reported $1 million over two campaigns for Obama, was on the Tesla board of directors was also probably totally irrelevant. Remember, this was the administration that was going to take government back from the special interests and give it to the people.

What happened instead was that billions of dollars came from the people and ended up in the pockets of the connected. And Musk's company was no different.

Just months after the party, Tesla bagged a $465 million loan, which was enough to rescue it from its financial troubles. Musk has claimed that, while his company received a lucrative loan from the Department of Energy, which was eventually paid off, what really helped Tesla was the investment from Daimler. In May 2009, Daimler invested $50 million into Tesla, purchasing a 10 percent share in the company.[6]

Now here's where it gets interesting. Two months later, Daimler turned around and sold 40 percent of its Tesla investment to an Abu Dhabi–based investment firm, Aabar Investments, and stated that such a move was "part of its original plan."[7] Three years later, the United Arab Emirates–controlled company sold its Tesla stake for a whopping $113 million[8] and then quickly bought a stake in an Iraqi power plant.[9]

All those transactions leave us with two ways of looking at Tesla's U.S. bailout:

LEFT'S GREEN GOD SAVED BY ARAB OIL MONEY
or
TAXPAYER-BACKED TESLA MAKES MILLIONS FOR ARAB COMPANY

Musk now argues for a different path forward for green businesses, one that would help protect his Tesla from upstart compelltors seeking the kind of seed money from taxpayers he scored. He tweeted that a "carbon tax would be a better way." Musk added: "Yes, am arguing against subsidies and in favor of a tax on the end. . . . Market will then achieve best solution."

But beyond killing off competitors, why would Musk take such a position?

Because Tesla also relies on California's carbon tax credit scheme to make any profits at all:

> Its first-quarter profit, a modest $11 million, hinged on the $68 million it earned selling clean-air credits under a California program that requires automakers to either produce a given number of zero-emission vehicles or satisfy the mandate in some other way. For the second quarter, Tesla announced a $26 million profit (based on one method of accounting), but again the profit hinged on $51 million in ZEV credits; by year's end, these credit sales could net Tesla a whopping $250 million. There are also generous tax credits and rebates for electric-car buyers: $7,500 from the federal government and up to $5,000 if you live in California.[10]

So California automakers who are profitable by selling cars that run on fossil fuels essentially prop up businesses like Tesla because they have to buy clean air credits, thanks to aggressive intervention by the government.

Sounds free market to me.

Musk insists he made his fortune without anyone's help.

SolarCity, run by Lyndon Rive, Musk's cousin, also had a healthy appetite for tax breaks and benefits. Turns out, their whole business model depended on continued access to the taxpayer piggy bank.

SolarCity was forced to admit as much in its third-quarter financial reports for 2013. "If, for any reason, we are unable to finance solar energy systems through tax-advantaged structures," the report warned, "we may no longer be able to provide solar energy systems to new customers on an economically viable basis. This would have a material adverse effect on our business, financial condition and results of operations."[11]

And while Musk maintains a good relationship with Obama, to whom he donated $100,000 for the 2012 campaign, that goodwill doesn't exactly extend throughout every branch of the federal government. See, the Treasury Department and the Department of Justice are investigating whether SolarCity inflated its investments in solar panels, which, as part of the stimulus, brought in direct grants from the Treasury. According to SolarCity's SEC filings, the IRS is now auditing them, looking into whether they received federal funds inappropriately.[12]

SolarCity admits as much in its SEC filings, warning investors, if "at the conclusion of the investigation the Inspector General concludes that misrepresentations were made, the Department of Justice could decide to bring a civil action to recover amounts it believes were improperly paid to us."[13]

So Tesla and SolarCity then both benefited from taxpayer giveaways. Those aren't Musk's only companies, though. Remember his tweets! He cofounded PayPal. That didn't get any money. And he's also founded a really cool-sounding company called SpaceX, which designs and manufactures spacecraft and rockets. Sounds pretty free market to me. I mean, what's more independent than sending yourself into space? Well, SpaceX also has a contract with the government agency NASA, reportedly worth over $800 million.[14]

But, you know, he's totally self-sufficient. Are we sure he's supposed to be Iron Man? Or is it Irony Man?

Sadly, Musk's story could be the sort of thing that we should want America to celebrate. Moving here from South Africa (via Canada) was the fulfillment of a long-held aspiration. "He was already dreaming of moving to the United States," a *Mother Jones* profile noted, "a land he associated with inventors, explorers, and free thinkers."[15] Sadly, he is now part of the movement that is flushing competition down the crapper.

American innovation has given way to taxpayer extraction. Musk, like so many others profiled in the book, had already achieved success on his own. Why, then, would he take the help? Because it is there.

Musk's latest idea is a plan he calls the Hyperloop, "a rapid-speed train that claims to be able to transport passengers from San Francisco to Los Angeles in 30 minutes." The plan will allegedly cost only $6 billion, which Musk happily says he will contribute toward. But who picks up the rest of the check? Musk opposes the planned high-speed rail system in California now because, he says, the project is on pace to far exceed budget projections. "I mean California taxpayers are not just going to have to write off $100 billion but they're also going to have to maintain and subsidize the ongoing operation of this train for a super long time, sort of California's Amtrak. And that just doesn't seem wise for a state that was facing bankruptcy not that long ago," says Musk.[16]

There's the Iron Man we love. I agree, Elon. It doesn't seem wise for a bankrupt government to throw money after a project that wouldn't exist without its support. But I bet that wouldn't stop him from seeking tax support for the project once it's off the ground, no pun intended. It sure didn't stop him from going after our money all those other times.

So how to explain the seemingly wild contradictions? Stanford professor Fred Turner says hypocrites like Musk are "not quite self-delusion[al], but there is a habit of thinking of oneself as a free-standing, independent agent, and of not acknowledging the subsidies that one received. And this goes on all the time in the (Silicon) Valley."

Delusional billionaires are nothing new, I guess. Howard Hughes certainly had his issues. What bothers me is that the definitions of self-reliance may be changing. And our country, and its greatness, are changing right along with it, faster than a taxpayer-funded Tesla.

27 Carlos Slim

When everybody else is better off, they can buy more, they strengthen demand, strengthen the market, strengthen the country.

—Carlo Slim

On August 15, 2012, the U.S. men's soccer team traveled south to play in one of the most intimidating environments in all the world. Estadio Azteca, located in the high altitude of Mexico City, had been a house of horrors for the U.S. squad, as host Mexico had never lost to their fierce rivals when playing there.

But that night, in a fairly meaningless match, the U.S. team scored in the eightieth minute, and held on for a historic win.

The handful of U.S. fans, protected on all sides of the stadium by Mexican police with riot gear, ignored the threatening shouts and dodged the bags of urine being flung in their direction as they cheered the win.

The Mexican fans (the ones not throwing the bags of pee) sat in utter devastation. Soccer fans are already an exuberant bunch, but allegiance tends to run particularly fierce in economically down-trodden areas. And Mexico, with nearly half its population living in poverty, fits the profile.

On the one hand, Mexico has given us tequila, chips and salsa, and Salma Hayek. On the other, it's given us a massive problem with illegal immigration and the ever-increasing threat of Mexico's violent drug cartels.

And it isn't like Mexico exists in a vacuum. The tens of millions of illegal immigrants currently hanging out in our country take jobs from Americans and drain our resources, which only increases our own poverty.

But that's okay with Carlos.

Unbelievably, Carlos Slim perpetuates, and profits, from poverty in both the United States and Mexico.

How did you think he became, at one time, the richest man in the world?

Even worse, while Slim is profiting from poverty, we're paying for it with our hard-earned tax dollars.

Carlos Slim Helú (his son is Carlos Slim Domit) bought out Mexico's state-owned telephone company in 1990. As part of the deal, the new company, Telmex, was given "what amounted to a seven-year guarantee of monopoly status at a time when phone companies around the world had the money—and will—to expand into new markets."[1]

Slim maintains a monopolistic stranglehold on the Mexican phone business today. Telmex has more than 80 percent of the fixed landline business in Mexico while corporate cousin Telcel, also owned by Slim, has more than 70 percent of the wireless business.[2]

It's a market share that has been extremely lucrative to Slim, whose net worth is now estimated to be $72 billion.[3] And it's been extremely costly to Mexico.

A report by the Organisation for Economic Co-operation and Development (OECD), an international agency that advises governments, found that Slim's monopolies were hurting Mexico in a very real way.

The report found, "The welfare loss attributed to the dysfunctional Mexican telecommunication sector is estimated at $129.2bn (between 2005 and 2009) or 1.8 per cent GDP per annum." OECD also found that Mexicans suffered from "the highest monthly subscription costs for basic broadband internet connections and the slowest advertised download speeds."[4]

Real Clear Markets estimated that Slim, by cornering the market and raising the prices, was reducing "average living standards of the Mexican family more than $600 per year. Mexico's backward telecom infrastructure also reduces GDP by $32 billion per year — a substantial loss in Mexico's $1.6 trillion economy."[5]

So Slim has overcharged his customers "with high fees disproportionately hitting the poor." And Mexico is mired in economic destitution. But it hasn't hurt Slim's bottom line, thanks in no small measure to our tax dollars.

The United States sends hundreds of millions in aid south of the border each year.[6] The money ostensibly goes to help fight the drug cartels and improve border security, as laughable as that may seem.

Then again, does Slim really want the border controlled? If immigrants allegedly come to this country to work, wouldn't stopping the invasion free up jobs for some of America's poor?

But that doesn't help Slim. Because in addition to profiting off policies that keep Mexicans poor, he makes money off low-income Americans, too.

One of the lesser-known welfare programs in America today is the Lifeline program. First enacted during the Reagan administration, its aim was to provide subsidized emergency support to certain low-income Americans who qualify. In the 1980s, we didn't have all those highfalutin cell phone technologies.

As cell phone technology increased, the Lifeline program adapted to include prepaid wireless devices. So now, in case the drug deal you arranged with your prepaid phone goes south and you get shot, you can use the same phone to call 911! Today, Lifeline still provides for emergency calling, but it can also provide 250 free minutes, 250 free text messages, and even a free phone.

Almost overnight, hundreds of prepaid cell companies—like TracFone and Sprint—started Lifeline divisions, offering eligible users subsidized phones.

TracFone is a prepaid wireless provider, and subsidiary of the Mexico-based telecom company América Móvil. América Móvil is owned by Carlos Slim.

So the subsidized phones, dubbed Obamaphones after a woman in Cleveland became an overnight YouTube sensation, turn a profit for Slim with every one that gets handed out. The more phones our tax dollars pay to have given out, the more money for Slim.

Because of campaign finance laws, Slim isn't allowed to donate to U.S. campaigns. But the head of Slim's America-based enterprises can. And has.

TracFone's owner, F. J. Pollak, and his wife, Abigail, became very interested in politics around 2008. Abigail Pollak has helped bring in more than $1.5 million for Obama, including working as a bundler in 2012, harvesting more than $632,000 for the president's reelection. F. J. Pollak also got in on the action, giving $156,500 to help elect Democrats in 2012, counting at least $50,000 toward Obama's victory.[7]

And just because they work in the phone business, don't think it's all done long-distance, either: "The Pollaks hosted Obama at their Miami Beach home in June for a $40,000-per-plate fundraising dinner, and hosted a similar event with Michelle Obama in July 2008. The couple personally donated a combined $66,200 to Obama's re-election effort that year."[8]

Clearly, Pollak and the Obama administration see eye to eye on the future of subsidized cell phones.

Pollak's political legwork hasn't hurt Slim.

TracFone's subsidized cell phone service, Safelink, has grown into the nation's largest Lifeline provider, servicing four million subscribers nationwide.

From 2008 to 2012, TracFone received more than $1.15 billion in tax money.[9]

Oh you didn't know you were being taxed for it? You ever closely inspect your own phone bill? I know how depressing it is, but if you look close, you'll see that you help pay for Slim's subsidies on every phone bill you get.

You're welcome, Carlos.

Of course, it's not just the taxpayer money that's so appealing to companies like TracFone. It's also the increased exposure.

The more customers, the more opportunities for new leads for their other services.

The FCC admits as much, spelling it out plainly in a memo, saying that TracFone invested "heavily" in 2010—$41 million—in advertising their Lifeline program.[10] With that kind of money pouring into ads, it's clear TracFone views the program as a major chunk of their business.

According to the company's own SEC filings, TracFone "revenues . . . continued to expand rapidly." This increase, in part, was due to the subsidized Safelink program.

In 2011 alone, their ranks of prepaid subscribers grew by 11.3 percent to around 19.8 million. With such swelling numbers, it's no wonder TracFone became interested in things that might cut down on enrollment.

You know, silly things like fraud enforcement.

Like most welfare programs, Lifeline is wildly susceptible to fraud. As Sharon Gillett, who led the FCC's Wireline Competition Bureau, reported, Lifeline's fraud problems really started when it opened up its prepaid cell phone plans.

No way.

But it's true. A survey conducted by the FCC spanning seventeen states and territories found that 9 percent of Lifeline users—nearly one in ten—were ineligible.[11]

Gillett's report points to "a substantial number of subscribers" who received two or more Lifeline phones, as well as multiple people in one household who received free phones.

In Alabama, New Hampshire, and West Virginia, the ineligibility rate was far worse, with nearly one in five receiving a taxpayer-funded phone they didn't qualify for.[12] And keep in mind that more than a fourth of users declined to answer the FCC's survey.

That study focused only on the people who got phones who shouldn't have. Anybody who has seen *The Wire* knows that so-called burner phones are also the go-to technological device for gang members and other criminals. So not only do our taxes go to support a Crapitalist like Slim, but they also subsidize drug dealers.

Someone call 911.

How did the program get this way? One thing to keep in mind: with every TracFone that gets handed out, Slim gets paid.

That's how math works for Crapitalists. Fraud is good. Waste is profitable. And the expansion of entitlements only pads the pockets of those who gobble up the contracts to provide them.

Why else do you think TracFone, as the *Washington Times* reported, lobbied against measures to reform the program?[13] Hell, the FCC recently proposed a $4.5 million penalty against Slim's company after its investigation concluded that TracFone "willfully and repeatedly" registered "ineligible consumers."[14]

Lifeline's numbers are surging. From 2008 to 2011, enrollment nearly doubled, topping 12.5 million Americans. And the cost went from $772 million to $1.6 billion.[15] In 2012, that tax, seen as the Universal Service Fund on your bill, cost us $2.2 billion.[16]

But with Lifeline's current enrollment standards, that means there're around 20 million more Americans who are potential customers of these free cell phones.

That would be almost one in ten Americans.

Much of which would end up back in the pockets of Mexico's Monopoly Man.

The *Wall Street Journal* once wrote that "it's hard to spend a day in Mexico and not put money in [Slim's] pocket."[17]

Slim's companies make up more than a third of the Mexican stock exchange, so it's fair to say he has more than a little ownership of the Mexican economy. But Mexico is almost certainly the worse for it. They even have terms for Slim's role:

George W. Grayson, a professor of government at the College of William & Mary, coined the term "Slimlandia" to describe how entrenched the Slim family's companies are in the daily life of Mexicans.

It's not a reverential term. Many Mexicans hoped privatization, which began in the early 1990s, would create competition and drive prices down drastically. That hasn't happened. "Slim is one of a dozen fat cats in Mexico who impede that country's growth because they run monopolies or oligopolies," says Grayson. "The Mexican economy is highly inefficient, and it is losing its competitive standing vis-à-vis other countries because of people like Slim." [18]

On the one hand, what Slim does in Mexico is, quite literally, his business. But because of the negative effects his monopolies have had on the Mexican economy, the U.S. taxpayer has had to come to the rescue. And now he's cashing in on America's poor, too.

Slim's bought his way into the American market and will only look to expand his reach, which has proven to be poisonous to the economies it infects. Crapitalists who profit from poverty have their own circle of free market hell. And Carlos Slim will sit in the center of it.

Conclusion
A Courtesy Flush Won't Do

As Princeton professor Martin Gilens and Northwestern professor Benjamin Page concluded in an exhaustive study of American politics, the country is rapidly devolving into an oligarchy where a few players dominate the nation's legislative agenda. "Economic elites and organized groups representing business interests," they write in the journal *Perspectives on Politics*, "have substantial independent impacts on U.S. government policy, while average citizens and mass-based interest groups have little or no independent influence."[1]

But after reading this book, that conclusion doesn't surprise you. While Crapitalists come in all shapes, sizes, and industries, their agenda remains the same: picking your pockets to pad their lifestyles.

So where do we go from here?

More legislation in Congress promising to "fix" the problem? Hardly.

Subjecting us to additional regulations, spanning thousands of pages, which a few "insiders" know how to navigate, will only swell the number of lobbyists descending upon Washington, D.C., and augment the notorious backdoor dealings that Americans despise.

Plus, we're overregulated as it is.

We need to be burning pages in the *Federal Register*, not adding to them.

What's the solution then?

The answer is simple, actually.

Remove the incentives for Crapitalism entirely. "Special" interests will subside if bureaucrats aren't in the business of selecting winners and losers.

Hey, if loons like Al Gore and Terry McAuliffe want to race their electric cars around the track to see whose catches fire first, fine, have at it. But the duo would probably think twice about lobbying for their portion of green government grants if, you know, those green government grants didn't exist in the first place.

They'd have to bring their product to market the old-fashioned way, which means a business plan that doesn't hinge on our "investment."

And if Gore and company turn a profit, good for them!

Unlike the Left, we don't begrudge those who become successful and even—gasp—rich by working their asses off. That's capitalism. It's the American way, and it's awesome.

But while the solution is easy, the road to restore constitutional order isn't.

Politicians are drunk with power and their pals are now addicted to corporate welfare. All this talk about "limited government" really scares the hell out of them. It's why Tom Steyer and other Crapitalists have pledged to spend "huge" sums of money over the next two elections opposing any efforts on the part of conservatives and libertarians to put Uncle Sam on a Weight Watchers diet.[2] To hear them tell it, our government isn't fat enough. They want *more* federal spending, if you can believe it, to boost economic growth and fight income inequality.

It'll work this time!

Pinky swear!

The irony of all this is that while our friends on the Left babble on and on about the "haves" and the "have-nots," their policies actually exacerbate wealth disparity, as the Obama presidency has demonstrated. Under this administration, income for the top 1 percent has increased by more than 30 percent, yet wages for the rest of us remain at a standstill.[3] As one writer in the *New York Times* put it, the "proportion of economic gains going to the very wealthy under the Obama administration is greater than it was under Mr. Bush."[4]

That's why Crapitalism is so dangerous and must be aggressively challenged. Its end goal is similar to that of socialism's: wealth redistribution.

The whole thing stinks.

I don't know about you, but I'm fed up and ready for change.

It's time to bust up the collusion between big business and big government.

It's time that ideas succeed or fail based on their merits, not taxpayer largesse.

It's time to liberate the free market system responsible for building the middle class and ushering in unprecedented prosperity.

What I'm saying is, it's time to tell all the Crapitalists to get lost.

This book gives you the ammo needed to unleash a hurricane of humiliation.

A courtesy flush won't do.

The entire system needs cleansing.

So get to work.

Notes

Introduction

1. http://www.rasmussenreports.com/public_content/political_commen
   tary/commentary_by_scott_rasmussen/government_has_no_business
   _dabbling_in_business.
2. http://www.qe.com/ar2008/letter.html.
3. http://www.politico.com/story/2014/04/wall-street-republicans
   -hillary-clinton-2016-106070.html.
4. http://www.forbes.com/profile/john doerr/.
5. http://www.nytimes.com/2009/11/03/business/energy-environment
   /03gore.html?_r=1&dbk.
6. http://online.wsj.com/article/SB125383160812639013.html.
7. http://online.wsj.com/article/SB120027887033287745.html.
8. http://www.time.com/time/magazine/article/0,9171,1969740,00.html
   #ixzz241cetnnK.
9. http://www.consumerreports.org/cro/video-hub/featured/featured
   -videos/100000-fisker-karma-breaks-down/17387256001/149620198
   7001/.

10. http://www.csmonitor.com/Business/Latest-News-Wires/2013/1126
    /Fisker-bankruptcy-Feds-to-lose-139-million-on-Fisker-Automotive.

11. http://espn.go.com/nfl/story/_/id/7914553/senate-approves-plan
    -new-minnesota-vikings-stadium.

12. http://www.voiceofsandiego.org/fact/article_8515e7c8-dda4-11e0
    -8172-001cc4c03286.html.

13. http://www.nytimes.com/interactive/2010/09/08/sports/20100908
    -stadium-sidebar.html.

14. http://www.forbes.com/profile/steven-spielberg/.

15. http://www.washingtonpost.com/blogs/virginia-politics/post
    /mcdonnell-confirms-the-obvious-spielberg-to-film-lincoln-movie-in
    -virginia/2011/05/04/AFfNMOnF_blog.html.

16. http://watchdog.org/78725/mcdonnells-trade-trip-itinerary-missing
    -specifics/

17. http://www.imdb.com/title/tt0443272/.

18. http://online.wsj.com/news/articles/SB1000142405270230366590457745
    0071884712152.

1. Representative Greg Meeks

1. http://www.nytimes.com/2010/03/20/nyregion/20meeks.html?_r=0.

2. http://sunlightfoundation.com/tools/expenditures/.

3. http://www.nytimes.com/2010/03/20/nyregion/20meeks.html?_r=0.

4. http://www.crewsmostcorrupt.org/mostcorrupt/entry/gregory-meeks.

5. http://www.fec.gov/press/press2008/20080204meeks.shtml.

6. http://www.crewsmostcorrupt.org/mostcorrupt/entry/gregory-meeks
    -report.

7. http://www.nytimes.com/2010/03/20/nyregion/20meeks.html?
    _r=0.

8. http://www.crewsmostcorrupt.org/mostcorrupt/entry/gregory-meeks.

9. http://nypost.com/2012/01/08/eyes-on-meeks-shady-house-sale/.

10. http://www.nytimes.com/2010/03/20/nyregion/20meeks.html?_r=0.

11. http://www.kaieteurnewsonline.com/2012/10/11/ed-ahmad-pleads
    -guilty-faces-10-year-minimum-jail-term-fines-totaling-us42-5m/.

12. http://www.crewsmostcorrupt.org/mostcorrupt/entry/most-corrupt
    -members-of-congress-report-2013.

13. http://nlpc.org/stories/2010/02/24/rep-gregory-meeks-blasted-bush
    -response-hurricane-katrina.

14. http://nypost.com/2010/03/15/meeks-second-story-on-katrina-fund
    -seems-all-wet-too/.

15. http://nlpc.org/stories/2010/02/07/rep-meeks-can%E2%80%99t
    -account-hurricane-katrina-money-firestorm-puts-spotlight-paterson.

16. http://www.nytimes.com/2010/02/15/nyregion/15newdirex.html? _r=0.

17. http://nypost.com/2013/01/08/racino-probe-targets-dems-high -rollers/.

18. http://www.nydailynews.com/new-york/deals-secret-lobbying -marked-aqueduct-slot-machine-operator-process-report-finds -article-1.190873.

19. http://nypost.com/2013/01/08/racino-probe-targets-dems-high -rollers/.

20. http://www.nydailynews.com/new-york/subpoena-aqueduct-enter tainment-group-probe-rev-floyd-flake-multimillion-dollar-empire -article-1.194354.

21. http://www.nydailynews.com/news/rep-gregory-meeks-sees-racism -aqueduct-racino-criticisms-rev-floyd-flake-darryl-greene-article -1.198760.

22. http://nypost.com/2009/12/29/meeks-not-so-blessed/.

23. http://www.nydailynews.com/new-york/records-show-rep-gregory -meeks-carribean-trips-wife-tab-artist-article-1.432359.

24. http://nypost.com/2009/12/29/meeks-not-so-blessed/.

25. http://www.nydailynews.com/new-york/sen-bribe-case-desperate -power-ex-aide-article-1.1307380.

26. http://nypost.com/2014/02/09/meeks-paid-47k-to-lawyers-despite -being-cleared-by-committee/.

2. Representative Maxine Waters

1. http://leftofthemark.com/speaker/maxine-waters.

2. http://www.realclearpolitics.com/articles/2011/08/25/kerosene _maxine_to_tea_party_go_to_hell_111079.html.

3. http://www.washingtonpost.com/wp-dyn/content/article/2010/09 /16/AR2010091606819.html.

4. Ibid.

5. http://www.crewsmostcorrupt.org/mostcorrupt/entry/Maxine-Waters -report.

6. Ibid.

7. http://www.breitbart.com/Big-Government/2012/10/01/Inside-the -Maxine-Waters-Ethics-Committee-Debacle.

8. http://www.washingtontimes.com/news/2010/nov/7/lobbyist-paid -15k-to-maxine-waters-husband/?page=all.

9. Ibid.

10. http://www.washingtonpost.com/wp-dyn/articles/A12322-2004Dec19. html?nav=rss_politics.

11. Chuck Neubauer and Ted Rohrlich, "Capitalizing on a Politician's Clout," *Los Angeles Times*, December 19, 2004.

12. http://www.legistorm.com/member_family/522/Rep_Maxine_Waters .html.

13. http://www.legistorm.com/earmarks/details/member/522/Rep_Maxine _Waters.html.

14. https://www.opensecrets.org/politicians/contrib.php?cid=N00006690& cycle=2010&type=I&newMem=N&recs=100.

15. http://www.nytimes.com/2013/05/12/business/in-house-maxine-waters -takes-new-tack-on-banks.html?amp;_r=0&adxnnl=1&;gwt=regi&page wanted=all&adxnnlx=1397433639-+OoPnFh/f8hoI8Ayb4LT8A.

16. http://www.politico.com/news/stories/0811/61828.html.

17. http://www.realclearpolitics.com/articles/2011/08/25/kerosene_maxine _to_tea_party_go_to_hell_111079.html.

18. http://www.breitbart.com/Breitbart-TV/2012/09/02/Maxine-Waters -World-Hated-Racist-America-Until-Obama%20-Elected.

19. http://www.humanevents.com/2011/08/27/top-10-outrageous-maxine -waters-quotes-2/.

3. Terry McAuliffe

1. Mark Leibovich, *This Town: Two Parties and a Funeral—plus plenty of valet parking!—in America's Gilded Capital* (New York: Blue Rider Press, 2013), 38.

2. http://www.startribune.com/templates/Print_This_Story?sid= 46265282.

3. Ibid.

4. http://www.washingtonpost.com/politics/greentech-formula-has-made -big-profits-for-mcauliffe/2013/09/21/3c6e332c-2136-11e3-b73c-aab60 bf735d0_story.html.

5. http://abcnews.go.com/Politics/complicated-legal-backstory-terry -mcauliffes-car-company/story?id=19959500.

6. http://www.washingtonpost.com/politics/greentech-formula-has -made-big-profits-for-mcauliffe/2013/09/21/3c6e332c-2136-11e3-b73c -aab60bf735d0_story.html.

7. http://www.breitbart.com/Big-Government/2013/11/03/DHS-Official -Who-Advocated-for-GreenTech-in-Internal-Emails-Lands-Job-With -Major-McAuliffe-Donor.

8. http://washingtonexaminer.com/political-cronies-keep-cash-flowing -to-terry-mcauliffe/article/2535330.

9. http://watchdog.org/130474/cabinet-confirmations-mcauliffe/

10. http://www.washingtontimes.com/news/2014/may/23/mcauliffe-vetoes
    -development-fund-ethics-bill/
11. Leibovich, *This Town*, 373.

4. Mike Ilitch—Pizza Pimp

1. http://www.huffingtonpost.com/2013/10/10/kwame-kilpatrick
   -sentenced-prison-detroit-corruption_n_4066248.html.
2. http://www.nbcnews.com/id/36665950/#.Uq9U741H3pU.
3. http://www.crainsdetroit.com/article/20090426/free/304269954/hot
   -n-steady-renewed-focus-on-value-keeps-little-caesars-cooking-at.
4. http://www.freep.com/article/20130625/BUSINESS/306250105/Top
   -7-pizza-chains-Little-Caesars-moves-up-a-notch.
5. http://articles.latimes.com/1995-09-03/business/fi-41725_1_pizza
   -hut.
6. http://www.michigandaily.com/content/source-ilitch-may-run
   -governor.
7. http://www.crainsdetroit.com/article/20120822/FREE/120829973
   /comerica-park-owner-to-refinance-remaining-61m-public-debt-on
   -300m#.
8. http://thefederalist.com/2013/11/05/stadium-euthanisia-will-houston
   -voters-sentence-astrodome-death/.
9. http://www.bloomberg.com/news/2012-09-05/in-stadium-building
   -spree-u-s-taxpayers-lose-4-billion.html.
10. http://www.theguardian.com/world/2014/mar/29/detroit-bankrupt
    -red-wings-arena-divides-community.
11. http://detroit.curbed.com/archives/2013/06/the-ilitch-effect-eddys
    tone-park-avenue-hotels-going-down.php.
12. http://www.freep.com/article/20140204/NEWS01/302040024/Detroit
    -council-votes-today-on-arena-deal-Ilitches-to-get-land-for-1.
13. http://www.thedailybeast.com/articles/2013/12/04/bankruptcy-hasn-t
    -stopped-detroit-s-plan-for-public-funding-of-new-sports-stadium
    .html.
14. http://www.wsws.org/en/articles/2013/12/17/dplr-d17.html.
15. http://michiganradio.org/post/detroit-gets-new-sports-and-entertain
    ment-district-not-without-controversy.
16. http://www.freep.com/article/20140204/NEWS01/302040024/Detroit
    -council-votes-today-on-arena-deal-Ilitches-to-get-land-for-1.
17. http://www.nytimes.com/2013/09/27/us/300-million-in-detroit-aid
    -but-no-bailout.html?_r=0.
18. http://www.deadlinedetroit.com/articles/3024/update_boot_marian

_s_car_ilitches_reportedly_owe_detroit_1_5m_in_back_taxes#.UrBEB o1H3pU.

19. http://www.wingingitinmotown.com/2012/12/26/3805440/do-the -red-wings-owe-the-city-of-detroit-70-million.

5. Chris Dodd

1. http://www.salon.com/2011/03/02/dodd_13/.
2. http://www.mpaa.org/about/ceo.
3. http://www.nytimes.com/2014/04/18/business/media/hollywood -begs-for-a-tax-break-in-some-states-including-california.html?_r=0.
4. http://www.cbpp.org/cms/?fa=view&id=3326.
5. http://www.nytimes.com/2012/12/04/us/when-hollywood-comes-to -town.html?pagewanted=all&_r=1&.
6. http://www.techdirt.com/articles/20111212/02244817037/congressional -research-service-shows-hollywood-is-thriving.shtml.
7. http://articles.latimes.com/2014/jan/02/business/la-fi-ct-onlocation -20140102.
8. http://articles.latimes.com/2013/jan/02/entertainment/la-et-ct-fiscal -cliff-tax-break-20130102.
9. http://www.creators.com/opinion/john-stossel/why-does-government -suppress-information.html.
10. http://www.thewrap.com/movies/column-post/lions-gate-goes-rogue -movie-futures-trading-16563.
11. http://www.opensecrets.org/politicians/industries.php?cycle=2010&cid =N00000581&type=I.
12. http://online.wsj.com/news/articles/SB122360116724221681.
13. Ibid.
14. http://online.wsj.com/news/articles/SB124545642440632999.
15. http://online.wsj.com/news/articles/SB123681364667801647.
16. http://www.courant.com/news/opinion/editorials/hc-rennie0222.art feb22,0,3796755.column.
17. http://www.opensecrets.org/news/2011/02/political-past-of-former -aig-executive-joseph-cassano.html; http://www.washingtontimes.com /news/2009/mar/30/aig-chiefs-pressed-to-donate-to-dodd/.
18. http://www.opensecrets.org/news/2009/03/before-the-fall-aig-payouts -we.html.
19. http://politicalticker.blogs.cnn.com/2009/03/18/breaking-i-was -responsible-for-bonus-loophole-says-dodd/.
20. http://www.journalinquirer.com/connecticut_and_region/dodd -defends-fannie-mae-freddie-mac-rips-bush-and-the/article_f5561ef1 -d4a4-54b6-bd5b-1424e9fd6819.html.

21. http://www.opensecrets.org/news/2008/07/top-senate-recipients-of
-fanni.html.
22. https://www.opensecrets.org/politicians/industries.php?cycle=2010&
cid=N00000581&type=C.
23. http://online.wsj.com/news/articles/SB1000142405270230441910457932
7043941676608?cb=logged0.9368546800687909.
24. http://thehill.com/blogs/hillicon-valley/personnel-notes/146769
-mpaa-names-former-sen-chris-dodd-chairman-a-ceo.
25. http://variety.com/2013/biz/news/chris-dodd-salary-2012-12008
37496/.
26. http://www.opensecrets.org/orgs/summary.php?id=D000027729.

6. Chuck Swoboda

1. "Keynote Address—Second International ALN1 Conference."
2. http://www.foxnews.com/leisure/2013/02/20/preparing-for-bulb
-ban/.
3. https://ladylibertytoday.wordpress.com/2011/07/15/67-oppose
-upcoming-%E2%80%98ban%E2%80%99-on-traditional-light-bulbs
-rasmussen-reports%E2%84%A2/.
4. http://www.opensecrets.org/lobby/clientissues_spec.php?id=D000049
849&year=2007&spec=ENG.
5. http://www.opensecrets.org/news/2011/06/ceo-6-14-2011.html.
6. http://www.digikey.com/en-US/articles/techzone/2010/may/vice
-president-and-energy-secretary-praise-cree-leds.
7. http://www.heraldsun.com/business/localandstate/x2119573766
/Cree-reports-86-9M-profit-for-2012-13.
8. http://washingtonexaminer.com/article/114959.
9. http://www.bizjournals.com/triangle/stories/2010/09/20/daily2
.html.
10. http://spectator.org/blog/22499/when-lights-go-down-it-aint-pretty.
11. http://nlpc.org/stories/2013/11/04/alternative-bulbs-another-phony
-market-propped-govt-mandates-subsidies.
12. http://www.washingtonwatch.com/bills/show/ED_34475.html.
13. http://www.digikey.com/us/en/techzone/lighting/resources/articles
/VP-Energy-Sec-Praise-Cree.html.
14. http://www.usatoday.com/story/news/nation-now/2013/12/27
/incandescent-light-bulbs-phaseout-leds/4217009/.
15. http://nlpc.org/stories/2013/11/04/alternative-bulbs-another-phony
-market-propped-govt-mandates-subsidies.
16. http://www.ledsmagazine.com/articles/2010/12/cree-opens-led-chip
-manufacturing-facility-in-huizhou.html.

17. http://homeguides.sfgate.com/clean-up-energyefficient-bulbs
     -break-78636.html.
18. http://www.dailymail.co.uk/news/article-1243138/Still-glowing
     -strong-109-years-worlds-oldest-lightbulb.html.
19. http://online.wsj.com/news/articles/SB100014241278873245394045783
     40711390906982?cb=loged0.426915317275651.

7. Vinod Khosla

1. http://www.nytimes.com/2009/03/15/business/15AIG.html?_r=0.
2. http://www.nbcnews.com/id/23148959/.
3. http://www.breitbart.com/Big-Government/2012/11/23/Peter
    -Schweizer-Obama-Admin-Uses-Green-Energy-Loans-To-Recycle
    -Money-Back-To-Donors.
4. Peter Schweizer, *Throw Them All Out* (New York: Houghton Mifflin Har-
    court, 2013).
5. http://rainmaker.apps.cironline.org/donors/vinod-khosla/.
6. http://www.breitbart.com/Big-Peace/2012/07/23/air-force-59-per
    -gal-biofuel.
7. http://beforeitsnews.com/politics/2012/10/soros-helps-pro-obama
    -pac-sprint-to-the-finish-2465966.html.
8. http://mediamatters.org/research/2011/11/18/throw-it-all-out
    -schweizers-doe-claims-rest-on/185882.
9. http://www.cbsnews.com/news/cleantech-crash-60-minutes/.
10. http://energy.gov/sites/prod/files/edg/recovery/documents/Recovery
    _Act_Memo_Idaho.pdf.
11. http://www.bizjournals.com/kansascity/print-edition/2012/05/25
    /nordic-windpower-sees-its-plans-for.html?page=all.
12. http://www.reuters.com/article/2012/07/15/us-usa-military-biofuels
    -idUSBRE86E01N20120715.
13. http://www.macon.com/2011/12/02/1808239/range-fuels-biorefinery
    -in-foreclosure.html.
14. http://www.lanzatech.com/sites/default/files/imce_uploads/rls
    _-_lanzatech_messina_2013_1.pdf.
15. http://www.biofuelsdigest.com/bdigest/2013/07/16/coskata-shelves
    -ipo-for-second-time/.
16. http://www.cbsnews.com/news/cleantech-crash-60-minutes/.
17. http://modernfarmer.com/2013/10/thomas-jeffersons-farming
    -failures/.
18. http://www.cbsnews.com/news/cleantech-crash-60-minutes/.

8. Neil Bluhm

1. http://www.forbes.com/profile/neil-bluhm/.
2. http://articles.chicagotribune.com/2013-12-17/business/chi-neil
   -bluhm-25-million-to-northwestern-20131217_1_law-school-legal
   -clinic-holocaust-educational-foundation.
3. http://dhbusinessledger.com/Content/Suburban-Trends-and-Issues
   /Suburban—Trends-and-Issues/Article/Rivers-Casino-dealmaker-eyes
   -next-big-project/87/172/2858.
4. http://www.chicagomag.com/Chicago-Magazine/March-2012/100
   -Most-Powerful-Chicagoans-Neil-Bluhm/.
5. http://www.opensecrets.org/pres08/bundlers.php?id=N00009638.
6. http://www.opensecrets.org/pres12/bundlers.php.
7. Lynn Sweet, "Clinton Brings Fund-Raising Muscle to Chicago; Bill Clinton Will Headline Fund-Raisers for Kerry and Obama," *Chicago Sun-
   Times*, July 1, 2004.
8. Rob Olmstead, "Des Plaines Wins Casino," *Daily Herald*, December 23,
   2008.
9. Ibid.
10. http://triblive.com/x/pittsburghtrib/news/s_583211.html#axzz2nr
    VQxNJB.
11. http://www.post-gazette.com/businessnews/2008/07/18/Those-not
    -in-on-Barden discussions-criticize-deal/stories/200807180125.
12. http://articles.philly.com/2008-08-15/business/25257866_1_gaming
    -board-casino-project-second-casino.
13. http://www.journal topics.com/news/article_9b53b2ae-5df4-11e3
    -b2eb-001a4bcf6878.html.
14. http://desplaines.patch.com/groups/business-news/p/rivers-casino
    -appeals-1057-million-property-tax-assessment.
15. http://pittsburgh.cbslocal.com/2012/03/06/rivers-casino-appeals
    -property-assessment/.
16. http://dailycaller.com/2012/04/02/gsa-shake-up-follows-stupid-and
    -infuriating-waste-of-taxpayer-dollars/.
17. http://www.nomabid.org/2010/03/gsa-leases-41000-additional-sf-at
    -constitution-square-in-noma/.
18. https://www.fbo.gov/index?s=opportunity&mode=form&id=dd4aa67c8
    6c7f6bcc79f2e8d057ef38c&tab=core&_cview=1.
19. http://www.nomabid.org/about-the-bid/administrative-documents/.
20. http://blumbergcapitalpartners.com/BCP-news/northwestern-mutual
    -picks-up-justice-department-hq-for-305m/.

9. Jay–Z

1. http://www.azlyrics.com/lyrics/jayz/bigpimpinextended.html.
2. http://rap.about.com/od/artists/p/JayZ.htm.
3. http:/hwww.grantland.com/story/_/id/7021031/the-nets-nba -economics.
4. http://www.supremecourt.gov/opinions/04pdf/04-108.pdf.
5. http://www.grantland.com/story/_/id/7021031/the-nets-nba -economics.
6. http://ksfm.cbslocal.com/2010/05/18/jay-zs-business-portfolio/.
7. http://www.suntimes.com/news/nation/18694439-418/jay-zs -4040-club-in-atlantic-city-closed.html#.U0wlZeZdVDg.
8. http://ksfm.cbslocal.com/2010/05/18/jay-zs-business-portfolio/.
9. http://www.dnainfo.com/new-york/20121123/prospect-heights /barclays-center-owner-drops-challenge-citys-741-million-appraisal.
10. http://observer.com/2013/10/forest-city-ratner-sues-the-city-to-get -even-more-atlantic-yards-tax-breaks/.
11. http://mediatakeout.com/62248/jay-z-releases-new-track-blasts -brooklyn-nets-fans-says-thanks-for-the-money-and-calls-them -f-ckin-dweebs-is-he-going-crazy.html.
12. http://www.politico.com/story/2013/08/jay-z-obama-hall-of-fame -inductor-95156.html#ixzz2qCqkRN4a.
13. http://www.salon.com/2011/10/25/the_jay_z_distraction/.
14. http://www.nytimes.com/2004/05/26/nyregion/different-design -soon-be-less-so-rethinking-atlantic-center-with-customer-mind .html?pagewanted=all&src=pm.
15. http://www.barclayscenter.com/premium-seating/the-vault.
16. http://nypost.com/2013/10/31/first-barneys-now-barclays-center -black-luxury-box-holders-targeted/.
17. http://www.salon.com/2011/10/25/the_jay_z_distraction/.
18. http://www.nydailynews.com/blogs/iteam/blogger-calls-jay-z -overstating-benefits-brooklyn-atlantic-yards-project-blog-entry-1 .1632128.
19. http://dddb.net/documents/economics/AtlanticYards091009.pdf.
20. Ibid.
21. http://atlanticyardsreport.blogspot.com/2013/11/average-affordable -2-br-in-first.html
22. http://www.huffingtonpost.com/matt-sledge/aqueduct-report-jayz -was-_b_774487.html.
23. http://nypost.com/2010/02/21/jay-z-stake-in-aqueduct-slots-deal -draws-scrutiny/.

24. http://www.huffingtonpost.com/matt-sledge/aqueduct-report-jayz-was-_b_774487.html.
25. http://www.nydailynews.com/news/jay-z-aqueduct-racino-pal-david-rosenberg-lawsuit-target-article-1.170831.
26. http://thegrio.com/2012/02/08/jay-z-reportedly-only-gave-6k-to-charity-in-2010-after-earning-63-mil/.

10. George Kaiser

1. http://reason.com/blog/2011/09/20/george-kaiser-2009-theres-neve.
2. http://www.greentechmedia.com/articles/read/solyndra-rolls-out-tube-shaped-thin-film-1542/.
3. http://sunlightfoundation.com/blog/2011/10/13/barack-obamas-other-billionaire-how-george-kaiser-turned-oklahom/.
4. http://reason.com/blog/2011/09/20/george-kaiser-2009-theres-neve.
5. http://www.whitehouse.gov/the-press-office/remarks-president-economy-0.
6. http://www.bloomberg.com/news/2012-11-02/solyndra-judge-s-approval-of-bankruptcy-plan-appealed.html.
7. http://www.forbes.com/forbes/2007/1126/042b.html.
8. http://sunlightfoundation.com/blog/2011/10/13/barack-obamas-other-billionaire-how-george-kaiser-turned-oklahom/.
9. Ibid.
10. http://www.forbes.com/sites/kellyphillipserb/2013/01/10/tax-code-hits-nearly-4-million-words-taxpayer-advocate-calls-it-too-complicated/.
11. http://answers.reference.com/information/terminology/how_many_words_in_the_bible.
12. http://www.bloomberg.com/news/2012-11-05/irs-loses-appeal-to-stop-solyndra-from-carrying-out-plan.html.
13. Ibid.
14. http://www.forbes.com/forbes/2007/1126/042b.html.
15. http://www.bloomberg.com/news/2013-05-03/billionaire-kaiser-exploiting-charity-loophole-with-boats.html.
16. Ibid.
17. Ibid.
18. http://thehill.com/homenews/administration/201595-white-house-casts-obama-as-warrior-for-the-middle-class.
19. http://www.usatoday.com/story/money/business/2013/12/09/household-wealth-thirdquarter/3932563/.

11. Sally Susman

1. http://investing.businessweek.com/research/stocks/people/person.asp?personId=4204108&ticker=PFE&previousCapId=23723165&previousTitle=ESSENTRA%20PLC.
2. http://thehill.com/blogs/pundits-blog/campaign/190411-like-father-like-daughter-one-bundler-begets-another.
3. http://www.opensecrets.org/lobby/top.php?indexType=i.
4. http://www.opensecrets.org/lobby/indusclient.php?id=H04&year=2009.
5. Visitor Access Records | White House
6. http://online.wsj.com/news/articles/SB10001424052702303830204577446470015843822?mg=reno64-wsj&url=http%3A%2F%2Fonline.wsj.com%2Farticle%2FSB10001424052702303830204577446470015843822.html.
7. http://www.forbes.com/sites/brucejapsen/2013/05/25/obamacare-will-bring-drug-industry-35-billion-in-profits/.
8. http://features.blogs.fortune.cnn.com/2011/07/28/pfizer-jeff-kindler-shakeup/.
9. http://www.nytimes.com/2011/10/28/us/politics/obama-bundlers-have-ties-to-lobbying.html?pagewanted=all&_r=2&.
10. http://washingtonexaminer.com/if-big-pharma-likes-your-healthcare-plan-you-can-keep-it/article/2538357.
11. http://www.nytimes.com/2012/02/15/us/obama-shift-on-contraception-splits-catholics.html.
12. http://www.forbes.com/sites/edsilverman/2013/12/26/will-the-affordable-care-act-give-drugmakers-a-boost/.
13. http://people.equilar.com/bio/sally-susman-pfizer/salary/559551#.U30e5a1dUT1.
14. http://www.pfizerplus.com/gi/health_care_reform.aspx.
15. http://abcnews.go.com/blogs/politics/2012/06/memos-unveil-how-white-house-worked-with-phrma-to-sell-obamacare/.
16. http://www.bloomberg.com/news/2012-05-31/drugmakers-vowed-to-campaign-for-health-law-memos-show.html.

12. Steven Spielberg

1. http://www.imdb.com/title/tt0443272/?ref_=nm_flmg_dr_1.
2. http://watchdog.org/37418/odw-watchblog-mcdonnell-cuts-pbs-subsidizes-spielberg/.
3. http://www.virginia.org/pressroom/release.asp?id=266.
4. http://www.ncsl.org/research/financial-services-and-commerce/silver-screen-dreams_sl-magazine.aspx.

5. http://www.washingtonpost.com/politics/gov-mcdonnell
-rejected-plea-offer-to-face-one-felony-spare-wife-any-charges-avoid
-trial/2014/01/23/96b53a62-83bd-11e3-8099-9181471f7aaf_story.html.

6. http://watchdog.org/78725/mcdonnells-trade-trip-itinerary-missing
-specifics/.

7. http://voices.washingtonpost.com/virginiapolitics/2010/12
/mcdonnell_and_spielberg_speak.html.

8. http://articles.dailypress.com/2011-05-04/news/va—lincoln-film
-20110504_1_bob-mcdonnell-doris-kearns-goodwin-book-mary-todd
-lincoln.

9. http://wamu.org/news/11/12/01/lincoln_biopic_film_incentives
_often_not_worth_cost.

10. http://watchdog.org/78725/mcdonnells-trade-trip-itinerary-missing
-specifics/.

11. http://online.wsj.com/news/articles/SB100014241278873237343045
78545530274694000#mod%3Dtodays_us_new_york%26articleTabs%3D
comments.

12. http://www.independent.ie/irish-news/budget-2014-spielberg
-inspires-tom-cruise-clause-that-will-bring-hollywood-blockbusters
-here-29667460.html.

13. http://www.nytimes.com/2013/11/08/us/politics/in-hollywood
-clintons-a-star.html?pagewanted=all&_r=0.

14. http://www.businessweek.com/printer/articles/30696-obamas-ceo jim
-messina-has-a-president-to-sell.

15. http://www.forbes.com/profile/anil-ambani/.

16. http://online.wsj.com/news/articles/SB100014240527487043346045753
38791530127472?mod=WSJ_hps_LEFTWhatsNews&mg=reno64-wsj.

13. Jeffrey Katzenberg

1. http://online.wsj.com/news/articles/SB10000872396390443571904577630430778711196.

2. http://www.politico.com/blogs/burns-haberman/2012/05/the-katzen
bergobama-connection-123186.html.

3. http://www.motherjones.com/politics/2013/05/jeffrey-katzenberg
-dreamworks-barack-obama-fundraiser.

4. Ibid.

5. http://online.wsj.com/news/articles/SB100008723963904435719045776
30430778711196.

6. http://www.nytimes.com/2011/03/24/business/media/24imax.html.

7. http://www.nytimes.com/2012/04/25/business/global/sec-asks-if
-holywood-paid-bribes-in-china.html.

8. http://www.motherjones.com/politics/2013/05/jeffrey-katzenberg
-dreamworks-barack-obama-fundraiser?page=2.

9. http://usnews.nbcnews.com/_news/2012/02/18/10439615-china-to
-ease-access-for-us-movies-biden-says?lite.

10. http://www.bloomberg.com/news/2012-08-07/kung-fu-panda-studio
-to-spend-20-billion-yuan-in-shanghai.html.

11. Interview with Jeffrey Katzenberg, *International Wire,* June 28, 2013.

12. Ibid.

13. http://sunlightfoundation.com/blog/2012/04/18/katzenberg/.

14. http://www.reuters.com/article/2012/04/24/us-sec-movies-idUS
BRE83N15V20120424.

15. http://www.newyorker.com/online/blogs/evanosnos/2013/02/holly
wood-and-censorship-in-china-revenue-and-responsibility.html.

14. Ronald Perelman

1. http://nymag.com/relationships/features/16463/.

2. http://www.crainsnewyork.com/article/20110123/FREE/301239973
/ron-perelman-vs-donald-drapkin.

3. Ibid.

4. http://nymag.com/relationships/features/16463/index2.html.

5. http://influenceexplorer.com/organization/macandrews-forbes/486d8
995a3da4e0789e3b94c1844b848?cycle=2008.

6. https://www.opensecrets.org/obama/inaug_2009.php.

7. http://news.yahoo.com/billionaire-ron-perelman-cantor-wife-just-latest
-board-060022457.html.

8. http://www.politifact.com/truth-o-meter/promises/obameter/promise
/30/end-no-bid-contracts-above-25000/.

9. https://www.fbo.gov/index?s=opportunity&mode=form&id=b655c001d
75069b1e245ec2d69f60690&tab=core&_cview=1.

10. http://articles.latimes.com/2011/nov/13/nation/la-na-smallpox
-20111113.

11. Ibid.

12. http://online.wsj.com/news/articles/SB100014240529702047071045780
91030386721670.

13. Joe Larsen, "ASPR: Resilient People. Healthy Communities. A Nation
Prepared," Biomedical Advanced Research and Development Authority,
U.S. Department of Health and Human Services, March 2014, p. 4.

15. Al Gore

1. http://www.nytimes.com/2009/11/03/business/energy-environ
ment/03gore.html?_r=0.

2. http://www.joesapt.net/superlink/shrg99-529/.
3. http://www.cbsnews.com/news/report-al-gores-net-worth-at-200
    -million/.
4. http://www.washingtonpost.com/politics/decision2012/al-gore-has
    -thrived-as-green-tech-investor/2012/10/10/1dfaa5b0-0b11-11e2-bd1a
    -b868e65d57eb_story.html.
5. http://finance.fortune.cnn.com/2013/06/03/energy-loan-silver
    -interview/.
6. http://www.washingtonpost.com/politics/decision2012/al-gore-has
    -thrived-as-green-tech-investor/2012/10/10/1dfaa5b0-0b11-11e2-bd1a
    -b868e65d57eb_story.html.
7. http://www.breitbart.com/Big-Government/2011/11/16/80—of-Green
    -Energy-Loans-Went-to-Top-Obama-Donors.
8. http://abcnews.go.com/Blotter/car-company-us-loan-builds-cars
    -finland/story?id=14770875.
9. http://www.forbes.com/sites/warrenmeyer/2011/10/20/update-fisker
    -karma-electric-car-gets-worse-mileage-than-an-suv/.
10. http://www.coyoteblog.com/coyote_blog/2011/10/ray-lane-in
    -2009-obama-administration-first-example-of-successful-government
    -venture-investment.html.
11. http://www.nytimes.com/aponline/2014/02/18/business/ap-us-fisker
    -bankruptcy.html?action=click&contentCollection=Automobiles&region
    =Footer&module=MoreInSection&pgtype=article&_r=0.
12. http://www.insidermonkey.com/hedge-fund/generation+investment+
    management/146/.
13. http://www.washingtonpost.com/blogs/post-politics/wp/2013/11/25
    /al-gore-goes-vegan-with-little-fanfare/.
    http://www.washingtonpost.com/blogs/erik-wemple/wp/2013/01/31
    /gore-im-proud-of-the-transaction/.
14. http://online.wsj.com/news/articles/SB100014240527023046551045791
    63663464339836.
15. http://oilprice.com/Energy/Energy-General/Al-Gores-Hipocrisy The
    -Climate-Crusader-Profits-from-Fossil-Fuels.html.
16. http://www.washingtonpost.com/business/economy/al-gore-stands
    -to-gain-about-70-million-after-selling-current-tv-to-al-jazeera/2013
    /01/04/4775e5d2-56a5-11e2-8b9e-dd8773594efc_story.html.
17. http://usatoday30.usatoday.com/news/washington/2007-02-27-gore
    -house_x.htm.
18. http://content.usatoday.com/communities/greenhouse/post/2010/05
    /how-green-is-al-gores-9-million-montecito-ocean-front-villa/1#
    .U0hdl61dVDg.

19. http://usatoday30.usatoday.com/news/opinion/editorials/2006-08
-09-gore-green_x.htm.

16. Zygi Wilf

1. http://www.nytimes.com/2005/08/19/sports/football/19vikings
.html.
2. http://www.oregonlive.com/business/index.ssf/2014/01/minnesota
_vikings_owner_zygi_w.html.
3. Ibid.
4. http://www.washingtonpost.com/wp-dyn/content/article/2011/01
/30/AR2011013004545.html?sid=ST2011013105801.
5. http://www.businessinsider.com/why-is-the-national-football-league
-given-tax-exempt-status-2012-3.
6. http://www.forbes.com/sites/kurtbadenhausen/2011/12/14/the-nfl-signs
-tv-deals-worth-26-billion/.
7. http://www.dailymail.co.uk/sport/nfl/article-2567263/Minnesota
-Vikings-stadium-demolished-huge-explosion-voted-worst-fans.html.
8. http://www.celebritynetworth.com/richest-businessmen/zygi-wilf
-net-worth/.
9. http://prod.static.vikings.clubs.nfl.com/assets/docs/stadium/DES
-funding.pdf.
10. http://observer.com/2013/10/big-bad-wilf-did-zygis-stardust-take-it
-all-too-far/3/.
11. http://www.minnpost.com/community-voices/2012/06/stadium-post
mortem-how-wealthy-nfl-owner-got-millions-taxpayers.
12. Ibid.
13. http://observer.com/2011/11/zygi-wilf-vikings-owner-tackles-19-m
-park-avenue-pad/.
14. http://www.twincities.com/sports/ci_25346902/nfl-winning-super
-bowl-bid-likely-include-tax.
15. http://www.twincities.com/ci_20915808/minnesota-vikings-stadium
-authority-name-ceo-at-1st.
16. http://www.forbes.com/teams/minnesota-vikings/.
17. http://www.minnpost.com/community-voices/2012/06/stadium-post
mortem-how-wealthy-nfl-owner-got-millions-taxpayers.

17. Tom Steyer

1. http://blog.sfgate.com/nov05election/2013/04/03/obama-on-climate
-change-at-billionaire-tom-steyers-home-the-politics-of-this-are
-tough/.
2. Ibid.

3. http://www.newyorker.com/reporting/2013/09/16/130916fa_fact_lizza?currentPage=all.
4. http://blog.sfgate.com/nov05election/2013/04/03/obama-on-climate-change-at-billionaire-tom-steyers-home-the-politics-of-this-are-tough/.
5. http://money.cnn.com/2008/09/17/news/newsmakers/lashinsky_steyer.fortune/index2.htm.
6. http://www.breitbart.com/Big-Government/2013/09/22/McAuliffe-s-Green-Billionaire-Supporter-Enriched-Himself-Through-Coal-And-Oil.
7. http://www.newyorker.com/reporting/2013/09/16/130916fa_fact_lizza?currentPage=all.
8. Ibid.
9. http://www.foxnews.com/politics/2013/06/27/critics-accuse-keystone-foe-hypocrisy-over-oil-investment-history/.
10. http://news.investors.com/ibd-editorials/062713-661681-obama-donor-benefits-from-keystone-demise.htm.
11. http://www.foxnews.com/politics/2013/06/27/critics-accuse-keystone-foe-hypocrisy-over-oil-investment-history/.
12. http://thelead.blogs.cnn.com/2014/06/19/who-is-tom-steyer/.
13. http://thehill.com/homenews/campaign/291559-greens-get-billionaire-ally-money.
14. Rick Daysog, "Democratic Donor Gives $5 Million to Prop. 23 Foes," McClatchy-Tribune News Service, July 27, 2010.
15. http://thehill.com/homenews/campaign/291559-greens-get-billionaire-ally-money.
16. http://completecolorado.com/pagetwo/2014/05/21/ritter-moderated-intimate-discussion-for-billionaire-climate-activist-and-other-elites/.
17. http://www.reuters.com/article/2013/02/25/us-nexen-cnooc-idUSBRE9101A420130225.
18. http://www.judicialwatch.org/press-room/press-releases/sued-obama-treasury-dept-regarding-possible-drilling-rights-collusion/.
19. http://www.washingtonpost.com/politics/tom-steyers-slow-and-ongoing-conversion-from-fossil-fuels-investor-to-climate-activist/2014/06/08/6478da2e-ea68-11e3-b98c-72cef4a00499_story.html.
20. http://www.institutionalinvestor.com/Popups/PrintArticle.aspx?ArticleID=1024622.
21. Ibid.

18. James Sinegal

1. http://www.politico.com/news/stories/0912/80834.html.
2. Ibid.

3. Remarks at the Swearing-in Ceremony, Great Hall, Frances Perkins Building, Washington, DC, September 4, 2013, Targeted News Service, September 4, 2013.

4. http://www.forbes.com/sites/timworstall/2013/03/06/of-course -costco-supports-a-higher-minimum-wage-it-already-pays-above-it/.

5. http://www.bizjournals.com/washington/blog/2011/04/nine-years -to-recoup-4m-for-wheaton.html.

6. http://www.chicagojournal.com/Blogs/Near-Loop-Wire/01-18-2011 /City_Council_approves_West_Loop_Costco_tax_break.

7. http://www.rbj.net/article.asp?aID=199871.

8. http://www.nola.com/news/baton-rouge/index.ssf/2013/05/costco _baton_rouge_incentive.html.

9. http://www.weeklystandard.com/Content/Public/Articles/000/000 /013/914tecyh.asp?page=2.

10. Ibid.

11. http://www.weeklystandard.com/Content/Public/Articles/000/000 /013/914tecyh.asp?page=2.

12. http://www.ij.org/in-their-own-words-bureaucrats-and-developers -come-clean-on-eminent-domain-2.

13. http://online.wsj.com/news/articles/SB1000142412788732470510457 81 49012514177372?mod=WSJ_Opinion_LEADTop.

19. Warren Buffett

1. http://www.forbes.com/profile/warren-Buffett/.

2. http://www.cbsnews.com/news/warren-Buffett-says-he-wont-donate -to-obama-super-pacs/.

3. http://www.motherjones.com/politics/2012/04/barack-obama-warren -Buffett-campaign-cash.

4. http://online.wsj.com/news/articles/SB1000142405270230363090 45 79418754090426372?mg=reno64-wsj&url=http%3A%2F%2Fonline.wsj .com%2Farticle%2FSB10001424052702303630904579418754090426372 .html.

5. http://money.cnn.com/2012/09/21/pf/taxes/romney-tax-return/.

6. http://www.nytimes.com/2011/08/15/opinion/stop-coddling-the-super -rich.html?_r=0.

7. http://www.bloomberg.com/news/2011-08-25/berkshire-hathaway-to -invest-5-billion-in-bank-of-america-shares-surge.html.

8. http://online.wsj.com/news/articles/SB1000142405311190433280457 6538580352785252?mod=googlenews_wsj&mg=reno64-wsj&url=http %3A%2F%2Fonline.wsj.com%2Farticle%2FSB100014240531119043 32804576538580352785252.html%3Fmod%3Dgooglenews_wsj.

9. http://www.usnews.com/opinion/blogs/nancy-pfotenhauer/2014/05/12/even-warren-buffet-admits-wind-energy-is-a-bad-investment.
10. http://www.thestreet.com/story/11446065/1/yes-Buffett-is-a-hypocrite-time-to-move-on-folks.html.
11. http://nypost.com/2011/08/29/warren-Buffett-hypocrite/.
12. http://www.davidmcelroy.org/?p=5950.
13. http://www.cnbc.com/id/100962421.
14. http://www.post-gazette.com/business/2013/12/24/Heinz-trims-retiree-health-care-contribution-Heinz-cuts-retiree-health-care-funding/stories/201312240033.
15. https://www.iscebs.org/Resources/Surveys/Documents/retmedTW2011.pdf.
16. http://www.americanthinker.com/blog/2013/11/obamas_pal_Buffett_enriched_again_by_govt_taxpayers_lose.html.
17. http://news.bbc.co.uk/2/hi/americas/1170874.stm.
18. http://www.economist.com/node/12414924.
19. http://dailyreckoning.com/warren-Buffett-hypocrite-extraordinaire/.

20. Jeffrey Immelt

1. Paul Krugman, "The Competition Myth," *International Herald Tribune*, January 25, 2011.
2. http://www.whitehouse.gov/administration/advisory-boards/jobs-council.
3. http://www.newyorker.com/reporting/2008/06/23/080623fa_fact_boyer?currentPage=all.
4. http://watchdog.org/59851/white-house-visitors-log-shows-a-list-of-rich-famous-and-powerful/.
5. http://www.theatlantic.com/business/archive/2013/04/the-case-against-cronies-libertarians-must-stand-up-to-corporate-greed/275404/.
6. http://www.nytimes.com/2011/11/12/business/energy-environment/a-cornucopia-of-help-for-renewable-energy.html?pagewanted=all&_r=1&.
7. Ibid.
8. http://www.opensecrets.org/orgs/summary.php?id=D000000125&cycle=A.
9. http://www.opensecrets.org/lobby/clientlbs.php?id=D000000125&year=2011.
10. http://washingtonexaminer.com/new-energy-department-grants-went-to-firms-giving-mostly-to-democrats/article/2538891.
11. http://www.washingtonpost.com/wp-dyn/content/article/2009/06/28/AR2009062802955.html.
12. http://www.nytimes.com/2011/03/25/business/economy/25tax.html?pagewanted=1&_r=2&partner=rss&emc=rss.

13. http://www.thestreet.com/story/11060496/1/general-electrics-harlem -horse-trade.html.

14. Ibid.

15. http://blogs.wsj.com/corporate-intelligence/2012/10/16/geloss/.

16. http://www.nytimes.com/2012/10/17/business/battery-maker-a123 -systems-files-for-bankruptcy.html.

17. http://blogs.wsj.com/corporate-intelligence/2012/10/16/geloss/.

18. http://www.electrificationcoalition.org/members.

19. http://watchdog.org/110844/subsidy-summit-seeks-political-juice-for -electric-carmakers/.

20. http://www.zerohedge.com/article/gasparino-confirms-jeff-immelt -scolded-cnbc-staff-being-anti-obama.

21. http://www.nytimes.com/2009/09/27/business/global/27spy.html? pagewanted=all&_r=1&.

22. http://www.ge.com/ar2008/letter.html.

21. John Podesta

1. http://www.opensecrets.org/revolving/rev_summary.php?id=24899.

2. http://washingtonexaminer.com/obama-hires-revolving-door-lobbyist -and-clinton-fixer-john-podesta/article/2540496.

3. http://www.politico.com/story/2013/12/center-for-american-progress -donor-list-101140.html#ixzz2pGeacexV.

4. Ibid.

5. http://thecable.foreignpolicy.com/posts/2011/10/24/john_podesta _stepping_down_as_head_of_cap#sthash.MJEyrReo.dpbs.

6. http://freebeacon.com/politics/progressives-for-sale/.

7. http://www.nytimes.com/2013/12/13/us/politics/new-obama-adviser -brings-corporate-ties.html?pagewanted=all&_r=0.

8. http://www.thenation.com/print/article/174437/secret-donors-behind -center-american-progress-and-other-think-tanks.

9. http://thehill.com/blogs/hillicon-valley/technology/198350-com cast-time-warner-execs-have-been-big-obama-supporters#ixzz2xwt AqL7j.

10. http://www.nytimes.com/2013/12/13/us/politics/new-obama-adviser -brings-corporate-ties.html?pagewanted=all&_r=0.

11. http://freebeacon.com/politics/podesta-group-clients-donated-to-podestas -center-for-american-progress/.

12. Mike McIntire and Michael Luo, "White House Welcomes Donors, and Lobbyists Slip in Door, Too," *New York Times*, April 15, 2012; http://www .nytimes.com/2013/01/20/us/medicare-pricing-delay-is-political-win -for-amgen-drug-maker.html?pagewanted=all.

13. http://www.forbes.com/sites/larrybell/2011/10/25/obama-kick-back
-cronyism-part-1-stimulating-green-energy-the-chicago-way/3/.
14. http://www.state.gov/s/p/fapb/185597.htm.
15. http://www.politico.com/magazine/story/2013/12/income-equality
-ripple-effect-john-podesta-100891.html.
16. Ibid.
17. http://www.huffingtonpost.com/2013/12/11/is-ufo-disclosure-on-the
-plate-of-john-podesta_n_4428119.html.

22. Harry Reid

1. http://www.newyorker.com/archive/2005/08/08/050808fa_fact?
printable=true.
2. http://www.judicialwatch.org/corrupt-politicians-lists/judicial-watch
-announces-list-of-washingtons-ten-most-wanted-corrupt-politicians
-for-2012/#reid.
3. http://www.reuters.com/article/2012/08/31/us-usa-china-reid-solar
-idUSBRE87U06D20120831.
4. Ibid.
5. http://www.lasvegassun.com/news/2013/jun/14/company-dumps-big
-laughlin-solar-project-says-mark/.
6. http://www.foxnews.com/opinion/2012/12/12/cronies-that-got-away
-in-2012/.
7. http://www.reviewjournal.com/news/las-vegas-city-officials-kick-soccer
-deals-reids-way.
8. http://www.realclearpolitics.com/articles/2014/04/25/harry_reids
_long_coattails_122414.html.
9. http://www.legistorm.com/member_family/79/Harry_Reid.html.
10. http://www.latimes.com/news/politics/la-na-earmarks13nov13,0,6626376
,full.story?coll=la-home-headlines#axzz2vbVN3tqZ.
11. http://www.nationalreview.com/articles/314025/how-did-harry-reid
-get-rich-betsy-woodruff.
12. http://freebeacon.com/dirty-harrys-clean-energy-cronyism/.
13. http://www.realclearpolitics.com/articles/2013/10; sh01/reid_supporter
_whittemore_gets_2_years_in_campaign_cash_case_120171.html.
14. http://www.politico.com/story/2014/03/harry-reid-koch-brothers
-104248.html.

23. Fred Hochberg

1. http://www.opensecrets.org/pres08/bundlers.php?id=N00009638.
2. http://fedsdatacenter.com/federal-pay-rates/index.php?n=hoch
berg&l=&a=&o=&y=2012.

3. http://www.fulbright.com.au/2013-fulbright-symposium-speakers /2013-fulbright-symposium-keynotes/558-tom-healy.

4. Fred Hochberg interview on Bloomberg, Analyst Wire, November 16, 2009.

5. http://www.exim.gov/about/whatwedo/successstories/Ex-Im-Bank-Helps -Small-Montana-Business-Export-Pet-Toys.cfm.

6. http://cbo.gov/sites/default/files/cbofiles/attachments/45383-Fair Value.pdf.

7. http://www.gao.gov/assets/660/655201.pdf.

8. http://www.exim.gov/about/library/reports/annualreports/2013; shFY%202013%20Authorizations%20by%20Market_revised%2012%20 03; pc2013.pdf.

9. http://www.pv-tech.org/news/solyndra_using_ex_im_bank_loan _guarantees_system_to_support_commercial_roof.

10. http://vencon1.wordpress.com/author/vencon1/page/2/.

11. http://dailycaller.com/2014/02/10/center-for-american-progress-first -solar-green-relationship/.

12. http://mercatus.org/publication/assessing-department-energy-loan -guarantee-program.

13. http://www.bloomberg.com/apps/news?pid=newsarchive&sid=am7fI7G YgEF4.

14. http://www.spacenews.com/article/satellite-telecom/35763satmex -7-satellite-not-dependent-on-ex-im-loan#.Ud1zJ_nfSHc.

15. http://web.archive.org/web/20071231015132/http:/www.wfaa.com /sharedcontent/dws/wfaa/localnews/news8/stories/wfaa071227_mo _bankdrugs.5adabe14.html.

16. Ibid.

17. http://www.exim.gov/about/library/reports/annualreports/2013 /highlights.html.

18. http://washingtonexaminer.com/is-boeings-bank-heading-for-a -jumbo-jet-bubble/article/2546100.

19. http://www.reuters.com/article/2013/02/14/us-usa-delta-lawsuit -idUSBRE91D01J20130214.

20. http://washingtonexaminer.com/gop-could-make-hay-by-opposing -ex-im-bank/article/1178346.

21. http://www.realclearpolicy.com/articles/2013/01/15/surprise_export -import_bank_promotes_crony_capitalism_399.html.

24. George Soros

1. http://www.newyorker.com/reporting/2012/08/27/120827fa_fact _mayer?currentPage=all.

2. http://www.breitbart.com/Big-Government/2011/11/21/George-Soros -Helped-Craft-Stimulus-Then-Invested-in-Companies-Benefiting.

3. http://www.newyorker.com/online/blogs/newsdesk/2012/02/george -soros-democrats.html.

4. http://www.opensecrets.org/outsidespending/summ.php?cycle= 2012&disp=D&type=V.

5. http://blog.heritage.org/2012/01/26/soros-may-benefit-from-white -houses-natural-gas-proposal/.

6. http://www.insidermonkey.com/blog/should-i-sell-westport-innova tions-inc-usa-wprt-223770/.

7. http://www.americanthinker.com/blog/2008/08/rank_hypocrisy _from_george_sor.html.

8. Ibid.

9. http://www.bloomberg.com/apps/news?pid=newsarchive&sid=a.V5sg GzdsQY.

10. http://cnsnews.com/mrctv-blog/mike-ciandella/universities-fcc -newsroom-probe-have-close-ties soros-got-37m-funding.

11. http://www.breitbart.com/Big-Journalism/2014/02/22/media-silence -explained-soros-fingerprints-on-fcc-newsroom-probe.

12. http://www.breitbart.com/Big-Journalism/2013/03/11/Raw-Numbers -Expose-Media-Bias-Against-Koch-Brothers.

13. http://www.mrc.org/articles/nbc-silent-73-million-soros-special -anchors-liberal-report.

25. John Doerr

1. http://www.sfgate.com/green/article/Venture-capitalist-says-U-S -losing-green-race-3255503.php#page-2.

2. http://nymag.com/news/media/twitter-2011-10/index6.html.

3. http://www.sfgate.com/green/article/Venture-capitalist-says-U-S -losing-green-race-3255503.php#page-2.

4. http://webcache.googleusercontent.com/search?q=cache:XLdgsNTVXCg J:russmitchell.com/wp-content/uploads/2008/11/portfolio_green_doerr .rtf+&cd=2&hl=en&ct=clnk&gl=us.

5. Ibid.

6. Ibid.

7. http://www.telegraph.co.uk/earth/energy/6491195/Al-Gore-could -become-worlds-first-carbon-billionaire.html.

8. Schweizer, *Throw Them All Out*.

9. Ibid.

10. http://www.pv-magazine.com/news/details/beitrag/hanergy-completes -acquisition-of-miasol_100009798/.

11. http://www.pv-magazine.com/news/details/beitrag/hanergy-completes-acquisition-of-miasol_100009798/#axzz2wQxwRRbx.

12. http://www.csmonitor.com/Business/Latest-News-Wires/2013/1126/Fisker-bankruptcy-Feds-to-lose-139-million-on-Fisker-Automotive.

13. http://dailycaller.com/2013/11/22/taxpayers-lose-139-million-on-fisker-automotive-loan/.

26. Elon Musk

1. http://www.forbes.com/sites/hannahelliott/2012/12/28/tesla-and-spacex-founder-musk-buys-17-million-bel-air-mansion/.

2. Ibid.

3. http://www.nj.com/politics/index.ssf/2014/03/motor_vehicle_commission_passes_anti-tesla_rule_1.html#incart_river.

4. http://www.teslamotors.com/blog/people-new-jersey.

5. http://www.motherjones.com/politics/2013/10/tesla-motors-free-ride-elon-musk-government-subsidies?page=3.

6. http://www.caranddriver.com/news/daimler-takes-10-percent-stake-in-tesla-motors-car-news.

7. http://www.greentechmedia.com/articles/read/daimler-sells-40-of-its-stake-in-tesla-to-aabar-investments.

8. http://www.bbc.com/news/business-17649821.

9. http://www.thenational.ae/business/industry-insights/energy/abu-dhabis-taqa-sells-tesla-stake-and-buys-into-iraq.

10. http://www.motherjones.com/politics/2013/10/tesla-motors-free-ride-elon-musk-government-subsidies?page=3.

11. http://www.foxnews.com/politics/2014/03/03/solarcity-skyrocketing-stock-dependent-on-government-tax-giveaways/.

12. http://washingtonexaminer.com/carney-green-stimulus-profiteer-comes-under-irs-scrutiny/article/2510619#.UN4rj6UudhM.

13. Ibid.

14. Ibid.

15. http://www.motherjones.com/politics/2013/10/tesla-motors-free-ride-elon-musk-government-subsidies?page=3.

16. http://www.forbes.com/sites/hannahelliott/2013/08/12/latest-update-elon-musk-will-start-the-hyperloop-himself/.

27. Carlos Slim

1. http://money.cnn.com/2007/08/03/news/international/carlosslim.fortune/index.htm.

2. http://www.aljazeera.com/indepth/features/2012/06/2012629203127549484.html.

3. http://www.forbes.com/profile/carlos-slim-helu/#.
4. http://www.aljazeera.com/indepth/features/2012/06/2012629203
127549484.html.
5. http://www.realclearmarkets.com/articles/2013/03/12/for_155m_did
_carlos_slim_buy_silence_from_the_times_100195.html.
6. http://www.oecd.org/internet/broadband/49536828.pdf.
7. http://www.myfoxdc.com/story/19792114/carlos-slim-worlds-richest
-man-gets-richer-supplying-obamaphones-to-poor#axzz2wXwYnUxn.
8. Ibid.
9. http://www.usac.org/li/tools/disbursements/results.aspx.
10. http://transition.fcc.gov/Daily_Releases/Daily_Business/2012
/db0601/FCC-12-11A1.pdf.
11. http://www.breitbart.com/Big-Government/2012/06/13/Spending-Off
-the-Hook-Free-Phones-Costing-Taxpayers-2-1-Billion-Per-Year.
12. Ibid.
13. http://www.washingtontimes.com/news/2013/feb/5/fraud-and-abuse
-grow-after-subsidized-telephone-pr/.
14. http://www.fcc.gov/document/45-million-penalty-proposed-against
-tracfone-wireless.
15. http://www.businessweek.com/magazine/how-an-fcc-free-phone-program
-went-rogue-02022012.html.
16. http://blogs.wsj.com/digits/2013/02/12/what-is-the-fccs-lifeline
-phone-subsidy-program/.
17. http://online.wsj.com/news/articles/SB118615255900587380?
mod=home_we_banner_left&mg=reno64-wsj&url=http%3A%2F%2
Fonline.wsj.com%2Farticle%2FSB118615255900587380.html%3Fmod
%3Dhome_we_banner_left.
18. http://money.cnn.com/2007/08/03/news/international/carlosslim
.fortune/index.htm.

Conclusion

1. https://www.princeton.edu/~mgilens/Gilens%20homepage%20materials
/Gilens%20and%20Page/Gilens%20and%20Page%202014-Testing%20
Theories%203-7-14.pdf.
2. http://www.politico.com/story/2014/04/democrats-democracy
-alliance-liberal-donors-105972.html?hp=t1.
3. http://www.nytimes.com/2014/01/27/us/politics/lets-talk-about-the
-wealth-gap.html.
4. Ibid.

Acknowledgments

Writing is a passion of mine. And to have been given the opportunity to see that passion manifest in the form of three books now, I am incredibly grateful and humbled.

I'm even more grateful to continue to work with the talented team at Threshold Editions. My editor, Mitchell Ivers, always makes my manuscripts better. And *Crapitalism* is no exception. Thank you! Louise Burke, the executive vice president and publisher, continues to believe in my ideas, and for that I am very thankful. Kristin Dwyer, my publicist, is excellent at her job and super fun to promote a book with. I'd also like to thank Tom Pitoniak and Natasha Simons for their insights and edits.

My agents, Glen Hartley and Lynn Chu: thank you for being in my corner.

Also a big shout-out to Eric Eggers, who assisted me with research.

To my mentor, you know who you are: you'll be around many more years, brother, and we'll always cause trouble together. Thanks for your guidance and friendship.

To my beautiful wife and best friend, Kendra: thank you for your constant encouragement and deep love. I'm blessed beyond words to be your husband.

To baby Bella, my little bundle of joy.

To my family, I love every one of you dearly.

And above all, thanks to my Lord and Savior Jesus Christ. I was lost, but now I'm found.

Index